FIRST

BLOOD

About the Author

Sidney Harcave is Professor of Russian History at Harpur College of the State University of New York. Born in Washington, D.C., he graduated from the City College of New York and received his Ph.D. at the University of Chicago.

Mr. Harcave's professional career has included appointments at Harvard, Wyoming, Vermont, and Michigan universities. And he has served as Chairman of the Social Sciences Division at Harpur College, where he is now Chairman of the History Department.

His service with the United States Government has been extensive. During World War II he was a foreign affairs analyst in the Foreign Broadcast Intelligence Service. He has also served as a research analyst in the Office of Strategic Services and in the Department of State.

He has written widely for scholarly journals and contributed many articles to various encyclopedias. His books include RUSSIA: A HISTORY.

FIRST BLOOD

The Russian Revolution

of 1905

by Sidney Harcave

THE MACMILLAN COMPANY, NEW YORK
COLLIER-MACMILLAN LIMITED, LONDON

First Printing

The Macmillan Company, New York
Collier-Macmillan Canada, Ltd., Toronto, Ontario
Library of Congress catalog card number: 64-22470
Printed in the United States of America

Preface

This short account of the Russian Revolution of 1905 is based mainly on published primary sources, many of which were made available by the Soviet government in 1925 and 1955 to mark, respectively, the twentieth and the fiftieth anniversaries of the revolution. These have been supplemented by unpublished materials in the official archives of England, France, and Germany; also by studies and evaluations of other relevant materials. All are listed in the bibliography. In the body of the book, footnotes and textual documentation are limited to essential annotation and identification of quotations.

Popular usage is followed in transliterating the Cyrillic alphabet of the Russian language; and dates are given in accordance with the Julian calendar, employed in Russia until 1918, rather than the Gregorian calendar of the West.

Translations of the programs supported by the most important political groups of this revolutionary period are given in the Appendix, along with pertinent official documents.

In the effort represented here, I was favored particularly by the encouragement of Professor Michael T. Florinsky and the assistance of my wife, Norah. It is a pleasure to acknowledge their association and, at the same time, to absolve them of any responsibility for the manner in which I have used it.

30 July 1964   S.H.

3

Contents

5

3

The Gaponovshchina: A Test of Positions

4

Development of the Revolution: First Phase
January 10–February 18

5

Development of the Revolution: Second Phase
February–August

6

Development of the Revolution: Third Phase
August–October

7

Development of the Revolution: Fourth Phase
October–December

8

The Settlement

APPENDIX

Documents Related

to the Russian Revolution of 1905

Maps

The "Two Russias"

There exist two Russias. . . . Were I to label these two Russias, I should designate the one as the Russia of Leo Tolstoy, the great writer; and the other as that of Plehve, the late minister of the interior. The former is the Russia of our "intellectuals" and of the people; the latter is official Russia. One is the Russia of the future, as dreamed of by members of the liberal professions; the other is an anachronism, deeply rooted in the past, and defended in the present by an omnipotent bureaucracy. The one spells liberty; the other, despotism.

> —Paul Milyukov (Russian historian and liberal leader), *Russia and Its Crisis*, 1905.

Among the falsest of political principles is the principle of the sovereignty of the people. . . . Thence proceeds the theory of Parliamentarism, which, up to the present day, has deluded much of the so-called "intelligence," and unhappily infatuated certain foolish Russians. It continues to maintain its hold on many minds with the obstinacy of a narrow fanaticism, although every day its falsehood is exposed more clearly to the world.

> —Constantine Pobedonostsev (Over-Procurator of the Holy Synod of the Russian Orthodox Church and adviser to Nicholas II), *Reflections of a Russian Statesman* (trans. of *Moskovskii Sbornik*, 1896).

A CRITICAL TEST of the positions stated above was made in 1905. The popular uprising which occurred in Russia at that time may properly be termed the first revolution in the country's history: "first" because there had previously been no such mass action having both organization and a political program;

"revolution" because it succeeded in forcing a change in the monarchy's traditionally autocratic rule.

The groups that worked to bring about the Revolution of 1905 pursued various and often conflicting ultimate goals; but they accepted a common immediate goal, the fundamental need to curb the power of the autocracy. It was clear that, whatever the ultimate goals—all of which involved change of some kind—they would remain unattainable as long as the regime held absolute power and used it to prevent change.

Tsarism and Bureaucracy

At the beginning of the twentieth century, more power was concentrated in the hands of the ruler of Russia than in those of any other person on earth. The ruling Tsar,[1] Nicholas II, who had come to the throne in 1894, exercised unlimited sovereignty over some 135 million subjects living in an area that included over a seventh of the world's surface; and he was resolutely committed to administer that sovereignty in such a manner as to preserve and perpetuate the political, social, and economic order he had inherited from his father, Alexander III. He was of the firm belief that autocracy was the only political system suited to the Russians and that, with the final

[1] Although informal usage has made it acceptable to refer to the autocrat as "tsar," his short formal title was "emperor," and his full formal title—as given in Article 37 of *Svod Zakonov* (Collection of Laws)—was an impressive composite: "By the grace of Almighty God, the Emperor and Autocrat of All the Russias, of Moscow, Kiev, Vladimir, Novgorod; the Tsar of Kazan, the Tsar of Astrakhan, the Tsar of Poland, the Tsar of Siberia, the Tsar of Tauride Chersonese, the Tsar of Georgia; the Sovereign of Pskov and Grand Duke of Smolensk, Lithuania, Volhynia, Podolia, and Finland; Prince of Estland, Livonia, Courland, and Semigallia, Samogitia, Belostok, Karelia, Tver, Yugor, Perm, Vyatka, Bolgaria and others; Sovereign and Grand Duke of Novgorod on the lower lands, of Chernigov, Ryazan, Polotsk, Rostov, Yaroslav, Belosersk, Udor, Odborsk, Kondiisk, Vitebsk, Mstislav and of all northern land the Ruler; and the Sovereign of all lands of Iveriia, Kartalinsk, and Kabarda, and of the regions of Armenia; of the Princes of Cherkassiya and Gorsk, and others, the Heir-Sovereign and the Possessor; the Sovereign of Turkestan; the Heir of Norway, the Duke of Schleswig-Holstein, Stornmarn, Ditmars and Oldenburg etc., etc.,"

touches added by his father, it was an inherently sound, though admittedly not perfect, form of government. To make any major changes in it would only result in making Russia dangerously susceptible to revolution, the dread disease that had been appearing sporadically in Europe for more than two hundred years, ravaging monarchy after monarchy—England, France, Prussia, Austria, Spain—and was still an infection against which a monarch should watchfully guard his country. Moreover, Nicholas II thought of himself as a guardian answerable only to God for his stewardship:

> In the sight of my Maker I have to carry the burden of a terrible responsibility and at all times, therefore, be ready to render an account to Him of my actions. I must always keep firmly to my convictions and follow the dictates of my conscience.[2]

Foremost among the institutions supported by the Tsar's conscience and convictions was autocracy, a basis of government established by the Fundamental Laws of the Russian Empire:

> To the Emperor of All the Russias belongs the supreme autocratic and unlimited power. Not only fear, but also conscience commanded by God Himself, is the basis of obedience to this power.[3]

Though autocracy, by definition, is intolerant of constitutional limitations on the power of the ruler—such as might be expected, for instance, from legislative bodies deriving their authority from his subjects—it does not preclude recourse to elective advisory bodies. Yet Nicholas II opposed the latter also, reasoning that they might prove to be breeding grounds for the germs of change, which could develop into the idea of elective representation in other areas. Within his government,

[2] Nicholas II to Maria Feodorovna, October 20, 1902, *The Secret Letters of the Last Tsar,* ed. by Edward J. Bing (New York, 1938), pp. 161-62.
  Of the meager direct sources useful in judging the personal feelings of Nicholas II, these letters are the most important. They will be cited hereinafter by the shortened title *The Secret Letters.*
[3] Russia, *Svod Osnovnykh Gosudarstvennykh Zakonov,* Art. I.

the body most nearly advisory in nature was the State Council, made up of experienced and respected bureaucrats, whose opinions he might—or might not—seek, and whose judgments he might—or might not—accept. The council members, appointed by the Tsar, could be depended upon to uphold autocracy, not to limit it. To sustain this regime inviolate, the ruler, as a matter of course, opposed any movement that allowed either criticism of the existing order or united action for the purpose of changing it. Accordingly, the time-honored system persisted; only the organizations of the nobility, acting through their respective marshals, were allowed even to petition the tsar; and the evidence of four centuries of autocratic rule in Russia warned them against the imprudence of presenting political petitions.

Traditionally, the tsar exercised his power through a large and consequential bureaucracy, hierarchically organized, uniformed in grand style, and secure in positions commanding servile attention from the public. Two classes of bureaucrats were particularly powerful: the ministers, who directed the various branches of the central government; and the governors-general, governors, and prefects, who directed the chief geographical subdivisions of the empire.

The ministers sitting collectively as the Committee of Ministers, a body instituted in 1802 for the consideration of routine administrative problems, had only very limited jurisdiction; but individually they could handle the duties of their positions with considerable freedom as long as they retained the confidence of the tsar. Among them the most important was the minister of interior, whose office was concerned with many of the vital aspects of the imperial rule: it administered the provinces into which the country was divided, also the districts into which the provinces were divided; it regulated the services of the land captains, members of the nobility who controlled the local administration of peasant affairs; it supervised the work of the associations of the nobility; it operated the postal and telegraphic services, the office of censorship, and the department of police; and it exercised veto power over the zemstvos.[4]

[4] *See* p. 16 below.

Whenever problems were outside the scope of ministerial routine and were of such a nature that the tsar's approval was required, he might, if he wanted to hear a discussion of them, call a meeting of the Council of Ministers. This body, established in 1857 and always presided over by the tsar, was composed of the ministers, other high officials, and special appointees of the tsar; and in it the ministers, as well as other members, were advisors only.

Extensive authority was delegated to the governors-general, governors, and prefects, each of whom was appointed by the tsar and required to report to the minister of interior. A governor-general administered a group of provinces, over which he exercised both civilian and military control; at the time of Nicholas II, there were nine of these groups, the populace in most of them being mainly non-Russian. A governor administered one of the ninety-six provinces of the empire. And a prefect administered one of the four cities specifically exempt from provincial jurisdiction: St. Petersburg, Odessa, Kerch, and Sevastopol. These officials exercised arbitrary power when the tsar, using the authority decreed by the Law on Exceptional Measures, of 1881, placed a city, province, or district under "reinforced protection," which gave its administrator limited emergency power to deal with any condition or situation that he considered a threat to law and order; or under "extraordinary protection," which extended the administrator's emergency power to include the right on his own authority to banish persons from the area, to close newspapers and factories, to arrest and fine individuals, and to prohibit any kind of private gathering. By the beginning of 1904, more than half of Russia, including most of her major cities, was under some form of "protection."

The police, subordinate to the Ministry of Interior, likewise exercised a direct and powerful control. There were political police and regular police, city police and rural police, factory police and railroad police. Nowhere in Europe were the police as numerous, as venal, or as powerful as those of Russia. Most unrestricted in their authority were the political police, consisting of the Corps of Gendarmes and the municipal security departments, which had wide discretion in apprehending, holding, and punishing persons believed to be dangerous to the political stability of the empire.

High in the ranks of those who held eminent positions in various phases of the autocratic administration were many members of the imperial family. Those who were children or grandchildren of a tsar bore the title of grand duke or grand duchess; and members of succeeding generations, the title of prince or princess of the imperial blood. With each of these titles went a munificent income, much of it derived from the extensive "appanage lands," held by the imperial family, collectively the richest landlord in the country. Although membership in the imperial family did not automatically confer power, members who had the inclination and a modicum of ability and who did not incur the displeasure of the tsar were likely to hold important positions. Among the grand dukes in positions of prominence as Russia moved toward her first revolution were Alexander Michaelovich, Director of the Merchant Marine; Alexis Alexandrovich, Chief of the Navy; Vladimir Alexandrovich, Commander-in-Chief of the Guard and of the St. Petersburg Military District; Sergei Alexandrovich, Governor-General of Moscow;[5] Constantine Constantinovich, President of the Academy of Sciences and Chief of Military Educational Establishments; Nicholas Nicholaievich, Inspector-General of the Cavalry; and Michael Nicholaievich, Chairman of the State Council. These men, uncles and cousins of the Tsar, were powerful reinforcements of autocracy.

Oddly enough, in the midst of this staunchly autocratic Russia, there were two institutions alien to the prevailing system: the elected district and provincial zemstvos and the elected municipal dumas, the former administering schools, roads, and public health services in the countryside of thirty-three provinces;[6] the latter administering similar services in

[5] Commonly, reference to a governor-general indicated the chief city (e.g., Moscow) or general area (e.g., Finland) rather than the various provinces under his control.

[6] There were no zemstvos in Congress Poland (an area given to the tsar at the Congress of Vienna), in the western provinces of European Russia, in the far north of European Russia, in Transcaucasia, in the Cossack regions, or in Asiatic Russia.

the cities. It is true that their power was limited and that they functioned under the unfriendly control of the imperial bureaucracy; yet their very existence was at times a problem. Both were inheritances from the reign of the popular Alexander II (1855-81), and later tsars had endured their existence, knowing that it would be as impolitic to destroy them as unwise to encourage them.

When Nicholas II, at the time of his accession, learned that the zemstvos were hopeful of his extending their jurisdiction, he labeled their optimism a "senseless dream" and added: "Let all know that, in devoting all My strength in behalf of the welfare of My people, I shall defend the principles of autocracy as unswervingly as My deceased father."[7] In that declaration, he was implicitly reaffirming the traditional and official doctrine of the tsarist state as embodied in the well-known phrase "autocracy, orthodoxy, and nationalism"—a phrase held almost sacrosanct by the government and its supporters and used in conscious opposition to the spirit of the French revolutionary triad, "liberty, fraternity, and equality."

TSARIST VIEW OF SOCIETY

Complementing the Tsar's political principles was his interpretation of the scheme of Russian society. In his thinking, based on the traditional training he had received, the major divisions of society were the nobility, the peasantry, and the Orthodox Church. All were servants of the state in a relationship that was not overly complex. The nobility was the chief servant, providing the personnel for the higher ranks in civil and military affairs; the Church served by propagating the true faith and by encouraging morality and loyalty throughout the empire; and the peasantry discharged its duties by tilling the soil and fighting the wars. He looked upon all of these as genuinely loyal to throne and fatherland; but, knowing that the spirit falters when the body is weak, he felt that the state was under obligation to help the nobles maintain their landed estates, to keep the peasants from becoming landless laborers,

[7] As reported in *Pravitelstvennyi Vestnik*, January 18, 1895.

and to protect the Church from losing the privileges it enjoyed as the embodiment of the established faith.

In general, official theory considered "the people" of the land to be Russian and rural. Yet there were within the country forty million or so non-Russians (for Russia counted among her subjects the inhabitants of Finland, Congress Poland, the Baltic provinces, Transcaucasia, Siberia, parts of Central Asia, and others of "foreign" origin) and about twenty million urban inhabitants. What of them? They were all subjects of the tsar, as Nicholas once reminded a governor who had excluded Jewish children from a patriotic procession, and they were required to be both loyal and useful; however, they were customarily accounted to be less worthy and less inclined to loyalty than were his rural Russian subjects. The areas inhabited by national minorities were considered sources of possible trouble involving particularly the issue of separatism, while the cities were adjudged havens of a rootless and turbulent proletariat. To thwart or redirect the inclinations of these two groups, the government had its special devices. Where tendencies toward separatism were observed among minority groups, the policy of Russification, based on intensive reeducation emphasizing the Russian language and the Russian Orthodox religion, was employed. And efforts were made to anticipate the potential turbulence of the urban proletariat and to forestall it by paternalistic laws.

Such was the tsarist notion of a stable and secure Russia at the turn of the century. It not only shaped governmental policies but also defined reality for the chief officials and for the tsar. Unfortunately, the official view of reality and reality itself were never entirely congruous. When he began his reign, Nicholas II, a sanguine monarchist, could see no reason that the state of apparent calm he found in Russia should not continue. Ten years later, however, even a sanguine monarchist could not overlook the fact that Russia faced problems of a very serious nature. The critical question, by that time, was whether or not these could be solved without changing traditional policies. The Tsar thought that they could be. He was mistaken, but he adhered to his interpretation of the situation as long as he was able.

THE AGRARIAN PROBLEM

The most nearly insoluble problem was the agrarian one, involving the approximately 115 million Russians whose income was derived from agriculture. Debate over its nature and causes was heated and prolix, but there was no question about its existence; it was inescapably palpable in the growing impoverishment of both the nobility and the peasantry. Each year thousands of nobles, finding themselves in debt, either mortgaged their estates to the Nobles Land Bank or sold their land piecemeal to municipalities, merchants, or peasants. Within the generation preceding 1905, the nobility sold off one-third of its holdings and mortgaged one-third of what remained.

Whereas the nobles' course was a direct one to economic ruin, that of the peasants was an almost hopeless maze. They were circumscribed by legislation that, although framed for their benefit, often brought them burdens instead of blessings. At the time of their emancipation from serfdom, the government had planned to make of them an economically stable, and hence politically conservative, landholding class. To that end, it had issued laws providing that peasants might purchase certain land owned by the nobility (that which they had been cultivating for their own use in return for dues-in-kind, cash, or labor), and pay for it through "redemption dues" over a period of decades. This land, known as "allotment land," was not to be owned by individual peasant proprietors, but by the commune, the village organization of the peasantry. The individual was given only the right to cultivate certain strips of land that were assigned to him under the open-field system, which required that each field be divided into striplike portions. He could not sell these strips, nor could he mortgage them. In practice, he could not even renounce his right to them: they were his whether or not he wanted them. And he was required to pay his share of redemption dues to the village commune, which was responsible for the collective payments of the whole village.

This postemancipation settlement had prevented the proletarianization of the peasants, but it had not given them enough land to provide for their needs. When they required more than their land would produce, they bought or rented land from the Church, the imperial family, or the nobility (their chief source) ; or they sought work as laborers in the field or in the cities. Even so, their earnings were often so small that they could neither buy the food they needed nor keep up the payment of taxes and redemption dues they owed to the government for their land allotments. By the tenth year of Nicholas II's reign, their total arrears in payments of taxes and dues was 118 million rubles (the ruble was then worth fifty cents by dollar-standard), a sum larger than the amount due annually from them. And, as things were going, the situation could be expected to grow worse rather than better. Evidence of the predicament had been increasing for years. Hordes of hungry and ragged peasants roamed the country, searching for work, sometimes walking hundreds of miles to get it. In years of poor harvests, such as 1901, the numbers of these wandering unfortunates in the "barefoot brigade" were greatly multiplied. And desperate peasants proved themselves capable of violence. In the provinces of Kharkov and Poltava in 1902, thousands of them, ignoring restraints and authority, burst out in rebellious fury that led to extensive destruction of property and looting of noble homes before troops could be brought in to subdue and punish them. Incidents of this nature brought no gain to anyone, but they served to attract more concern to the agrarian problem.

When the government finally became alarmed at the state of affairs, it appointed and instructed numerous committees of investigation, who collected data that proved both staggering in volume and depressing in nature. They found that, while no part of the countryside was prosperous, some parts, particularly the fertile areas known collectively as the black-soil region, were in a state of decline. Though the acreage under cultivation had been increased in the last half century, the increase had not been proportionate to the growth of the peasant population, which had doubled during that period. Moreover, the price of grain, to which 97 percent of the land was sown, had declined. And adding to the general hardship was a condition that has always beset Russian agriculture—low yield. This situation, of course, affected the whole economy, but it weighed most heavily on the peasantry and on the less fortunate nobles who lacked not only capital but also, in many cases, both skill and interest in agriculture.

For the difficulties their investigations revealed, the official committees could find no remedies that were both sensible and acceptable to the government. Acceptable ones were those that would not weaken the position of the nobility nor change the position of the peasants in the social order; and remedies cut to those specifications were, naturally, so devitalized as to be mere palliatives.

THE NATIONALITY PROBLEM

In addition to the agrarian problem, there were three other major ones menacing the stability of the empire: they concerned the national minorities, labor, and the educated class. The government finally recognized these problems also, even though in a myopic and astigmatic way; Minister of Interior Plehve stated in 1903 that, after the agrarian problem, the three most serious ones plaguing the country were those of the Jews, the schools, and the workers—in that order.

For generations, the Jews had been considered a special problem in Russia. The official view had come to be that they were enemies of Christianity, exploiters of the peasantry, and the fountainhead of the revolutionary movement. Constantine Pobedonostsev, Over-Procurator of the Holy Synod of the Russian Orthodox Church from 1880 to 1905, asserted that the Jewish problem would be solved only when one-third of the Jews had emigrated, another third had been converted to Russian Orthodoxy, and the rest had disappeared. That was a view mistaken both in diagnosis and prognosis. The Jews were capable of being useful subjects of the empire if given the opportunity; and, despite generations of persecution and harassment, they still numbered over five million, half of the Jews in the world. Except for a few who were exempt, they were restricted to residence in Congress Poland and the Pale of Settlement, fifteen provinces east of Congress Poland. There they lived generally miserable and circumscribed lives, forbidden to settle or acquire land outside the cities and

towns, legally limited in attendance at secondary and higher
schools, virtually barred from the legal profession, denied the
right to vote for municipal councillors or zemstvo deputies,
and excluded from service in the Navy or the Guards. Consequently, their potential loyalty was, in many cases, turned
to enmity.

Actually, the government's treatment of the Jews, though
considered an issue apart, was only one aspect of a policy followed in dealing with all national and religious minorities, a
policy that succeeded only in aggravating or producing in
those groups a feeling of general disloyalty, the very evil it was
intended to prevent. Among the forty million non-Russians
(including, along with less numerous groups, Poles, Finns,
Jews, Letts, and Armenians) and even among Ukrainians and
White Russians, officially classified as Russians, there was a
spirit of restiveness, of growing impatience with inferior status, of resentment against Russification; and, among some of
them, the spirit of nationalism was quickening. This development, watched closely by the government, was matched by an
ever increasing severity of suppressive measures. Any semblance of adjustment under such conditions could be no more
than temporary.

THE LABOR PROBLEM

The labor problem elicited less passion from the government than did the nationality problem—but unfortunately, no
more practical understanding. In handling labor, as in handling other groups, the official policies were often self-defeating. The government's paternalism, expressed through the
designing of laws to protect workers in some respects and the
appointment of inspectors to enforce those laws, had failed to
convince the nearly three million factory workers, railroaders,
and miners that the government was on their side. The "protective" laws, when set beside the persistent abuses, seemed
inadequate despite the fact that they had brought a degree of
improvement in some conditions. They prohibited the industrial employment of children under the age of twelve and,
except for night work in glass factories, limited the employ-

ment of those between twelve and fifteen to eight-hour days and excluded them from work on Sundays and holidays. They prohibited the practice of charging workers for the lighting of shops and plants. They required that workers be paid in cash, not kind, "at least once a month." They limited the size and bases of fines for workers' tardiness (before 1886, in some plants, the fine for a fifteen-minute tardiness was a day's wages). Yet the workers felt justified in their belief that the laws had not done enough to free them from unfair and often inhuman treatment by owners, managers, and foremen; and they could point to many practices in support of their belief. They could be forced to work beyond the maximum eleven and a half hours per day that the government had decreed in 1897. They were still subject to what seemed arbitrary and exorbitant fines for tardiness, absence, or mistakes in their work. They had to accept the abuse of foremen. And they had to live on what were probably the lowest wages in Europe. Though the cost of living also was low in Russia, the average worker's 15 rubles per month could not buy the equal of what the French worker's 110 francs (41 rubles—less than the amount received by a German or a British worker) would buy for him. Moreover—and this was the situation that was turning the workers' dissatisfaction to desperation—there was open to them no legal means by which to appeal for redress or improvement: the "protective" laws prohibited their organizing trade unions and forbade their resorting to strikes. They could not be expected to look to the maker of those laws, the government, for relief; rather, they could be expected to listen the more sympathetically to the radical ideas, then becoming current in the urban environment, that appeared to accord with their needs.

In 1901 a police report on the state of labor asserted:

Agitators, seeking to realize their goals, have achieved some success, unfortunately, in organizing the workers to fight against the government. Within the last three or four years, the easygoing Russian young man has been transformed into a special type of semi-literate *intelligent*, who feels obliged to spurn religion and family, to disregard the law, and to defy and scoff at constituted authority. Fortunately such young men are not numerous in the factories, but this negligible handful terrorizes the inert majority of workers into following it.[8]

Although the report exaggerated some details (Russian labor had not yet broken the mold of traditional beliefs), it indicated a very important fact: there was a beginning of recognizable change. Some workers were daring to defy constituted authority through illegal strikes, and here and there a few were joining secret revolutionary groups. But, since the legalization of trade unions and strikes was inconsistent with established policy, the government continued to rely principally on the old methods, arresting labor agitators and enacting more of what was intended as paternalistic legislation.

One new method, introduced in 1900 by Sergei Zubatov, head of the Moscow security department, and labeled "police socialism" by its critics, was given a cautious trial. As conceived, it seemed feasible: workers' societies were to be formed, with police approval, to provide healthful, fraternal activities and opportunities for cooperative self-help together with "protection" against influences that might have an inimical effect on loyalty to job or country. Such groups were organized in Moscow, Odessa, Kiev, Nikolaiev, and Kharkov; but conditions proved unfavorable to their success as planned.

Between 1900 and 1903, a period of industrial depression, many firms became bankrupt and employment was generally cut as a result of the reduction in orders from the steel industry's chief patron, the government. The workers were therefore in a state of unusual restiveness and were liable, when a legal organization was opened to them, to turn it toward an end not envisioned by its sponsors. The societies attracted a satisfactory number of members, but they did not serve to prevent strikes; in fact, radical workers found them to be ready-made bands through which to organize strikes or from which to draw support for striking workers outside the societies. One strike, begun in 1902 by workers in the railroad shops in Vladikavkaz and Rostov-on-Don, stirred such a response that,

[8] I. Kh. Ozerov, *Politika po Rabochemu Voprosu v Rossii za Poslednie Gody* (Moscow, 1906), p. 131.

by the following summer, some 225,000 in the various industries of southern Russia and Transcaucasia were on strike.
These, to be sure, were not the first illegal strikes the country
had experienced; but their stated aims, broad and indicative
of political awareness, in addition to the fact that they attracted support from nonworkers as well as workers, made
them more disturbing to the government than earlier ones had
been. Therefore what had seemed an inspiration to its crea-
tors was soon adjudged a very serious mistake. All the societies
were closed by the end of 1903, Zubatov was exiled, and the
idea of "police socialism" was disavowed by the government.
(That it was reintroduced within a few weeks was characteristic of the indecisiveness of the government's attempts to
handle the labor problem.)

THE EDUCATED CLASS AS A PROBLEM

Plehve, speaking for the government, had correctly designated the problem of the schools as one of the country's most
pressing, but he had failed to evaluate the situation that had
produced it—the antigovernment stirrings among the entire
educated class.

Those involved in that part of the situation recognized by
Plehve were the students of the universities, other schools of
higher learning, and occasionally also those of secondary
schools and theological seminaries. Throughout the empire,
they were concerning themselves with matters that the government considered quite unrelated to their proper employment,
and they were taking part in open, often disorderly, displays
of defiance and radicalism. There were many politically-con-
scious malcontents among them who might turn any class,
club, or association into a protest meeting or demonstration in
denunciation of some aspect of police conduct, governmental
policy, or administration. To express their feelings, students
often resorted to the boycotting of examinations, rioting or
arranging marches in sympathy with strikers or political prisoners, circulating petitions, or writing antigovernment propaganda. This exuberant disorder was at first interpreted by the

government merely as vexatious evidence of a lack of proper training in the precepts of patriotism and religion. Officials were disturbed to learn that the condition was widespread and that it was disrupting even the work of Russia's oldest and most distinguished seat of education, the University of Moscow; but they were confident that they could design measures for changing it. Some felt that a toughening-up of curricula and administrative practices was the answer; yet the situation showed little improvement after such measures as increasing the emphasis on classical languages and mathematics in the secondary schools and curbing the autonomous rights of the universities. Nor did expulsion, exile, or forced military service break up the spirited activity of the students. In fact, when the official decision to overhaul the whole educational system was finally made, in 1904, and to that end Vladimir Glazov, head of the General Staff Academy, was selected as Minister of Education, the students had grown bolder and more resistant than ever.

"SOCIETY" VERSUS "GOVERNMENT"

The expressions of discontent among the students were basically symptoms of a condition prevailing not only in the educational institutions but also far beyond their walls. It was a condition that marked one of the "two Russias," the one commonly called "society," made up of those among the educated whose principles were irreconcilable with the regime's and who, by their own definition, were the spokesmen for the *real* Russia. The other of the "two Russias" was, in popular reference, "government."

The gulf between society and government had begun to appear in the late eighteenth century, when certain men educated in Western modes and ideas, having examined Russian life and found it wanting, decided that the government was the actual bar to progress. Later, in the comparatively halcyon days of the reforms of Alexander II, there was some promise of reconciliation among the discordant conceptions of what was good for Russia, but it had receded when Alexander III established a policy freezing the existing order. And that was the policy on which the government was standing fast at the beginning of the twentieth century. Meanwhile, among the educated, growing in number and ambition, many had become alienated from, and increasingly frustrated by, a government apparently incapable of governing and unwilling to surrender a position it was unfit to occupy.

The spokesmen of society argued that Russia was culturally and materially backward not because she lacked the capacity for progress but because she lacked the freedom to realize her potential capacity. If government would only hearken to society or, perhaps, capitulate to it, Russia could resume the journey toward enlightenment and liberty that had been begun several times in the country's history (notably with the reforms of Peter the Great, Catherine II, Alexander I, and Alexander II) and then been interrupted.

The phrase "two Russias," identifying the opponents in the general political conflict of this period was a convenient one, and it has remained popular because of its brevity; but it should always be used with a consciousness of its limitations. Actually, there was not a clear-cut dichotomy in Russia—"society" on one hand and "government" on the other. Things-as-they-were did not conform to such a simple classification. Those among the educated who presumed to speak for all of Russian society were glossing over certain facts: the 74 percent of the population who were illiterate and the 19 percent who were barely literate were almost wholly unconcerned with the principal debate between conflicting factions; the clergy and the merchant class generally adhered to old traditions and had little interest in current trends; and a great part of the nobility was aligned by both heritage and interest with government. However, while the dichotomy itself was unreal, the belief in its existence was real; and that belief helped to sharpen differences between the government and the opposition by providing each with a definite image of itself and of its adversary. "Society" thought of itself as an idealistic fellowship of dedicated men and women struggling for truth and justice, and of the government as an organized group of bureaucrats who kept the country shackled by tradition and whose administration preserved unchanged the conditions of an outlived past. "Government," on the other hand, conceived of itself as the legitimate guardian of truth and justice, and of its opponents as a group of addled chatterers.

The opposition kept the government conscious of the problems; but problems, even such as those facing Russia at the turn of the century, do not necessarily lead to revolution. Revolution must be born in the minds of men; its very essence is the rejection of the legitimacy of constituted authority by a large part of those subject to that authority, and rejection is psychological rather than physical. Before 1905, only the self-deceived could believe that most of the Russian people had consciously broken with tsarism. Visible evidence argued the contrary. The hundreds of thousands who joined in mass demonstrations of devotion and loyalty whenever the Tsar visited the Kremlin, officiated at public formalities, or traveled anywhere in his empire testified to the popular inclination to venerate him as if he were a divine figure. Their affection might be described by some as only skin deep, but there was no way of proving it either genuine or superficial except by tests such as war or rebellion—and those tests were yet to be made. There was evidence, however, that antipathy toward existing authority was growing: slowly among the peasantry, at a faster rate among workers as well as among some of the national minorities, and most vigorously among the educated.

It was the educated, and particularly that element among them known as the "intelligentsia," heirs of a long tradition of intellectual probing of Russian life, who were critical of, and intermittently in conflict with, tsarism. The position of the most radical among them was often stated in some paraphrase of the harsh words that one of their number, Dmitri Pisarev, had written in the 1860's:

The dynasty of the Romanovs and the Petersburg bureaucracy must perish. . . . What is dead and rotten must of itself fall into the grave. All we still have to do is to give a last push and cover their stinking corpses with dirt.[9]

[9] D. Pisarev, *Select Philosophical, Social and Political Essays* (Moscow, 1958), p. 147.

The least radical believed that tsarism was legitimate and that it might be viable if it acted in time to rid itself of the bureaucracy and admit the people to a share in the government. In the preceding century, they had counselled patience, believing that it was the tsar's prerogative to initiate reforms and the subjects' obligation to carry out their duties in such a manner as to prove worthy of the reforms. But by 1904, even the hitherto patient were beginning to believe that reforms were past due, that time was running out for the regime.

ORGANIZED OPPOSITION TO THE GOVERNMENT

As the fateful year of 1905 approached, the illegal opposition facing the government was, all told, greater than any in the previous history of Russia. It was led by, and to a large extent composed of, *intelligents* (as members of the intelligentsia were called) : students enrolled in the universities and other institutions of higher learning, expelled students, and members of the professions. The "people" in whose name they spoke were at first poorly represented among them, but workers—and occasionally peasants—were beginning to recognize oppositional organizations as instruments capable of giving form to their discontent and strength to their aspirations.

The size of the opposition as it developed could not be taken as an accurate measure of its strength. It was divided into a bewildering variety of parties and groups—numerous enough to inspire the exaggeration that, for every Russian, there were two parties—and division is debilitating. The differences among some of these groups were clear only to the initiated. But all of them were aligned with one or the other of two opposition movements: the *revolutionary*, seeking to overthrow the regime by violence, replacing it with a democratic republic that at some future date would be supplanted by a socialist society; and the *liberal*, dedicated to the establishment of civil liberties and representative government by peaceful means.

Those in the revolutionary movement (mostly socialists but

including a few anarchists) agreed on a common goal but
were in such disagreement over tactics and doctrine that they
became divided into two major parties, the Russian Social
Democratic Labor Party[10] and the Russian Socialist Revolutionary Party.[11] The SD's were wedded to Marxism, with its
emphasis on the leading role of the working class and the
importance of mass revolutionary action. The SR's were affected by Marxism but eclectic in their philosophy. They gave
the peasantry a place of importance in their program and believed that revolution could be effected in a number of ways.
One of those methods, far removed from the mass action favored by the SD's, was based on terrorizing the government by
the assassination of its leading officials; to employ this method,
they formed a special branch known as the Fighting Organization. Within each party there were factions, which disagreed
over seemingly minor questions concerning tactics and organization: among the Social Democrats the factions were labeled
Bolshevik (majority) and *Menshevik* (minority) at an early
date, while the factions among the Socialist Revolutionaries
were not sufficiently defined to merit names until the end
of 1905.

Associated or affiliated with the two major revolutionary
parties were numerous national minority parties and groups.
Some of them—for instance, the Jewish Bund, the Lettish Social Democratic Party, and the Georgian Socialist-Federalists—
though differing with their Russian comrades over aspects of
the revolutionary program for the nationalities, agreed with
them that the overthrow of tsarism was necessary and that
cooperation among its opponents was feasible to a certain extent. However, other non-Russian socialist organizations preferred to dissociate themselves from the Russian revolutionary
movement and go their own ways toward the overthrow of
tsarism, for they wanted to be free of any possible interference
in other phases of their nationalistic programs. Among these,

10 This party is frequently called the RSDLP; and its members,
Social Democrats or SD's. For its program, *see* Appendix, p. 263.
11 Members of this party are commonly called Socialist Revolutionaries or SR's. For the party program, *see* Appendix, p. 268.

the most prominent was the right wing of the Polish Socialist Party—usually called the PPS, for *Polska Partia Socjalistycna*.

The revolutionary movement, despite the many differences among its leaders and the irregularity of its operations, had been a conscious concern of the government since 1881, when it had overreached itself in the assassination of Alexander II. After that, those who had been recognized as revolutionaries and apprehended had been granted no quarter. Many had been imprisoned in the Fortress of St. Peter and Paul or at Schlüsselberg, and many had been exiled to Siberia or remote parts of European Russia. Others had fled the country and found refuge abroad, most of them in Switzerland, France, or Germany, where many Russian students—not exiles, but young malcontents who were hostile to the regime—were attending various universities. For these self-exiles and political refugees, Geneva had become the revolutionary headquarters and favorite place of residence. So, while the movement within the country was being so policed that its activities were limited, localized, and generally ineffective, it was receiving inspiration and some direction, inconstant and irregular though they were, from the revolutionaries who were working at a distance and biding their time until they could return to Russia and to more immediate activity for their cause.

Of course the dedication and effectiveness of these out-of-country revolutionaries varied. And by no means did they agree on the reasons, procedures, or goals for the changes they proposed to effect in Russia. The majority of them argued incessantly about theory and tactics, defended various positions, contended for precedence, and often dissipated their usefulness in polemic and intrigue. But there were some whose energy and perseverance were to bring them to prominence and eventual leadership either in the Revolution of 1905 or in the covert revolutionary efforts that continued in its wake, finally to be resolved in 1917. In Geneva, there were the Social Democrats Plekhanov, Martov, Lenin, Trotsky, Dan, and Axelrod as well as the Socialist Revolutionaries Chernov and Gotz; in Paris, the Social Democrats Steklov and Ryazanov. Others, living apart from the centers of concentration, made personal efforts to spread an understanding of the revolutionary cause, and themselves became widely known champions. Typical of these was Catherine Breshkovskaya, who, with many years of imprisonment and Siberian exile behind her, was visiting the United States in 1904 and 1905 on behalf of the Socialist Revolutionaries.

By 1901, the revolutionary movement had managed to acquire a sufficient organization and following to justify an increased watchfulness in Russian officialdom. It was able, now and then, to make plans and get them into operation before the police were aware of them. However, it was to continue for some time to express itself in fits and starts. Mass response was undependable, and the police were able to contain whatever disturbances it could produce.

The liberals, even before they were organized, were divided into moderates and extremists. The moderates identified themselves from the beginning with the zemstvos (the municipal dumas, which might have been expected to favor the liberal opposition, stayed aloof until 1904). They were ably led during the period of their greatest influence by Dmitri Shipov, who between 1893 and 1904 occupied the most important zemstvo post in the country, that of Chairman of the Moscow Provincial Zemstvo Board. A member of the landed nobility and a monarchist by conviction, he was prominent among those who sought to convince the Tsar of the need for reform and of the advisability of expressing confidence in the people by permitting them to elect a national consultative assembly. Men of Shipov's conviction were committed to the use of legal means for achieving their ends. The zemstvos provided that means, and zemstvo leaders from various parts of the country often met to discuss common needs and aspirations. When the Ministry of Interior issued a ban on such meetings, in 1902, declaring them illegal because of their political nature, they were discontinued; but the idea of a national zemstvo organization survived in an organizational bureau, headed by Shipov, and was revitalized in 1904. National zemstvo meetings being prohibited, Shipov and other moderate liberals, including the Princes Peter and Paul Dolgorukov, formed a group of forty men called *Beseda* (Conversation) that met from time to time in Moscow to discuss zemstvo work and exerted an influence far greater than their limited number would suggest.

As early as 1901, the moderates among the liberals were being challenged by the extremists, who decried both the moderates' tactics and their aspirations as timid. One of the most prominent exponents of the extremists' position, Ivan Petrunkevich, had so repeatedly aroused official disfavor that for many years he had not been allowed the freedom necessary for leadership; yet there were plenty to help keep the group both prominent and vigorous. The majority of the extremists came from professional groups, though some came from the zemstvos. All of them, affected by the revolutionary example, wanted organization and action. Their first notable step was the founding, in 1901, of an illegal, liberal newspaper, *Liberation,* which was published in Germany and smuggled into Russia. It fulfilled its purpose as a means of organizing the liberals by helping to establish the Union of Liberation, which held its first congress in January, 1904.[12] Although the Union was designed as an organization for liberals of all kinds, it was dominated from the first by the extremists, a leader among whom was Paul Milyukov (quoted on p. 11 above). The principal aim of the Union was the establishment of a constitutional government elected by means of what became popularly known as four-tail suffrage—universal, equal, secret, and direct.

The Union of Liberation spoke for the majority of liberals, but certainly not for all of the people. Yet, of the different organizations claiming to speak for all, it had the greatest initial advantages: it represented a belief that was common to all in the opposition, that political freedom was the first step required in the regeneration of Russia; and its leaders, being dedicated to action, were more likely to be acceptable as coordinators of a general movement than were those who supported what many interpreted as temporizing tactics. This generally favored position of the Union of Liberation may be credited with the fact that the public's collective efforts to

[12] For the program of the Union of Liberation, *see* Appendix, p. 273.

establish liberty and representative government came to be
known as the "liberation movement."

The liberals' chances of success seemed slight, however,
despite their organization and program. The use of force
being denied by their own doctrine, they limited themselves
to peaceful—though not always legal—persuasion, working
through the zemstvos, professional associations, their own underground organizations, and whatever other means they
might contrive to spread the idea of liberalism. Their activities, adequate as they were to keep up their spirit and hopes,
did not seem strong enough to effect any change in the regime.
But the liberals were not therefore convinced of any need for
altering their course, their rationale being that, if "society"
were sufficiently outspoken, "government" would in time be
frightened into concession.

PLEHVE AND THE POLICY OF REPRESSION

At the beginning of 1904, however, the government was
showing no signs of responding as predicted. The Tsar's most
important minister, the vigorous Plehve, was keeping well informed, through his secret agents among the political police,
of the extent of the oppositional movement; but he was not
alarmed by it. He had changed his earlier attitude toward the
opposition as well as his methods of handling it, and he felt—
mistakenly, it was to be shown—that he now had it under control. When he had taken his post, two years earlier, replacing
the assassinated minister Dmitri Sipyagin, he had been full of
enthusiasm for his plans to solve the major problems and to
eliminate the visible signs of unrest by liquidating the oppositional organizations. When he could make little headway at
either, however, he had begun to rely on the repressive
strength of the police state to maintain order: putting the
affairs of more provinces under emergency "protection," using
the powers of censorship more indiscriminately, and directing
the political police to employ greater severity in quelling disorders and making arrests.

Measures such as these had silenced the opposition in the

years following the assassination of Alexander II, in 1881, and
had given Russia the superficial look of calm that Nicholas II
had observed in 1894. But the opposition was no longer so
easily intimidated by them. The two years of Plehve's tenure
of office saw the rapid spread of illegal organizations, the serious outbreaks among the peasants of Kharkov and Poltava,
the bitter—almost revolutionary—strikes in Transcaucasia and
southern Russia, and continuing student disorders. Such evidences of unrest and the government's failure to alleviate the
conditions producing them caused a greater number of "society" to feel that active opposition was legitimate, indeed
necessary, under the circumstances. And their feelings came to
be concentrated in hatred of Plehve, who, as Minister of Interior, was director of the state police and the symbol of "government." He was charged with gratuitous malevolence in the
Kishinev pogrom of 1903, in which forty-five Jews were mur-
dered in the presence of soldiers and police; and, although
the charge was only partially justified, it was accepted by the
opposition as wholly true and was used as an argument in
proving that the government was lost to humanity. And some
of his later official acts were to bring them to the conclusion
that the government was lost to reason also.

It is easy, with the gift of hindsight, to review the situation
in Russia at the beginning of 1904 and to conclude that she
was on the verge of inevitable revolution; to support that conclusion with defensible evidence would be far from easy. To
be sure, even if antigovernment activity reached a crest and
subsided, as it had in the past, the country's critical problems
would remain unsolved until the regime altered its course.
How soon that point would have been reached under prevailing circumstances, however, no one can say. If Russia had not
become involved in the war with Japan in 1904, affairs might
have taken a different turn; but the war came, and with it
a situation immediately favorable to revolution.

2

Shadow of Revolution

1904

May God bless Russia with peace and prosperity in the coming year.

> —Nicholas II, in a telegram to the Russian armed forces in the Far East, January 1, 1904.

With all Russia I believe that the hour of Our victory is approaching and the Lord God will bless My beloved army and navy with renewed strength to crush the enemy and to support the honor and glory of Our Fatherland.

> —Nicholas II, in "Order of the Day" to the Russian armed forces, January 1, 1905.

THE YEAR 1904 was a portentous one for the Russian monarchy. Yet Nicholas II, though he finally acknowledged some signs of danger and acted to avert immediate disaster, was able to retain his apparent complacency through the months of turmoil and to look ahead with confidence.

OUTBREAK OF WAR WITH JAPAN

A major part of his concern was forcibly drawn to affairs in the Far East, where Japan was proving a hindrance to the Russian government's reckless policy of imperialism in Manchuria and Korea. Neither country sought war; but Russia did not fear the prospect, and Japan, mindful of the threat to her national security as well as to her own imperialistic designs in Manchuria and Korea, was willing to fight if necessary.

The Tsar could not take seriously the possibility that a

small Asiatic country, just beginning a program of moderniza-
tion, would dare to break the peace with the mightiest land
power in the world. Consequently he could not believe that
the failure of the mid-1903 negotiations between Russia and
Japan regarding their respective interests in Korea and Manchuria might serve as a prelude to war. Yet, at the beginning
of 1904, although the Tsar had yielded on a few points, the
two countries were still far from agreement, and Japan was
becoming more threatening. At the traditional New Year's
Day reception for the diplomatic corps, Nicholas spoke "very
earnestly and sternly" (his own words) to the Japanese minister, informing him that Russia was "quite conscious of her
strength" and that there was a limit to her patience. He felt
that his words made the desired impression and that the
Japanese would soon adopt a more pacific tone.

The Russian military advisers predicted that, if Japan were
insane enough to go to war—though they still insisted that her
increasingly bellicose attitude was mere bluffing—Russia could
easily counter any of her moves. Japanese troops would probably be landed in northern Korea, which would then be used
as a staging area for a combined military and naval assault on
Port Arthur, the Russian naval base in southern Manchuria.
Some lighthearted optimists in the War Ministry saw no need
to anticipate even so much action: "One flag and one sen-
tinel," they said, "and the prestige of Russia will do the rest."
But soberer officials were willing to consider plans for a possible conflict, however improbable it might seem. Their plans
were based on the assumption that Japan would have an initial numerical advantage in her land forces but a slight inferiority in naval power; the Russian command in the theater
of operations would therefore use defensive tactics until reinforcements could arrive from European Russia; then, with
vastly superior numbers, Russia could begin offensive operations that would drive the "insolent Asiatics" into the sea and
permit the dictation of a crippling peace to the defeated
enemy. Acceptance of this attractive exaggeration led newspapers to depict the Russian army as defeating the inferior
Japanese by "snowing them under with their caps."

The early planning accepted certain premises that were to

be proved disastrously mistaken: that, against Russia's war strength of three million men, Japan would be able to put a maximum of only five hundred thousand into the field—a figure too small by one million; that Russian officers were superior to the Japanese; that Russian naval superiority in the Pacific would engage Japanese attention long enough for the movement of Russian troops to reinforce those already in Manchuria; and finally—most disastrously mistaken of all— that, if war should come, it would be fought with the support of a united and enthusiastic civilian population.

The unexpected war began on the night of January 27, 1904, the opening attack preceding even the formal declaration of war; and it brought with it the test not only of Russian military plans but also of the morale of the Russian people. The Japanese opened hostilities, not by landing in northern Korea as expected, but by engaging the Russian Pacific squadron at Port Arthur and, with the advantage of surprise, sinking many of the vessels and destroying Russia's boasted naval superiority in the Pacific area.

It was customary for Russian rulers to announce the country's entrance into war at a special ceremony in the Kremlin of the "old capital," Moscow. Nicholas II omitted this traditional act at the opening of the war with Japan; yet the people throughout the country responded to the news of the attack on Port Arthur as they had always responded to a formal, official announcement. In the streets of the cities, crowds demonstrated patriotically, cheering the assembling soldiers and singing "God Save the Tsar." The first shock of war impressed even the students of the University of St. Petersburg, who made a patriotic march to the Winter Palace. The Tsar was buoyed up; he wrote to his cousin William II of Germany that the outbreak of hostilities had "stirred the generally sleepy nature" of his people. The war was expected to be a short one, and many were imaginatively savoring the taste of an early victory. Admiral Alexeyev, in command of all Russian armed forces in the Far East, expressed the fear that the Tsar would let the war end too quickly, allowing the Japanese an easy peace after only a slight pinch of defeat. As it turned out, the war was neither short nor victorious. And the initial fervor of patriotism that caused the temporary shifting back of many into the traditional feeling for tsar and fatherland was quickly dissipated, having provided the government with only a brief respite from domestic troubles. The familiar problems remained, and soon there was no foreseeable chance that the people might again return of their own accord to a conciliatory mood.

THE ASSEMBLY OF ST. PETERSBURG FACTORY WORKERS

The one notable venture into domestic problem solving at this time was, in reality, a renewal of what had been officially stamped as a fiasco at the end of the preceding year: "police socialism." That it was given a second trial was due to the insistence of a St. Petersburg priest, Father George Gapon, who, as a young prison chaplain (he was now in his early thirties), had been closely in touch with the great undercurrent of discontent in the country. Believing that there had been unrealized promise in the government's first attempt to alleviate this discontent by making legal provisions for workers' meetings and group activities, he persuaded the Prefect of St. Petersburg, General Nicholas Kleigels, to allow him to start in that city a labor society similar to those that had been so peremptorily disbanded in 1903. Then with the approval of the succeeding prefect, General Ivan Fullon, and the sanction of Minister of Interior Plehve, he proceeded to promote the organization throughout the factories of the city.

In February, 1904, Plehve approved the charter of the newly organized body, the Assembly of St. Petersburg Factory Workers, and two months later, the first branch of the Assembly was officially opened. Membership was limited to workers of Russian nationality and the Christian faith, since they were believed to be the most reliable. The aim of the Assembly, from the official point of view, was the same as that of the previous experiment in "police socialism": to immunize the workers against revolutionary ideas and to maintain and strengthen monarchist and nationalist sentiments among them. They were to have an association in a wholesome, moral, nationalist, and Orthodox environment, where they could improve their lot in a number of ways. They might set up their own stores and tea rooms, establish mutual-aid funds, attend lectures and concerts, or take part in group recreational activities. In addition, they were to have legally approved opportunities for discussing their needs and legitimate grievances. However, they would not be permitted to discuss political matters or to organize trade unions. All activities were to be in charge of Gapon, who would report secretly to the prefect, occasionally receive funds, and be under constant surveillance by numerous police agents.

Despite the government's hopes and the diligence of Gapon, the initial response of the workers was not an enthusiastic one. In the first half of the year, the Assembly had but a modest following, somewhat over a thousand. The early months of the war were not a propitious time for organization.

DECLINE IN MORALE

However, when month after month passed and Russian forces were still not able to open the offensive that was supposed to drive the Japanese from the Manchurian area in which the war had become concentrated, labor as well as the people at large, having lost their earlier patriotic elation, began turning to matters of more personal concern and again becoming critical of the government. Those first months of fighting could be interpreted on the home front only as a period of defeat and humiliation: most of the Russian Pacific squadron sunk, Port Arthur besieged, the Japanese pushing relentlessly north after landing in southern Manchuria, needed reinforcements limited by the inadequacy of the Trans-Siberian Railroad, which could carry four military trains a day, only two of which were troop trains. It was not a heartening picture.

The Tsar looked upon the war as the country's only proper employment at the time and, despite difficulties and disappointing turns, he was prepared to see it through to the last Russian soldier and the last kopeck in the imperial coffers. But it was becoming evident that his dedication and purpose were not generally shared. The men in Manchuria fought stolidly and uncomplainingly, but with little notion of why they were there; the average soldier could not be expected to believe that the object of his fighting was this distant and, to him, worthless Manchuria. Also, among those not engaged, there was practically no understanding of the goals of the war, for insufficient effort was being made to give them any acquaintance with its nature or to arouse their concern. Most of the country's soldiers remained in Europe during the war, their only active experience being gained through the quelling of disturbances by strikers and demonstrators. The sailors in the Black Sea Fleet, prohibited by various treaties from leaving the Black Sea, were mindful only of fleet affairs; and those of the Baltic bases and the Baltic Fleet, until the latter were sent to the Far East, were as remote from the war in spirit as in body. Even the guards regiments were relatively untouched by it. Moreover, from neither the guards regiments nor the line regiments in the rear did many officers volunteer for service in Manchuria; the few who did so were regarded as oddities.

As the war continued, a bizarre situation developed: here was a country engaged in one of the bloodiest wars in history, giving little evidence of involvement. True, the Tsar reviewed troops destined for the front, groups of reservists were seen at the stations as they left their families to entrain for the front, aristocratic ladies rolled bandages, occasionally a wounded soldier would be seen. But, except for the suspension of the Court's social program, life went on as usual. Most able-bodied men were in civilian clothes, and most men in uniform had no contact with the war. News from the front was printed and read; but its effect was not the sparking of patriotism, rather the reinforcement of antigovernment propaganda pointing out that those who ruled Russia were inefficient and corrupt.

The war's effect was damaging also to the domestic economy. When hostilities had broken out, the country was just recovering from the economic depression of 1900-1903. And, whereas some wars supply economic impetus by providing extra employment and increasing civilian income, the Russo-Japanese War actually retarded the recovery that had begun the year before its outbreak. Some industries, notably the metallurgical and leather, benefited from an increase in government orders. But the textile industry, Russia's largest, declined because the call-up of reservists cut civilian income, and thereby the demand for textiles, to an extent not offset by increased governmental demand. Consequently in many textile centers, particularly in Lodz, employment dropped. The managements of even the more fortunate industries seldom passed any of their increased profits on to the workers; more often they required overtime work without overtime premium, all the while holding wage rates to the low prewar levels. Thus the net economic effect of the war was to extend, rather than reduce, areas of tension. And labor, now fortified in some industries with the experience gained in the mass strikes of 1902 and 1903, grew more restive, more hostile to management, and more contemptuous—if concerned at all—with the country's war effort. In almost every industrial center, there was the scent of trouble, though actual evidence of it was often difficult to detect; and, until it manifested itself, no particular effort was made to root it out.

In the countryside the effects of the prolonged conflict were less marked but, where evident, were mainly negative. The call-up of reservists, most of them peasants, was not large enough to upset the peasant economy seriously, but it had an adverse effect on morale. With each reported defeat in Manchuria, peasant enthusiasm for the war decreased; and the number of reservists failing to report for duty increased each month. The situation, though not yet alarming, was significant; peasant response might be slow but, if directed, it could become a stubborn force with which to reckon.

Gradually, even among the military personnel, what had been chiefly indifference was taking on a more serious aspect here and there. The Social Democrats began in 1904 to organize their first circles among the troops, those in the capital and at the Kronstadt naval base. And, in the first half of that year, ninety-seven soldiers were tried for political offenses—a small number, but greater than in preceding years. Yet there was no general or coordinated disaffection among the armed forces, for they were too numerous and too widely dispersed to be readily influenced even if they had been receptive to subversive persuasion. In all, over a million reservists were summoned to service during the war, the reserve battalions and regiments being assimilated into existing divisions. Their strength might have been coveted by the antigovernment leaders, but it was a force not readily attainable. The elite guards regiments in St. Petersburg seemed impervious to propaganda as did also the troops at the front, who were scarcely touched by dissension as long as the fighting continued. The prisoners of war in Japanese camps and the troops in the rear were the ones most likely to be reached and affected. The reservists particularly, men just taken from the farm, factory, or office, were much more responsive to antigovernment propaganda than those in the standing army. Although there were few socialists among them, many of those able to read were ready to accept and study the antiwar leaflets distributed by the socialists. Also, many of them were affected by being used against strikers and rioting crowds with whom they were personally sympathetic. But, on the whole, authority was respected and effective among the troops until well into 1905.

As for the organized groups of the political opposition, their programs were still far too disparate to allow their realization of gains they might have made against a government under stress. The socialists, of course, denounced Russia's position as imperialistic; but, as long as there was a measure of public enthusiasm, an antiwar position was a hindrance rather than a help to its proponents. The liberals were weakened and more widely divided by the beginning of the war. The moderates among them, while deploring the foreign policy that had involved the country in conflict, thought it impolitic to argue about the wisdom of it and unpatriotic not to support the fatherland. The extremists, on the other hand, regarded the war as a disguised blessing, for it would decrease the power of their political "enemy"; they felt—as did many others privately—that the worse the war went for the government, the better the ultimate results would be for the people. Between the moderates and the extremists were other liberals who, though not in accord with the turn of events, felt that patriotic sentiment coupled with pleas for reform would be

more effective in bringing change than would open opposition.

On the whole, the effect of the first three months of the war
was to retard the growth of the liberation movement, even
while providing conditions that would later favor it. A different government might have used that early opportunity to
court the more moderate of the opposition; but official opinion, as expressed through Plehve, upheld domestic-policy-as-
usual. And, since the government regarded public support as
something to be commanded rather than sought and won, it
succeeded in destroying whatever patriotic good will the war
had initially aroused.

First came the further alienation of the zemstvo liberals by
Plehve. Shortly after the Japanese attack, they attempted to
form an all-zemstvo organization, with Prince George Lvov as
chairman, to aid sick and wounded soldiers as well as the
families of those who were killed. Plehve demanded that, before any work was begun, the names of the personnel involved
should be submitted for his approval. His order was disobeyed, and he retaliated by refusing—as was his right—to confirm the February election of several zemstvo chairmen, the
most prominent among whom was Dmitri Shipov, who had
been elected for his fifth term as chairman of the Moscow
Provincial Zemstvo Board. To that rebuff the Moscow zemstvo
replied with an act of defiance—which just happened to succeed: the election, as successor to Shipov, of Fedor A. Golovin,
who was closer to the extremist Milyukov than to the moderate Shipov and therefore likely to be the more antipathetic
to Plehve's policies. The results only emphasized the widen-
ing breach: the government continued to believe that the
zemstvos were using the war as an excuse to increase their
power, and the zemstvo liberals now believed that the government would rather lose the war than cooperate with "society."

Plehve's refusal to confirm Shipov's election came in April,
a month that may be taken as the turning-point in the wartime relations between the "two Russias." The period of so-
called good will was now definitely on the wane, and antago-
nisms were rising.

Among the national minorities there had been no particular

reason for any change in attitude. In Finland, the intensity of
the Russification policy that had turned most of the people
against the Russian government was unabated; in Congress
Poland, while thousands of Polish reservists were joining their
units to serve Russia, no change was being made in the much-
resented official policy; in Transcaucasia, the turmoil that had
begun nearly seven years earlier, with the imposition of a
Russification policy on the Armenians, continued and bitterness spread; and in Jewish communities, despite the fact that
a greater number of Jews were fighting in Manchuria than
was consistent with the Jewish proportion of the population,
there was no mitigation of the anti-Semitic campaign with
which Plehve's name was linked.

It would have been difficult to determine the exact focus of
the hatred that was being built up throughout the empire,
but a few prominent men were select targets. Plehve, blamed
personally for most of the obnoxious domestic policies, was
one of them. And, as might be expected, the men who represented the regime's arbitrary control over the areas under
"protection" were often hated with intensity not only by those
subject to their authority but also by revolutionaries at large;
they were convenient symbols of the government's excesses
and repression. Singled out for particular vindictiveness because of the severity with which they administered reactionary
and anti-Semitic policies were the Grand Duke Sergei Alexandrovich, Governor-General of Moscow; the Grand Duke
Vladimir Alexandrovich, Commander-in-Chief of the St.
Petersburg Military District; General Nicholas Kleigels, Governor-General of Kiev since early in 1904; General Viktor von
Wahl, former Governor of Vilna and, since 1902, Assistant
Minister of Interior and Commander of the Corps of Gendarmes; and Prince Gregory Golitsyn, in command of both
civil and military affairs in Transcaucasia.

Equally detested was Governor-General Nicholas Bobrikov
of Finland, who became one of the first in 1904 to pay the
tragic cost of intolerable government. After nearly five years of
determined and brutal effort, he had not succeeded in forcing
the Finns and the Swedes (who formed an upper-class minority in Finland) to accept Russification; nor had he re-

treated from his position. With the situation thus deadlocked in June, young patriot Eugen Schaumann decided to relieve it by sacrificing both Bobrikov and himself. To that end, he shot and killed the governor-general and then committed suicide, leaving behind him a message to the Tsar in which he called attention to the "grave evil" existing not only in Finland but also in other parts of the empire. His effort was in vain: the Tsar felt that he had lost a valuable servant difficult to replace; but he continued to feel, as he had when he appointed Bobrikov, that the Finns were being misled by a minority of troublemakers, whom a firm hand applied long enough would convert to right-mindedness. In choosing a successor, he was not as interested in severity as in strength of will, the determination to perform a task properly, however unpleasant. He chose Prince Ivan Obolensky, a man not quite as strong as Bobrikov but one who, as Governor of Kharkov, had distinguished himself by the dispatch with which he had put down the peasant troubles of 1902. Thus one target of hatred was replaced by another.

By the middle of 1904, Nicholas II, then at his favorite summer residence, Peterhof, was facing an accumulation of troubles that seemed almost insurmountable. He was sending Obolensky to Finland, but he knew that the situation there was still an uneasy one. He had just received from Golitsyn a disturbing report of an equally uneasy situation in Transcaucasia. The Tsarina, his beloved Alix, was in the last month of pregnancy, desperately hoping that, after four girls, she would bear a son, who could inherit the throne. And his waiting for a good report from Manchuria was prolonged and unrelieved; the land forces, in charge of General Alexis Kuropatkin,[1] were not yet ready to begin the promised offensive.

---

[1] At this time, all operations were still under the superior command of Admiral Alexeyev, to whom Kuropatkin often showed such insubordination that the Tsar had to intervene. In October, when Alexeyev was finally recalled from the Far East, at his own request, he was not replaced; and thereafter, Kuropatkin was left with the sole responsibility of commanding the land forces.

REACTIONARY POLICY CHALLENGED

But even such troubles were temporarily eclipsed for the Tsar on July 15 by the morning report of his palace commandant: in St. Petersburg, a bomb thrown by a revolutionary had just taken the life of Minister of Interior Plehve. It was not the first time that the opposition had struck so openly and directly at his government; two years earlier Plehve's predecessor, Sipyagin, had been killed by a Socialist Revolutionary, and dozens of lesser officials representing "government" had been assassinated in the past five years. But the thrusts were becoming more frequent. The Tsar was not given to demonstration; and, though saddened, he showed no evidence that he was alarmed by the incident. The day's entry in his diary stated simply, "In the person of my good Plehve I have lost a friend and an irreplacable Minister of Interior."

Popular response to Plehve's death was of a different order. There were both sympathy and acclaim for the one who threw the fatal bomb, Egor Sazonov, an expelled university student and member of the Fighting Organization, terroristic arm of the Socialist Revolutionary Party. Plehve had been chosen by the revolutionaries as a particularly odious official whose death, it was hoped, would help to put fear into the government and arouse in the populace a revolutionary spirit. The results were not as planned; but, when news of the assassination spread, the perpetrators must have received some satisfaction from the public demonstration of hatred for their victim. A man had been blown to bits, his coachman and horse killed, an accompanying officer severely wounded; and thousands cheered because the object of the atrocity represented their oppressors. The newspaper *Liberation* expressed the view of most of the opposition in its statement that the killing of the minister was the logical culmination of the policies the government had been following since 1881—policies which, it implied, had to be renounced. Even some police officials felt that Plehve's death, though deplorable, was opportune since his repressive policies could not be enforced indefinitely.

For more than five weeks, the ministerial post remained
vacant; and public anxiety mounted day by day, for no official
indication was given concerning the steps being considered,
whether further repression, more arrests, or—less likely—some
kind of change in the government. During that time, many
loyal servants of the crown insisted that the government must,
as it had in 1880, temper the policy of repression and make
some effort to win back popular support. Prince Vladimir
Meshchersky, one of the most reactionary journalists in the
empire, spoke of the late minister as a representative of the
"atrophying spirit of St. Petersburg bureaucracy." Whether or
not the Tsar himself took the tragic incident and the people's
reception of it as a sign that there was a need for a policy
change cannot be determined by evidence. It is reported that
he first decided to replace Plehve with Boris Stürmer, a man
of similar views; and that, only through the intervention of
his mother, the Dowager Empress Maria Feodorovna, was he
convinced that he should appoint a man who would regain
public support. It is not known whether his final decision was
a response to advice or an expression of his personal judgment; however, during the waiting, there occurred a suggestion of change in his estimate of the situation. On August 11,
to mark the christening of his son, the Tsesarevich Alexis, he
extended some unusual gratuities to his people: the abolition
of the right of peasant courts to impose corporal punishment,
the ending of corporal punishment in the army, and the granting of minor improvements in the status of the Jews—for example, the right of veterans of the current war to live outside
the Pale. Though these concessions did not represent any
great change in conditions, they served to heighten the anticipation of the public waiting for news of the new appointment.

BEGINNING OF POLITICAL "SPRING"

On August 25, Nicholas offered the post of Minister of Interior to Prince Peter Svyatopolk-Mirsky, and on the following
day the appointment was announced officially. Public suspense
was relieved, and the response was gratifying to official ears.

Articulate leaders proclaimed that the day was the beginning of a liberal "spring"; and everywhere there was a visible easing up of tension among the people.

In a formal record, the new minister would seem a most unlikely harbinger of spring. His background and experience were impeccably aristocratic, military, and bureaucratic. He was a graduate of the courtly Corps of Pages, veteran of the Russo-Turkish War of 1877-78, alumnus of the guards regiments, former Director of the Department of Police in the Ministry of Interior; and, since 1902, he had been Governor-General of Vilna and Commander of the Vilna Military District. There were dozens of men with almost identical backgrounds in the empire, men with no political philosophy except that based on service to the throne. What distinguished him from the others was a difference, not in philosophy, but in attitude. And the evidences of that attitude had won him a wide public approval. He had left the Ministry of Interior in 1902 because of lack of sympathy for the tactics of Plehve. Moreover, he had gained a reputation for mildness as Governor-General of Vilna, where large numbers of Poles, Jews, and Lithuanians had made for a long history of conflict between government and residents.

Svyatopolk-Mirsky opened his term by removing General von Wahl and others of Plehve's lieutenants from important posts in the ministry and announcing that his program would be designed to demonstrate official confidence in the people and to eliminate the conditions separating the people and their government. The hopes that these first acts and words aroused were totally disproportionate to his intentions and certainly to those of his sovereign. Nevertheless, with his taking office, the change in public attitude was indeed like a spring thaw after a long, hard winter. Even the conservative *Novoe Vremya* expressed hope for the coming of a rapprochement between government and society that would strengthen the country in its struggle with the enemy on the battlefield and with the subversive elements at home.

The two who were expected to interpret and direct the anticipated policy changes, Nicholas II and Svyatopolk-Mirsky, though congenial in many respects, were not so constituted as to be comfortably paired for the new course. The Tsar, in the ten years of his reign, had achieved a public reputation that was quite prejudicial to his leadership. He was generally believed to be without firmness of character or will, yielding to the advice of the person he had last seen, and especially subject to the influence of the ultra-reactionary "grand ducal party" (a popular designation for those members of the imperial family who had earned public ill will through their severity in discharge of official duties). The reputation was undeserved. Plehve had come much nearer to a proper evaluation of the Tsar when he described him to a new minister as "soft, but stubborn," responding to pressure and persuasion only to a limited degree. In fact, he was a man of courage, of definite and—unfortunately—unchanging convictions, one who admired strength, consistency, and decisiveness but gave the impression of having none of these virtues. His soft-spoken, kindly manner, his aversion to emotional demonstration and dramatic conduct, and his average physical make-up put him in strong contrast to other members of the Romanov family, which tended toward big men of decided character, high-mettled, and of aristocratic aspect. But he might have changed the popular impression if he had understood, at the time, the basic nature of the new course, appreciated its gravity, and attended differently to the business of pursuing it. His failure to do so, though understandable, was unfortunate. Trained to be a tsar and kept apart from the people, he had no conception of public opinion; he understood neither its importance nor the devices for handling it. He had agreed reluctantly to make some gestures of appeasement after Plehve's death; but he had no intention of changing any of the government's basic policies, in which he believed with deep sincerity. He simply hoped that the gestures would pacify the dissatisfied and permit the country to return to its immediate and most important duty, winning the war with Japan.

Svyatopolk-Mirsky, with all his good will and honest intentions, was soon to recognize the awkwardness of dealing with both the Tsar's reluctance and the public's urgency to get new policies under way. To keep the confidence of the Tsar and to gain and hold the support of an over-expectant public would

have taxed an effective administrator and a strong leader—and
he was neither. His position was made the more difficult because he could make some conciliatory moves, but the limits of
those moves were not defined; and he could make some concessions, but they must not be such as to allow any public
participation in the affairs of state or even any public discussion of them. However, Svyatopolk-Mirsky was a hopeful man,
and he set about his new duties with vigor.

For a while Russian affairs seemed to be improving everywhere. Even the fortunes of the dishearteningly dragging war
with Japan became more favorable. On September 22, General
Kuropatkin began the long-deferred offensive against the
main Japanese forces, at Shaho, south of Mukden. Six days
later, the Baltic Fleet left its berth for a journey of 18,000
miles to Port Arthur with the aim of relieving the besieged
port and destroying Japanese control of the sea. The Tsar was
kept occupied for weeks with receiving, visiting, and reviewing
military and naval units—in the capital, in Odessa, Suwalki,
Revel, Dvinsk, Vitebsk.

Meanwhile the Minister of Interior was carrying on a campaign on two fronts. On the one, he was drafting and urging
the bureaucracy's acceptance of legislation he deemed necessary to remove causes of discontent; on the other, he was seeking to reestablish contact and good relations between the
government and society. His initial efforts were well received
by the public. The press wrote enthusiastically and confidently
of things the "spring" held in store for the country. And many
writers shared the inspiration of the poet who found the air
pleasant with ". . . warmth and light/ And everything . . .
gowned in the garments of spring."

The new minister based much of his activity on the conviction, ardently supported by such men as Shipov, still head of
the zemstvo organizational bureau, that the zemstvos spoke for
society and that the way to civic peace was through good governmental relations with them. One of his first acts, therefore,
was to end the Plehve policy of harassment of the zemstvos.
He rescinded the restrictions and punishments that had been
imposed on their leaders and thereby won respect for the sincerity of his announced intentions. Among those affected by

these acts was one of the veterans of zemstvo liberalism, the
sixty-year-old Ivan Petrunkevich, who had often been arrested
and exiled for his outspoken opinions and who, for twenty
years, had been deprived of the right to live in the capital. In
further acknowledgement of the importance of the zemstvos,
Svyatopolk-Mirsky expressed his belief that they were needed
in those provinces where none had been organized, and he
was responsive to the idea of adding to the State Council men
elected by the zemstvos.

All considered, it was as if a family dispute were being
settled, the Minister of Interior acting on behalf of the government; Shipov, on behalf of society as represented by the
zemstvos. Through Alexis Lopukhin, Director of the Department of Police (followed later by Sergei Herbel, Head of the
Chief Administration for the Affairs of Local Economy), the
minister negotiated with Shipov until the latter was both encouraged and impressed with the possibilities he envisioned
for the future.

GROWTH OF LIBERATION MOVEMENT

But Svyatopolk-Mirsky, as it turned out, did not in fact
speak for the government; and Shipov did not speak for society. What had seemed a family matter proved to be a con-
geries of internal conflicts. The new course as it was conceived
could not bring domestic peace. However, by showing that the
government would retreat under pressure, it provided the
impetus needed by the liberation movement; and by giving a
measure of freedom to the expression of public opinion, it
provided the opportunity for the movement to transform itself
into open political action.

The liberals remained divided, however, on the question of
procedure. Shipov and his followers saw the political "spring"
as a time for talking freely and rationally with the government in order to bring it to its senses. The extreme liberals
following Milyukov, on the other hand, had no faith in the
government's honor or wisdom and believed that it would
yield only to pressure. For them the "spring" was a time to
organize the entire opposition for political action to force con-

cessions. Though still unfavorable to armed uprising and general strike, they were now willing to threaten by indicating them as possibilities. Then, they reasoned, if the government should still refuse to yield, and revolution should ensue, the government would have only itself to blame.

For the revolutionaries the "spring" brought an opportunity and an embarrassment. Restiveness was still widespread, for many of its deep-seated causes were untouched by the changes being made; and, since police restrictions had been relaxed, it was stirred the more easily into organized activity. Antiwar and antigovernment propaganda were now being dispensed with greater facility and strikes were on the increase. Study circles (small, organized groups of revolutionaries) were flourishing. In addition, the Fighting Organization of the SR's, encouraged by the effect of its last action, continued planning; the assassins were to aim next at the Grand Duke Sergei Alexandrovich, the Grand Duke Vladimir Alexandrovich, and General Nicholas Kleigels. Yet, despite the fact that their activities were being carried out under unusually propitious conditions, the revolutionaries could not agree on their immediate aim—and therein lay the source of their great embarrassment during the "spring."

One of the initial reasons for this lack of agreement was the fact that most of the leadership was remote from the scene. Still "wanted" by the political police, most of the leaders remained abroad, deeply involved in the early and difficult stages of organizing their respective parties, still arguing theory and tactics. In some instances, particularly among the Social Democrats and their feuding Menshevik and Bolshevik factions, there seemed to be more concern with party politics than with events in Russia. However, since the revolutionaries had a following of potential value in Russia, they were constrained to divert some attention from argument to the determination of a position with respect to the "spring." They did not see it as a prelude to revolution but—agreeing with the extreme liberals—as an opportunity for exerting political pressure on the government. They agreed with the liberals also on the first goal to be sought: the establishment of a democratic regime. But, at that point, interparty agreement broke down.

The Bolsheviks, as well as a few Mensheviks and SR's, had little faith in the "liberal bourgeoisie"; the lesson of history as they interpreted it was that the liberals would betray the revolution and sell out to the government for political privileges that would benefit only themselves; therefore it behooved the revolutionaries to work alone toward the establishment of a democratic republic. Most Mensheviks and SR's, however, could see some utility in joining hands with the liberals.

They held that the revolutionaries could use different tactics, maintain their own organizations, aspire to the ultimate establishment of socialism and, at the same time, accept the liberal goals for the immediate future and even cooperate with the liberals in their political actions. The two approaches —of the Bolsheviks on the one hand and of the Mensheviks and SR's on the other—continued to affect the reaction of their respective adherents to the successive stages of progress toward revolution. However, as time went on, factional and interparty differences often manifested themselves more sharply in word than in deed; and the lines between factions, between one revolutionary party and another—even between the revolutionary and liberal movements—were often crossed, for the belief persisted among members of the opposition that the liberation movement was a common one.

To make a practical application of that belief, a conference of socialist and liberal parties and groups was called. Meeting in Paris from September 30 to October 9, it considered and attempted to define the points of mutual concern among them. Those participating were an impressive representation of the extent of the organized opposition: the Union of Liberation, the Polish National League, the Finnish Party of Active Resistance, the Socialist Revolutionary Party, the Lettish Social Democratic Party, the Polish Socialist Party, the Georgian Socialist-Federalists, the Armenian Revolutionary Federation. Also impressive was the program upon which they agreed. It emphasized their common determination to

1) "speed the inevitable fall of absolutism,"
2) abolish "the autocratic regime" and replace it with "a free democratic one based on universal suffrage,"

3) reestablish Finnish rights,
4) remove restrictions on national minorities,
5) insure "the right of national self-determination."[2]

The program contained some rather equivocal phraseology, part of it deliberate. "Regime" rather than "republic" was intended to be acceptable to those liberals who favored a monarchy, and yet not be repugnant to those who preferred a republic. "The right of national self-determination" could be —and indeed was intended to be—construed according to the preference of the reader. Of course, equivocal phraseology did not remove political differences, but it obscured differences that would not have to be settled in the immediate future. It would be a long time before the question of "republic or monarchy," for instance, would be a real one; and, in the meantime, calls for such things as the abolition of "the autocratic regime" could well serve as rallying cries for the entire opposition.

Soon the extreme liberals were not only finding allies outside the liberation movement but also capturing the movement from its distinguished moderate leaders. The latter achievement had its beginning within a month after the Paris conference. Encouraged by the appointment of Svyatopolk-Mirsky, the zemstvo organizational bureau, led by Shipov, had decided in early September to promote a countrywide congress in Moscow for the purpose of considering zemstvo problems and rights and making an effort to regain for the zemstvos the strength that Plehve had taken from them. The bureau's aim, as first decided upon, had been a modest one. But when Svyatopolk-Mirsky announced, a few days after their decision, that he intended to demonstrate the government's confidence in society, the majority of them, all of whom were either members of the Union of Liberation or its sympathizers, raised their sights. If the government wished to show its confidence in society, they reasoned, it should agree to *political changes* indicating that the confidence was warranted; and they forthwith began drawing up "theses" to be presented to the congress as suggestions of political changes for which they would

[2] *Revolyutsionnaya Rossiya*, December 5, 1904.

agitate. Shipov found himself a minority of one in opposing the change in the scope of the proposed congress. And Svyatopolk-Mirsky, who had gained the Tsar's assent to the meeting as first planned (if it were held in St. Petersburg), looked askance at the proposal that its agenda be broadened to include political problems. However, when he could get neither the Tsar's approval for a changed agenda nor the zemstvo organizational bureau's agreement to alteration or postponement, he declared that if the congress would meet in private quarters rather than in a public hall, no law would be broken and no police action would be taken against it.

So, for four days beginning on November 6, the congress met in various private homes in St. Petersburg. Shipov, still the revered leader, was chosen as its chairman; but the honor soon proved to be only a formal one. The assembly at once took a rebellious stance, making the adoption of a political program its principal business. Among its leading figures (men such as Ivan Petrunkevich, Prince Peter Dolgorukov, Fedor Rodichev, Prince Dmitri Shakhovskoi, Prince George Lvov, Nicholas Lvov, Yuri Novosiltsev, Count Peter Heyden, and Sergei Muromtsev) there was no patience with any idea of expressing humble wishes; they thought of themselves as speaking for the nation at a fateful time, a time after which it would be too late for the Tsar to make peace with the people.

Having discussed and reached majority agreement on certain amendments to the theses proposed by the bureau, the congress expressed its stand in the succinct terms of eleven theses.[3] The essential points of the adopted theses concerned the need for the government to heal the rift between itself and society by establishing the legal equality of all citizens of the empire and by permitting the people to participate in the governmental process through 1) the election of representatives to take part in the legislative work of both central and local government and 2) by the exercise, under guarantee, of such basic rights as the freedom of press, speech, religion, association, and assembly.

A year later, these theses would seem timid; but, in Novem-

[3] For the text of the Eleven Theses, *see* Appendix, p. 279.

ber, 1904, they were dramatic, bold, and militant. They did not satisfy all of the opposition, of course: the moderate liberals felt that they were too ambitiously demanding, and others felt that they touched too lightly on the agrarian, nationality, and labor problems. For the months immediately following the congress, however, these overt declarations by a part of the nobility were to serve generally as the minimum program of the opposition.

Having committed the initial act of defiance, the congress then called upon all local zemstvos to send petitions to the Tsar supporting the Eleven Theses, thus creating in effect a national political association. But it was a vague and divided association: a minority at the congress had followed Shipov in opposing some of the theses, and they had no intention of capitulating. Moreover, it lacked the tradition and the united will for a political campaign carried beyond the zemstvos. That was to be the work of the Union of Liberation, many of whose leaders—men such as Petrunkevich, Peter Dolgorukov, and Shakhovskoi—were also powerful figures in the left wing of the zemstvo movement.

Meeting illegally, but without interference, in St. Petersburg at the end of October, the leaders of the Union of Liberation had come to an agreement on the operation of the political campaign to the aim of which they were already committed: the replacement of the autocracy by a democratic regime. They planned to work through meetings of district and provincial zemstvos; meetings of municipal dumas; the anticipated November zemstvo congress; unions, to be formed in the various professions and ultimately to be united in a union of unions; and banquets of a political nature, the first ones of which were to be held on November 20 (ostensibly to celebrate the fortieth anniversary of the legal reforms through which Russia had been granted a modern system of courts). On the tactical side, the plans were equally definite: in the designated bodies, meetings, and banquets, the Liberationists (members of the Union) would propose petitions calling on the Tsar to provide for a popularly elected national assembly that would frame and adopt a democratic constitution.

The aim of all this concerted action was to mobilize the

entire educated class of the country and to convince the Tsar
of the need to submit. And the Liberationists were confident
that their tactics would prove effective. Certainly they had no
urge to use revolutionary means. A few weeks earlier, however, they had made an alliance—very tenuous, to be sure—
with the revolutionaries at the Paris conference; and, by that
alliance, whether they approved or not, they were morally ob-
ligated to support revolution if peaceful persuasion failed.
Such a step was completely abhorrent, of course, to the moderate liberals. But in November and December of 1904 the
possibility of revolution seemed remote, and the opportunity
for peaceful political campaigning was better than it had ever
been.

The Liberationists and their allies used the opportunity
well. In late November and early December, Russia was the
scene of activities that had never before been conceivable
there. It appeared that almost the entire middle and upper
classes—that is, the educated classes—were speaking out against
the government. The clergy was apparently unaffected by the
general agitation, as were many members of the merchant
class, so far; but their support was scarcely missed in the prevailing enthusiasm. At district and provincial zemstvo meetings as well as at sessions of municipal dumas throughout the
country, resolutions and petitions supporting the Eleven
Theses in part or whole were adopted and sent to the Tsar—
who at once pronounced them representations of insolence
and impropriety. Even at district and provincial meetings of
the nobility, where no voice of protest had been raised in
forty years, liberal nobles championed, and often gained support for, such resolutions and petitions. Many assemblies of
nobility adopted liberal addresses to the throne, usually somewhat milder than the Eleven Theses. And shortly after the
zemstvo congress, at a Moscow business meeting of twenty-four
provincial marshals of nobility, twenty-three of them signed
and sent to the Minister of Interior a memorandum declaring
the current situation to be abnormal and suggesting, as a
means of restoring harmony between the Tsar and the people,
the enlargement of the State Council by elected representatives. To be sure, there were also opposing voices: some assem-

blies of the nobility and some zemstvo meetings went against the tide and sent messages of support to the Tsar. But their words were practically lost in the clamor for change.

The clamor was even louder and more demanding at the political banquets that were held on November 20 and in the weeks that followed. In St. Petersburg, Moscow, and other important cities (among them: Kiev, Saratov, Odessa, Kaluga, Rostov-on-Don, Baku, Kostroma, Tiflis, Nizhny Novgorod, and Tashkent) the *intelligents* banqueted and declared their convictions. Sometimes they assembled by profession—medicine, law, journalism, education, or engineering—and sometimes, regardless of professional affiliation, merely as men with a common purpose. Though most of them affected the purpose of honoring the fortieth anniversary of court reforms, ingenious liberals found additional occasions for banquets—the anniversary of the founding of the Medico-Surgical Academy in St. Petersburg, perhaps, or the sesquicentennial of the opening of the University of Moscow. Almost any anniversary provided the excuse for a banquet; and a banquet, the opportunity for long and impassioned antiregime speeches and strongly worded resolutions. The outcome was usually the endorsement, not only of the reforms embodied in the Eleven Theses of the zemstvo congress, but also some of those espoused by the Liberationists, particularly the calling of a constituent assembly elected on the basis of four-tail suffrage and the granting of amnesty to those under sentence for political or religious offenses.

The opposition had never been so outspoken, nor had the attack on the regime and its policies ever been so open. Scarcely any opportunity for collective declaration was overlooked. Public statements enumerating intolerable official policies and demanding freedom were soon coming from every corner of the country, some from quite unlikely sources—one from a group of educators at a conference on technical education, another from a university faculty committee dealing with student disorders. Student groups, of course, were highly vocal sources. And they often followed word by deed; in Moscow a group of students protesting the life sentence given to Plehve's assassin, defied the police, and several of them were killed before their demonstration was ended. It was evident that the liberation movement was sweeping toward revolt. So pervasive had its influence become that the socialist organizations were overshadowed by it. Some of the latter, notably the Mensheviks and the SR's, supported the burgeoning campaign, but the Bolsheviks denigrated it and kept doggedly to their own program.

CONCLUDING DAYS OF POLITICAL "SPRING"

The government, though it continued the political police activities against the revolutionaries, was generally tolerant of the open defiance of the liberals for a time. Svyatopolk-Mirsky still believed that he could negotiate with the moderate zemstvo liberals and that he could eliminate the chief sources of opposition by ameliorative legislation. He was confident that, once his proposed program was under way, there would be a favorable response to the changes it would provide: the limitation or repudiation of official resort to arbitrary action in areas under "protection," the enlargement of the State Council by the addition of some members elected by public institutions, the granting of a greater degree of freedom in speech and press, the extension of the jurisdiction of the zemstvos, and the removal of some of the disabilities on religious minorities.

While his program was being considered by the bureaucracy during the fall of 1904 and details were slowly being worked out so that a fairly finished draft might be presented to the Tsar, events elsewhere were moving rapidly. The Tsar was spending much of his time seeing troops off to the Far Eastern front and much of his diplomatic energy endeavoring to appease England over the Dogger Bank incident, in which Russian men-of-war fired on English fishing boats. At the same time, within the ranks of officialdom itself, dissatisfaction and dissension were spreading. At court and among the higher bureaucracy (including even the Ministry of Interior), Svyatopolk-Mirsky's course was causing controversy. It was considered by many to represent an unnecessary capitulation since

the opposition of the intelligentsia, they felt, though a thing to
be expected, was not to be feared: it was mere idle talk nowise
representative of Russian thought. Some went so far as to at-
tribute ulterior motives to the minister himself, seeing his
program as a means by which he planned to enhance his personal power. A few thought that he was both right and honest.
The November zemstvo congress and its consequences helped
to bring matters to a head, for they indicated clearly that the
country—or at least the educated part of it—was not only rest-
less but also getting dangerously out of hand. The government
had either to stop the proliferating meetings and petitions or
to adopt some of Svyatopolk-Mirsky's proposals. For a while
the internal tug-of-war continued; and on November 21, when
the pull against him seemed too great, the minister offered to
resign. However, the Tsar came to terms with him and began
a series of meetings, over which he himself presided, for the
serious consideration of the reform proposals.

The result was the Imperial Ukase of December 12,[4] instructing the Committee of Ministers to make proposals for
ending emergency measures in "protected" areas, removing
some of the disabilities from national and religious minorities,
easing restrictions on the press, and establishing government
insurance for workers. While the ukase embodied most of the
Svyatopolk-Mirsky program, it omitted one of the program's
crucial proposals, that elected members be added to the State
Council; and that fact weakened its appeal to the opposition.
Another thing that limited its possible ameliorating influence
at the time of its issuance was the public knowledge that, if
past bureaucratic performances were used as criteria for pre-
diction, months—even years—might be expected to pass before
the proposals were put into operation.

For the Tsar and his close advisers the ukase of December
12 was a major policy retreat, and they expected results to be
proportionate. In their estimation, since reforms had been
promised, the opposition should be satisfied. It should also be
quiet: the ukase was followed by an official announcement
that no more meetings and gatherings in violation of the law

---

[4] For the text of this ukase, *see* Appendix, p. 282.

would be permitted; and zemstvos, municipal dumas, and all other bodies were to confine their future deliberations to matters relevant to their own affairs. As far as the Tsar was concerned, a chapter was closed. His Committee of Ministers would draft some reforms, the hubbub would cease, and he could give his undivided attention to the war. A few days after the signing of the ukase, he left Tsarskoe Selo for a week's trip to inspect the Third and Fourth Army Corps, about to leave for the Far East.

The "spring" had come to an end. The antigovernment forces had increased their demands and advanced their aims so far during the preceding four months that the ukase, which at one time would have represented gratifying concession on the part of the government, now seemed of little significance. Its most important omission, reference to any kind of law-making participation by elected representatives, made clear the fact that the Tsar refused to budge from his often-repeated policy of adherence to autocracy as interpreted by his father. Svyatopolk-Mirsky was again in a position of discredit, having been unable to satisfy either side.

Diffusion of Unrest

For the opposition, the question was "What next?" The moderate liberals had given up hope of peaceful negotiations with the Tsar and his ministers; but tradition, conviction, and habit commanded their acceptance of what they had received. And since they could not condone illegal opposition, they resigned themselves to a course of truculent passivity.

The Liberationists, however, did not yield. Following the course set at their October meeting, they continued efforts to organize professional unions, to keep alive where possible the militancy of the zemstvos, and to hold political banquets whenever any excuse for such an affair presented itself. The extreme liberals could thus continue their policy of open opposition and retain the support of a considerable part of educated Russia as long as the police did not implement the Tsar's orders of December 12 to stop all illegal meetings. And, during the interval between that date and the next crisis, on

January 9, 1905, the police felt that enforcing the order against liberals would be unwise—after that, inexpedient. The extremists were further favored by the now apparent logic of their contention that the government could not be "persuaded," but must be "compelled." The same logic fortified their belief that an alliance with the revolutionaries was necessary to end autocracy.

However effective the Liberationist tactics might be in keeping alive and even, perhaps, strengthening the opposition, they offered scant prospect of forcing the government to capitulate. Nor did the revolutionaries as yet have an ordered plan for overthrowing the government in the near future. For the present, they were concentrating on efforts to organize, propagandize, start and gain control of industrial strikes, and to penetrate the armed forces; in short, to prod and probe, using both the growing unrest and the weaknesses of the regime wherever they found them. As the end of 1904 approached, their efforts were favored by a variety of developments.

The outlook in the war with Japan remained a somber one, though the Tsar and some of his generals still hoped for a turn in military fortunes, counting on the steady stream of troops being sent to Manchuria to give Russia the needed superiority on land; and the Baltic Fleet, en route to Port Arthur, to give superiority at sea. So far, the reinforcements had not added sufficient strength to halt the Russian army's retreat northward; and discerning minds had judged the Baltic Fleet to be a motley group of warships on which to pin hopes of changing the balance of sea power. Moreover, there were now indications that the disaffection on the home front was becoming more serious. The number of reservists ignoring the call to active duty was still on the increase, and "incidents" attending the departure of those who did report were now more frequent. In Tambov, the Seventh Reserve Cavalry Regiment refused to entrain for the East and had to be compelled; and there were similar occurrences in Pskov and Archangel. In Mogilev, Kherson, and Vitebsk, reservists rioted through the streets, even broke into Jewish stores and destroyed property.

In Transcaucasia, the Baltic provinces, Finland, and Congress Poland, efforts to establish order had been futile; dissidence in those areas was, in fact, growing faster than ever. In December, Prince Golitsyn returned from Transcaucasia and asked to be relieved of his duties. He reported that parts of the area were on the verge of open revolt. In addition to the usual trouble with the Armenians, there was trouble with the Georgians, the Moslems, and even the Russian minority; and it was breaking out both in the cities and in the countryside. In Finland also the situation had worsened, and the newly appointed Governor-General Obolensky faced both antiwar and anti-Russian agitation as well as the disturbing fact that the Finnish Party of Active Resistance was accepting financial aid from Japan. In Poland, the Polish Socialist Party (the PPS) was taking Japanese help and making every effort to capitalize on the growing antipathy for the war. A November demonstration inspired by the PPS in protest against the mobilization of reservists was fired upon by troops. And this incident, the first Russo-Polish clash in forty years, marked the beginning of an extended campaign of terror against the authorities.

It is true that much of the unrest throughout the country was apolitical, elemental, and often (as in the case of anti-Semitic outbursts) actually unfavorable to the opposition. Discontented workers, for example, with their particular interest in economic improvement, were still largely unresponsive or hostile to attempts to draw them into antigovernmental manifestations. By the end of 1904, however, the political ideas of the liberals and socialists were more easily crossing the cultural barrier that had separated the educated from the uneducated, the antigovernment intelligentsia from the monarchist masses; and some workers were responding. That was illustrated by a December strike in Baku, where, in addition to the usual demand for shorter working days and higher wages, fifty thousand disaffected workers made the unusual demand for a constituent assembly and civil rights. This strike, in which Social Democrats had a hand, was quite successful; at its end the workers signed a collective agreement with the management of the struck factories and refineries whereby they were granted a nine-hour day and a wage increase. Naturally, they were impressed by the advice they had received from the Social Democrats; and though nothing came of their political demands, they now had some feeling of kindliness toward those who had suggested them.

Even in the officially approved Assembly of St. Petersburg Factory Workers, which was expected to keep workers safe from the influence of antigovernment troublemakers, there were evidences that the barriers were being crossed occasionally. In the latter part of the year, the Assembly began to overcome its earlier inertia and to display a growth, liveliness, and overt propriety most gratifying to those under whose supervision it had been operating—Father Gapon, Prefect Fullon, and the police. Comprising eleven branches in the various workers' districts, it could now claim about nine thousand members and a following of perhaps one hundred thousand— more than half of the factory workers in the city. Its popularity had developed with the revival of labor discontent following the initial distraction at the outbreak of the war with Japan, as the workers had gradually been led to appreciate the organization not merely for the congenial atmosphere, the entertainment, and the tea-rooms it provided, but also for the legal status it gave to their meetings and discussions.

The spirit at the branch halls was outwardly orderly, patriotic, and respectful of both civil and religious authority; and the police agents noticed with approval that socialist agitators —usually students, sometimes Jews—were often forcibly ejected by the members. Apparently the Assembly was functioning in the officially approved manner, providing thousands of workers with respectable and correct activities and putting them out of the reach of socialists. However, though appearances remained consistently satisfactory, both spirit and thought began gradually to change among the workers during the fall of 1904. This was due, in part, to the effectiveness with which some of the leaders scattered throughout the branches were beginning to point out the need for substantial changes if working conditions were ever to be improved. The workers were responding also, unwittingly in many cases, to the careful prodding of individual socialists in the Assembly (most of them SD's, supplemented by a few SR's) who, without revealing their real convictions and purpose, sought to direct the organization toward militancy.

The degree and nature of Gapon's involvement in this change of atmosphere is difficult to determine. He has been pictured as a conscious and willing tool of the opposition and, conversely, as a provocateur always discreetly acting for the police. But neither picture will stand close inspection. Though his ambition and self-confidence led him into irregular paths and though his actions seemed ambiguous at times, there is no reliable evidence to prove him dishonest in his dealings or disloyal to his ideals at this time. He was a man deeply interested in the conditions of labor, sympathetically affected by the injustices he saw, and sincerely dedicated to their correction. As such he was accepted among the St. Petersburg workers. By the end of 1904, he had a following more tightly organized and more concentrated than that of any other individual in the empire. And his influence was likewise unparalleled: handsome, eloquent, impassioned, he was revered by thousands of followers. His position attracted the attention, but not the official support, of the socialists. Some of them accepted the view that he was a police agent and should, therefore, be closely watched; others dismissed him as a "naïve idealist." Some were willing enough, individually, to work for socialist ends among his followers. But all condemned his tactics and deplored his influence—which they could not begin to match.

Whether he was leading or being led in allowing or advocating changes in the Assembly, the fact remained that, by the late fall, he was sympathetic to many of the political ideas of the liberation movement, in contact with some of its members, and agreeable to the idea of having the Assembly adopt petitions supporting the Eleven Theses of the zemstvo congress. He was not yet ready to support action, though he was not wholly unsympathetic to revolutionary ideas—if allowed his own interpretation of them. What he was evolving, with a small inner group of workers whom he met privately, was a synthesis of monarchist, liberal, and radical ideas. He was beginning to see the need for popular government; and he felt that it could be gained, not through revolution or repetitious harangues at political banquets, but through persuasion of the Little Father, Tsar Nicholas II.[5] He believed that the Tsar held the people close to his heart but that, in his treatment of them, he had been misled by a selfish bureaucracy operating in the interest of employers and landlords, not of workers and peasants. His belief and hopes were known to a group of thirty or so leaders in the Assembly but, as far as can be determined, unknown to the police. Had the officials been particularly alert, they could have noticed a suggestion of changing policy when some members of the Assembly took part in strikes at the Kozhevnikov and Novo-Sampsonievsky textile mills of St. Petersburg in the first weeks of December, but apparently they saw nothing amiss.

ON THE EVE

As a matter of fact, labor was not the government's preoccupation at that time: as usual, the war was the center of concern, and it was still going dishearteningly. Russia's position was weakened and her prestige further depressed by the news that Port Arthur had surrendered on December 20. Even among the otherwise indifferent, there had been admiration for the tenacity of the garrison which had held that city for five months, at the cost of seventeen thousand lives, against the murderous assaults of the Japanese, who had spent the lives of one hundred thousand in the siege; and its surrender, by General Stoessel, was widely believed to be an act of cowardice. A. S. Suvorin, a conservative editor, was moved to ask whether or not the Russians were any longer "a great people," while many of the people themselves openly and heatedly questioned the ability of a government that would allow such a debacle.

However, with the approach of Christmas, the surge of anti-

[5] There is evidence that, in November, 1904, Gapon suggested at a meeting of Assembly leaders the organization of a peaceful march for the purpose of petitioning the Tsar on February 19, 1905, the anniversary of the emancipation of the serfs—a suggestion on which no immediate action was taken. *See* M. Mitelman, B. Glebov, and A. Ulyanskii, *Istoriya Putilovskogo Zavoda* (Moscow, 1941), pp. 158-59.

government feeling seemed to be dying down once again; and except for infrequent and scattered incidents, the country gave the appearance of returning to normal. In the cities, the stores were busy, and the theaters and restaurants full. Quiet returned to the universities with the departure of students for the Christmas holidays, and factories were closed in order that workers also might have the traditional days of rest.

But in one small area of St. Petersburg the calm was unexpectedly broken. During the recess from work, the men of the Putilov Ironworks (with its nearly thirteen thousand workers, one of the largest enterprises in the country) became disturbed by the report that four of their number—workers Fedorov, Sergunin, Subbotin, and Ukolov—had been discharged because of their membership in the Assembly. Adding this alleged injustice to others of which they considered themselves victims, the workers seized upon it as the climax of an insufferable situation. On December 27, about three hundred and fifty of them, each an Assembly member, met and decided to send delegates to the management of the plant with demands for two actions: 1) the reinstatement of the four workers and 2) the removal of foreman Tetyavkin, an intensely disliked man, whom they held responsible for the dismissals. They designated Sunday, January 2, as the date for the report of the delegation. And, with that, they returned to their quarters and whatever there remained for them of the holiday mood, not realizing that they had just given the first thrust to what would become a very potent weapon.

3

The Gaponovshchina:

A Test of Positions[1]

Government by bureaucracy has devastated the country, has involved it in a horrible war, and is leading it further and further into ruin. . . . Russia is too great, its needs too varied and profuse, to be governed by bureaucrats alone. Popular representation is essential. The people must help themselves and govern themselves.

> —The Gapon petition, intended to be presented on January 9, 1905.

I trust in the Almighty and my people. It is absolutely necessary to put a stop to the active revolutionary party and to show the simple and honest workmen that they are misled by enemies of their country.

> —Telegram from Nicholas II to William II, January 12, 1905.

[1] The inner history—that is, the aspect involving personal motives, designs, and involvements—of the period of crisis (the Gaponovshchina) that developed through the organization led by Father Gapon must be pieced together from highly unsatisfactory sources, most of them circumstantial secondary accounts that contradict one another at very vital points. Of the few primary sources, the fullest is Gapon's *The Story of My Life* (London, 1905); and it is suspect because it was composed at a time when he was trying to convince the Russian socialists that he had been consistently on their side, a demonstrably false contention. If any record of deliberations and proceedings was kept by the Assembly of St. Petersburg Factory Workers, it has not been discovered. However, for a general account of the crisis, there is a considerable body of reliable official evidence. For examples, see Akademiya Nauk, SSSR, *Nachalo Pervoi Russkoi Revolutsii* (Moscow, 1955) and "K Istorii 'Krovavogo Voskreseniya' v Peterburge," *Krasnyi Arkhiv*, LXVIII (1935), 39-68. Such evidence may be used as a basis for the evaluation of some of the secondary accounts.

NEW YEAR'S DAY OF 1905 was, to all appearance, a calm one throughout the country, given over primarily to religious services in observance of the Feast of Circumcision. In St. Petersburg, it seemed particularly quiet since, in keeping with the wartime moratorium on Court social functions, the traditional reception for the diplomatic corps had been omitted from the holiday calendar. Tsar Nicholas was with his family at their customary winter residence, Alexander Palace in Tsarskoe Selo, some 15 miles from the capital, relieved to have escaped the official formalities of receiving the diplomats. Relatively few in the capital had even heard of the unpleasantness at the Putilov plant and, beyond the workers' quarters, it was of concern only to the few factory inspectors and police officers for whom it was, at most, an inescapable minor irritation and inconvenience. Nowhere was there any premonition of serious domestic trouble.

DEVELOPMENT OF THE PUTILOV STRIKE

About six hundred of the disaffected workers, Gapon now with them, gathered on Sunday, January 2, in the Narva hall[2] of the Assembly to hear the report of the men who had been delegated on December 27 to present their complaints to the plant management. It was a brief report, the heart of which was a statement made two days earlier by the plant manager, S. I. Smirnov, asserting that the workers had no grounds for grievances: of the four men whose alleged mistreatment was the basis of the complaints, only Sergunin had been dismissed —for faulty work; Subbotin had left of his own accord; Ukolov was to have been dismissed for unauthorized absence from work, but he had been retained after promising not to repeat the offense; Fedorov was still employed. Moreover, Smirnov had declared, he did not consider the Assembly of

2 So called because of its location in the Narva district, where there was a larger concentration of workers than in any other district of the city. The hall had formerly been a cheap tavern known as "Old Tashkent."

St. Petersburg Factory Workers authorized to negotiate with him.

Such rebuffs were familiar to the Putilov workers, and they had often accepted them resignedly. But, this time, their response was different. By appointing and instructing the delegates to represent them before the plant management, they had taken a step in the championship of what they considered justice; and while waiting for results, they had developed (with some purposeful encouragement from certain leaders in their branch organizations) a stubborn dedication to the achievement of what they had requested. Now, they refused to credit Smirnov's statement and, in the heat of their anger, quickly identified themselves with a "cause." Their "martyrs" were to be Fedorov, Sergunin, Subbotin, and Ukolov; their "persecutors," Smirnov, the factory inspectors, "that dog" Tetyavkin, and St. Petersburg Prefect Fullon (who also had refused to hear their case). When the alternatives were put before them, to submit passively to the rebuke or to press on, they were in no mood to hesitate or consider the cost. They responded with resounding approval when it was proposed that delegates be sent once more to Smirnov and that, in case he again refused to accede to their requests, *they would strike until he did.*

Thus began the Gaponovshchina, a week-long turbulence steered by Gapon, with the aid of his confidants among the Assembly leaders, and reaching far beyond the Putilov plant. Initiated as a limited protest by a few hundred unhappy workers prepared to break the law by striking but still considering themselves loyal Russian Orthodox subjects of the Tsar, within seven days it had become so widened in scope, increased in animation, and changed in purpose that it signalized crisis to the government.

On the morning after the Narva hall meeting, the workers' representatives presented their demands to plant manager Smirnov. As might have been expected, he refused to accede to them. And, as planned, the call to strike went around the plant; and virtually the entire work force, ignoring the efforts of a few policemen to stop them, quietly left the premises.

Many of them assembled at the nearby Narva hall; others simply went home.

By afternoon, word of the daring move had reached other plants and, when Putilov workers met in the Narva hall at a call from Gapon, they were joined by a number of interested men who customarily met in other halls of the Assembly. With that meeting, the workers began to display a willingness to resort to a powerful but hitherto untried weapon, the general strike. The words "general strike" were not used at the time, but their meaning was implicit in what was said and done. Gapon's fiery address to the workers and his proposal of extensive amendments to their demands effected a change in mood and program. He proposed that they exact of management those conditions that had long been the center of their discussions and wistful thinking but for which they had never dared to make a definite demand: an eight-hour day, an increase in the minimum daily wage from 60 kopecks to a ruble (100 kopecks) for men, an increase from 40 to 75 kopecks for women, the improvement of sanitary facilities, and the provision of free medical aid. When he read off the items to the strikers, some expressed the feeling that the demands were too strong: a one-third reduction in the work day and a two-thirds increase in the minimum pay seemed to them unattainable and likely to reduce the chance of any success. But so appealing were the suggestions and so effective their presentation that most of the workers could not resist, and the supporters soon outnumbered and shouted down the opposers. Acceptance was almost unanimous. The workers were committing themselves to a long, hard struggle, for the Putilov management was certain to reject such ambitious demands, and an extended strike was certain to bring hardships. Still, their action would not have been of such significance had it not immediately touched off a response-in-sympathy among others. Some of those attending this meeting agreed to a suggestion that other plants should be asked to join the Putilov strike; and, from there, the idea of a general strike was to grow and spread.

It seems that some aspects of the ensuing general strike

movement are destined to remain beclouded. There is insufficient evidence to determine whether it developed according to a predetermined plan; whether it was manipulated solely by Gapon (as he later claimed); whether its promotion was handled primarily by that inner group, directors of the several Assembly branches, with whom Gapon maintained such close contact and who are often represented as the "brains" of the Gaponovshchina; or whether it received its stimulation from the *sub rosa* efforts of the few socialists working in the Assembly. But there is no doubt that Gapon was a major force. He had the faithful following, the ability to contrive and execute, and the self-confidence necessary for the role. Assuredly it was he who prompted the initial move of the Putilovites which led directly to the Assembly's taking on the implicit character of a labor union and to its transformation into a quasi-revolutionary body. In the Narva hall, on January 3, he eschewed his duty as a priest and as an agent of the government when he did not disown the strike and use his influence to get the men back to work. And he courageously compounded the impropriety by assuming leadership of the strike, using that leadership to turn a limited, plant-wide strike with no economic demands into one that not only made economic demands but also provided the impetus for a general strike.

It should be noted, however, that at this stage Gapon did not suggest to his followers that they turn their economic strike into a political one nor that they make common cause with the liberal or revolutionary movements. On the contrary, he instructed them to tear up, unread, the leaflets that students were even then distributing among them in promotion of the revolutionary aim to "reduce autocracy to dust." Furthermore his continual exhortations against the use of violence were so effective that, throughout the Gaponovshchina, despite its almost uncontrollable growth, the workers were remarkably reluctant to use physical force.

With an apparent feeling of complete security in what he was doing, Gapon took the responsibility of heading the delegation that, on Tuesday, January 4, carried to Smirnov the

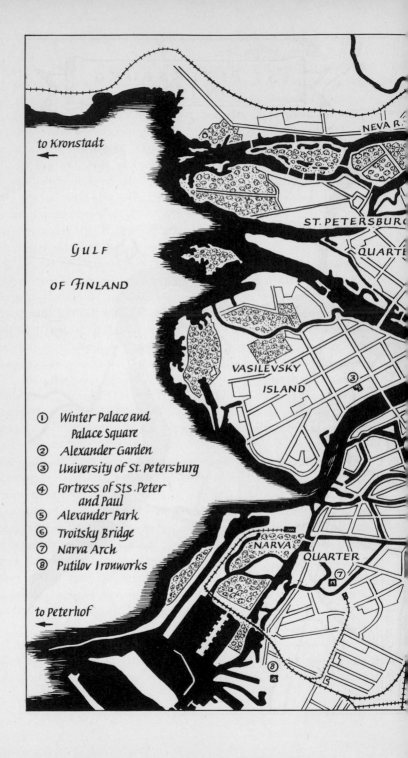

to Kronstadt

GULF

OF FINLAND

NEVA R.

ST. PETERSBURG

QUARTER

VASILEVSKY

ISLAND

③

① Winter Palace and
   Palace Square
② Alexander Garden
③ University of St. Petersburg
④ Fortress of Sts. Peter
   and Paul
⑤ Alexander Park
⑥ Troitsky Bridge
⑦ Narva Arch
⑧ Putilov Ironworks

NARVA

QUARTER

⑦

to Peterhof

⑧

demands adopted by the workers on the previous day. By this time further demands had been added to the original ones, some of them reflecting general practicability, others quite casual complaints: among the former, the demand that management accept a standing committee to be elected by the workers and authorized to present grievances and make final decisions about dismissal of workers; among the latter, the demand that the medical personnel of the plant be required to show more courtesy to the workers. Gapon, dressed as always in his priestly robes, read the demands before Smirnov, pausing after each to turn to the delegation with *"Ne tak li, tovarischi?"* (Right, comrades?) and to receive in reply the assurance of their accord. When he had finished, Smirnov again repeated his criticism of all such demands and the presumption of those who presented them, but he agreed to present them to the owners of the plant.

While their representatives were thus engaged, some of the strikers, having waited to talk to the workers of the nearby Franco-Russian Shipbuilding Plant during their free time, were successful in persuading 2,000 of them to lay down their work. And on the following day, Putilov workers induced nearly 11,000 at four other plants to join the strike. By the middle of the week some 25,000 were on strike, all making practically the same demands, those of the Putilov strikers being the models. Every branch hall of the Assembly was crowded with aroused workers speculating on the outcome of what they had begun, and Gapon hurried from one hall to another, exhorting, guiding, or conferring with his lieutenants.

Oddly enough, this altogether unusual activity by and among the workers aroused little outside concern at first, even among members of the bureaucracy whose responsibilities included the direction and overseeing of relations between the parties involved. The Minister of Interior, Svyatopolk-Mirsky, was currently apathetic and dispirited over the failure of his program for the country at large and was not inclined to concern himself actively with what he considered a minor aspect of it. The Ministry of Finance, which controlled the factory inspection system and received reports of the workers' doings, apparently saw no reason for alarm. Minister of Finance Kokovtsev was probably cheered by the prospect of reporting the situation to the Tsar as yet another muddle of the Ministry of Interior, which had for years been seeking to snatch from his ministry the control of the inspectors. And when he reported to the Tsar at Tsarskoe Selo on January 5, he was careful to indicate that Interior's attempts at "police socialism" were to be blamed for the present unfortunate state of affairs. In his account, which was, as far as record shows, the first one presented to Nicholas II, Kokovtsev reviewed the first three days of the strike, pointing out the harmful nature of the Gapon Assembly, the illegality of the strike and the strikers' demands, the unreasonableness of such demands during a war, and the general culpability of the Ministry of Interior. He emphasized his position that, although the workers had some justice on their side, they should not have attempted to negotiate with the factory owners nor resorted to striking, but should have depended on the Ministry of Finance to deal with the problems in controversy. But he expressed no anticipation of serious difficulties in righting matters.

Others in positions of authority were equally slow in recognizing the potential threat of the speed with which the strike movement was picking up momentum. St. Petersburg Prefect Fullon and the police seemed to be guided by the assurance that Gapon's leadership was to be trusted as the surest means of handling the strikers. They had become convinced that he alone could keep the discontented workers of the Assembly from going over to the revolutionaries. And even after the strike began to spread and it became evident that Gapon was set on his maverick course, ignoring his superiors in both church and government and actually promoting the strike movement, General Fullon held to a laissez-faire policy toward him, fearing that opposition or restraint might drive him to release his followers to the revolutionary camp and thus confront the police with a force they would be unable to handle. Taking what comfort he could from that position, during the first days of the strike the Prefect gave most of his attention to the city's plans for Thursday, the sixth, when the

Tsar was scheduled to take part, along with other high dignitaries of church and state, in the annual ceremony of the Blessing of the Waters.

"BLESSING OF THE WATERS" INCIDENT

January 6 was a general holiday, and most of St. Petersburg was in characteristic mood for such a day. When the Tsar and his entourage arrived from Tsarskoe Selo by train, they were received in the city by massed crowds that lined the two-mile route from the station to the Winter Palace and saluted the royal procession with enthusiasm and respect. At the palace, members of the imperial family, priests and prelates, members of the diplomatic corps, ranking military officers, and civilian officials—all resplendent in court dress—solemnly joined the Tsar in the first part of the traditional ceremony that blended the magnificence of the imperial court with that of the Orthodox Church. Then followed the procession of the Tsar and other participants through the palace and out to the banks of the Neva, where, standing under a canopy with a few dignitaries, Nicholas observed the climax of the ceremony, the formal blessing of the waters by Metropolitan Anthony of St. Petersburg. When the last words of the blessing were intoned, an artillery battery stationed offshore on Vasilevsky Island fired its customary salute—customary except for the fact that one cannon fired, in the direction of the ceremonial canopy, a live charge that had been inadvertently left in it, wounding one policeman and spattering shot against a wall near the spot where the Tsar was standing. Nicholas, as usual in moments of stress, remained calm and, as the ceremony was concluded, the procession returned in orderly fashion to the palace. The incident was given hardly any immediate publicity. Intrinsically, of course, it was of little importance except as an illustration of bureaucratic inefficiency, noteworthy in this instance because the Tsar was involved. But it is worth mention here as the first disquieting event officially recognized as such in what was to be one of the country's most disquieting years. When the Tsar and his family had returned to Tsarskoe

Selo that afternoon, St. Petersburg gave the outward appearance of a city in which the only concern of the day had been the observance of a traditional festival and the smooth execution of an important ceremony, both carried out with dignity and propriety.

EXTENSION OF THE PUTILOV STRIKE

But the atmosphere of the Assembly halls was far different from that in the heart of the city. Workers had begun to assemble early in the day, and by afternoon the halls were packed with strikers and potential strikers, all of them animated by the developments of the past few days and the anticipation of those to follow. The chief topic among them was the means to be employed in spreading the strike during the next day, when the plants would be reopened after the holiday. Another, and more important, one (though the average worker was less stimulated by it) was the announcement by Gapon that the time had now come for the strikers to make a direct appeal to the Tsar for political, as well as economic, reform. He carried with him, as he went from group to group, a copy of the proposed appeal in the form of a petition, which he read to the men and urged them to approve by signing—an act that for many of them meant simply marking it with the illiterate's cross. As usual, most of them were willing and eager to accept both his words and his direction, with little thought for the significance of what they were doing.

The strikers' acceptance of the petition marked the beginning of another phase of the Gaponovshchina, the political phase—and one of serious import. But historians may never be able to record accurately where and how all the ideas incorporated in that document originated. Months earlier some socialist members of the Assembly had drafted a political program based on the explicit argument that economic amelioration required the overthrow of autocracy, and the Gapon petition resembled that program in its acceptance of the need for political change as a prelude to economic change (a need that Gapon, three days earlier, had refused to admit). Yet it differed from the socialist proposal in one very significant re-

spect: it was not antimonarchist. It was a strange mixture of
Orthodox, monarchist, liberal, and socialist sentiments and
goals.[4] And whatever its background, many of its features
were characteristic of Gapon. It begged an autocratic tsar to
call a constituent assembly, to grant civil rights, and to declare a political amnesty, to separate church and state, to decree an eight-hour day, to recognize the right of labor to
organize, and to bring the war to an end.

Regardless of the extraordinary nature of the petition they
were endorsing, most of the strikers were primarily concerned
at the time with the transformation of their limited strike
into a general one. And on Friday, January 7, they came close
to that goal. Men from the Putilov Ironworks, the Franco-
Russian Shipbuilding Plant, the Ekaterinogof Mill, the Neva
Spinning Mill, and other industrial establishments went in
groups from one place of employment to another, wherever
there was a concentration of workers within the city, calling
the employed ones out to join in the fraternity of strikers.
The purpose of the strike was not entirely clear to all who
joined; some required no reason beyond the fact that workers
elsewhere were striking. However, most of them responded
readily enough to the call to lay down their work. Thus the
general strike, a type of tactic so dear to the hearts of socialists, was being brought about by monarchist, Orthodox workers (though some of their leaders were evidently swayed by
socialist views, the mass of workers was yet untouched by
them) —a bit of historical irony.

Only here and there did the strikers meet any resistance.
The Naval Guncotton Factory on Vasilevsky Island remained
at work, and two companies of sailors stood ready to turn
back any strikers who sought to come onto its premises. At the
print shops of the Senate and the Ministry of the Navy, the
printers, who refused to quit work, exchanged blows with outside strikers. But such instances were exceptions; on the
whole, the day was an orderly one with practically no violence or threat of violence. Nevertheless the promotional
methods of the strikers were demonstrably effective: by sun-

[4] For text of the petition, *see* Appendix, p. 285.

down, the industrial life of the capital was almost completely immobilized. All but 25,000 of the city's 175,000 workers were out. Shipyards, steel plants, textile mills, chemical plants, piano factories, chocolate factories, furniture factories, and breweries were shut down. In the industrial parts of the Narva Quarter (where it all started), in the Alexander Nevsky Quarter, the Vyborg Quarter, the St. Petersburg Quarter, and on the Vasilevsky Island, virtually all workers were idle.

Yet in the central districts of the city, normal services were continuing without interruption. Trains and streetcars ran on schedule, banks and stores were open, and in police and military quarters routine duties were performed. It was still possible to sit in the administrative offices, where clerks were as deferential as ever and services as efficient or inefficient as ever, and to overlook the seriousness of the runaway strike, perhaps to interpret it as a storm that would blow itself out. But even from such viewpoints, the picture soon darkened.

PREPARATIONS FOR THE WINTER PALACE MARCH

Gapon and his lieutenants were continuing their rounds of the Assembly halls, reading the petition and calling on workers who had not already indicated their acceptance of it to do so. In addition, during Friday and Saturday, they were putting the final touches to an ambitious plan to have tens of thousands of St. Petersburg workers and their families participate in a march, its columns forming at various Assembly halls, some converging at designated points, and all meeting in the square before the Winter Palace to demonstrate their support of the petition when it should be presented to the Tsar on Sunday afternoon. The workers' response to the plan was highly satisfactory. The scene at the end of the march, as it was put into their minds, was to be a dream come true: their Father Gapon presenting their petition to the Little Father, and they themselves falling to their knees in gratitude when he acceded to their humble requests. They were beginning to give themselves wholeheartedly to the anticipation of the good things that lay ahead for them, convinced that the day of deliverance from exploiting factory owners and callous bureaucrats was at hand. Had they not already stood up successfully in defiance of injustice? And were they not about to go out, shoulder to shoulder, break through the wall of deceit that prevented the Tsar from knowing the needs of his loyal people, and carry their petition directly to him?

That most of the strikers had any clear understanding of the petition that they were preparing to present or that they had ever consciously aspired to the political changes requested in it is most doubtful. They were discontented, to be sure, and bound by conditions that promoted desperation, as the rapid spread of the strike showed; but, for the most part, they still shared the average Russian worker's unconcern with political aims and were, in fact, generally antipathetic to political discussions. Their signing the document was, for the majority of them, only a manifestation of faith in their revered leader. That he subscribed to it and that it made reference to their own practical needs were sufficient to win their support. However, to say that Gapon was taking advantage of his followers' credulity and loyalty by promoting a liberal program disguised in monarchical terms, assuredly acceptable to them, would be unfair. As far as can be judged, he saw no illogic in the scheme he proposed. He apparently believed sincerely that, as Patriarch Philaret had guided Tsar Michael, the first Romanov, through troubled times some three hundred years earlier, he himself could use his influence to guide the present Romanov.

When the St. Petersburg authorities could no longer ignore the threatening growth of the movement among the workers, they began a series of desultory gestures toward it. The nature of their efforts supports the charges that Nicholas II did not use his autocratic power to provide Russia with a unified executive branch having a clear and consistent policy, and that he left too much to the discretion of inadequately instructed officials while he himself remained in the background. In this particular instance, there was some justification for the Tsar's distance from involvement: the information given him had not indicated that matters were at a critical point, simply that some kind of "socialist-priest" had misled a large number of workers into striking and that the misdeed would be summarily and appropriately dealt with. But the fact was that just now, in his government, there was not one perceptive and energetic official with definite and ample authority to handle the situation. Sergei Witte, former Minister of Finance (1892-1903) and now Chairman of the Committee of Ministers, was the man most fitted for such a task; but he was where the Tsar wanted him to be, in an office of little consequence and less power.

Of those whose duties included the handling of matters such as the growing strike, the Minister of Interior was the one with greatest responsibility. But Svyatopolk-Mirsky, at best, a relatively weak administrator, continued to follow the growth of the Gaponovshchina with little energy. His inertia was matched by that of Prefect Fullon, chief of St. Petersburg. In many ways like Svyatopolk-Mirsky—educated, well-bred, of pleasant personality—Fullon lacked both strength and initiative under stress. His responsibility was shared by the Grand Duke Vladimir, Commander-in-Chief of the St. Petersburg Military District;[5] but the latter's duty was to support, not dominate civilian authority, and he was slow in expressing concern about the present situation. When action seemed no longer avoidable, on January 7, both the prefect and the commander began to bestir themselves; and troops were ordered to the capital from as far away as Revel and Pskov to reinforce police and military units being detailed to guard railway stations and government buildings against possible disorder. But their efforts were not directed toward dealing with the source of the potential trouble or organizing any schemes to check its development. Vladimir was fitted both by position and relationship (he was Nicholas' uncle) to act more effectively than he did on this occasion. Certainly he could have pressed upon the Tsar the need for decisive and coordinated action by the government. However, though known for his direct manner and his whiff-of-grapeshot approach to civil disorder, he refrained from offering advice on the handling of this crisis.

[5] A large area including the provinces of St. Petersburg, Pskov, Novgorod, Livonia (except for the Riga district), Olonets, and Archangel.

(His attitude may well have been due to the fact, known to all in the imperial family, that the Tsar was more than likely to oppose any unsolicited suggestion from one of his uncles.)

For all concerned, January 8 was a critical day in the Gaponovshchina. Gapon himself informed the government of the proposed march of the workers and their families, underlining its peaceful character and asking that the Tsar receive him at the Winter Palace in order that he might present the workers' petition. With that, the matter of the strike had at last been brought to the door of the government and could no longer be ignored. Still, the Tsar was not alerted to the seriousness of the imminent showdown nor, as far as can be determined, even advised that his presence might be required in the capital on the following day.

Faced with the necessity of making some kind of response, Svyatopolk-Mirsky roused himself sufficiently to order that Prefect Fullon have Gapon arrested. But the order was not executed, Fullon declaring that his police force was inadequate to handle the turmoil that would surely follow if Gapon were arrested. For the same reason he failed to execute a later order of the Minister of Interior to arrest nineteen of Gapon's lieutenants. He was well aware that the government could not permit a mass demonstration against autocratic authority, as his police agents' reports indicated the march in support of the petition to be, and that the career of any responsible official who permitted such a demonstration would soon be ended. He was aware also that the police had confidence in a report that the revolutionists hoped to turn the march into an armed uprising, and he naturally feared that possibility. Clearly it was his duty to take action, but he continued to hesitate.

Finally, on Saturday evening, Svyatopolk-Mirsky, at a meeting with Fullon and various other civilian and military officials, sat down in desperation to devise some method of handling the problem. The members of this group could not hope to plot any course that would have the approval even of all their colleagues in government, from whom there had already come a variety of opinions and suggestions. Some favored drastic means; others had expressed the opinion that it would be expedient to receive Gapon and his petitioners. The Procurator of the St. Petersburg Superior Court had submitted a memorandum to the Minister of Justice, suggesting that a member of the imperial family receive Gapon personally. He urged above all the avoidance of bloodshed, pointing out that if blood were shed, one hundred thousand or more marchers, with revolutionary support, could be expected to react with violence. But for the Minister of Interior and those with him that evening, there were no alternatives to be considered—they must decide how to thwart the workers' plans, not how to make adjustments to them. Unauthorized marches were illegal activities and must be treated as such—using force if necessary.

The only moot question facing the planners concerned the tactics to be used. After the event, it seemed that the tactics they agreed upon were those that would result in the greatest shedding of blood and therefore, presumably, insure the most lasting intimidation. While there is no evidence that they intended such results, neither is there any evidence that they sought to avoid them. They made no adequate effort to reach the workers' leaders, to demand that the instructions for the march be rescinded, or to check in any other practical way the anticipated action before it should require forcible restraint. The plans adopted were, willy-nilly, the ones that would create the worst possible impression of the government. After the meeting, Svyatopolk-Mirsky hurried to Tsarskoe Selo to communicate the plans to the Tsar and receive his approval.

While the Minister and his colleagues were planning to use force, at least one definite effort was being made in the city to solicit some kind of insurance against it. Logically enough, that effort came from the political opposition, which, like the government, had reacted to the great, unpredicted strike slowly and hesitatingly. The movement had caught the leaders unprepared; it was none of their doing, and they had found themselves unable to control it. In recent days, some Social Democrats had distributed leaflets attacking the idea of a march and a petitioning of the Tsar as chimerical, but they had made no impression. Now, on the eve of the 9th, a delegation of ten men—nine *intelligents* and one worker—took a

definite stand on the immediate issue between government
and the workers, the march and the petitioning. Among them
were individuals whose words might be expected to carry
weight—men such as I. V. Hessen of the liberal *Pravo* and
Maxim Gorky. Their declared purpose was to persuade the
government to allow the proposed march in order to prevent
the bloodshed that would be inevitable if it were opposed by
force. That theirs were the only voices raised openly on this
question was a reflection not only of the fact that the public
was poorly informed but also of the fact that the Russian
people were not accustomed to expressing preferences or declaring positions in the hope that they would influence, one
way or another, any particular official act or plan. The ten
men first sought an audience with Witte, who informed them
that he had no jurisdiction over the problem with which they
were concerned. Then they tried to see Svyatopolk-Mirsky—
with no success. Thus impeded, without having gained even a
hearing for their views, they could only withdraw and join
the vigil of those who privately deplored what they expected
of the coming day. Their single achievement had been to
provide the opposition with additional evidence to support
antigovernment agitation.

Meanwhile, throughout the city, police and military preparations were under way. Although the government's plan to
stop the expected march was ostensibly a police action with
military support, responsibility for the execution of it was
placed in the hands of General Prince S. I. Vasilchikov,
Commander of the Guards. Official arrangements were that
mounted police, mounted gendarmes, infantry, and cavalry be
deployed near the several areas that had been designated by
Gapon (with no effort at concealment) as the places at which
the march, certain columns of which having converged, would
begin the final advance to Palace Square. It was understood
by those in command at each point that, when the marchers
reached the government forces, they should be told to disperse. What if the marchers refused? It was standard procedure for mounted police and cavalry (usually Cossacks), free
to use *nagaikas* and the flats of their sabers, to ride down
recalcitrant crowds and force them to disperse. What if these

measures failed? Commanding officers could order their men to fire warning volleys; and if these did not bring compliance, they could then order that the firing be directed into the crowds.[6]

Apparently ignorant of the significance of the plans being made for their reception, the strikers continued their efforts, under the close guidance of their leaders, to have everything ready and in order for their day of days. They had no reason to expect that violence would be used against them. On the contrary, they had many reasons for considering their position a safe one: their Father Gapon was an intimate of important officials; under his direction, they had begun and developed an extensive strike with no overt punitive action by the police; and their leaders had been neither restrained nor arrested. After all, they were at odds with the bureaucracy, not with the Tsar; and it was incredible that the Tsar would allow his troops to use force against his subjects in the act of presenting a humble petition. Of course, in the petition, they had agreed to the declaration that, if the Tsar did not order his officials to fulfill their requests, they were prepared to die before his eyes. But, to them, that was just a manner of speaking: they did not expect to bare their breasts and face martyrs' deaths in the Palace Square any more than they expected to meet violence at the hand of the Little Father.

At a later date, Gapon stated that he had been prepared, if the Tsar should refuse him, to join his forces with those of the revolutionaries and go to the barricades in defense of his position.[7] But evidence does not support that statement. He made

[6] The lives of lower class Russians were held in low esteem by their superiors; and officers often ordered their men to fire into unarmed crowds on what would have been considered, in the West, less than justifiable provocation. Not quite two years earlier, forty-five strikers in a Zlatoust plant in Ufa province had been shot to death when they refused to disperse.

[7] The socialists (there were some seven hundred SD's in the capital, probably as many SR's) would have liked to make the march a prelude to an armed uprising. But they lacked influence, still being treated with hostility by Assembly members; and they could have provided very few weapons for arming either themselves or others at this time.

no provision of firearms or other weapons for the marchers, and they did not meet force with force. Everything pointed to the fact that he was as confident as ever on the eve of the march. He knew, as did most of his followers, that his arrest had been ordered; but that fact was understood to indicate only that the bureaucracy, angered—and perhaps frightened— by his defiance of their authority, were trying desperately to keep him from taking his pleas directly to the Tsar. And care was being taken, in every workers' district, to forestall the possibility of his arrest; he had a regular and devoted guard of two hundred men. Without interruption, he continued to shuttle from one Assembly hall to another, keeping up the general enthusiasm, reviewing plans for the following day, and finally, exhausted, falling asleep in one of the rooms of the Narva hall. There was no indication that he expected the next day to bring anything but what he had predicted—that in the afternoon he would stand beside the Tsar, looking down on a happy crowd in Palace Square.

BLOODY SUNDAY

The day that brought the divergent preparations to focus, Sunday, January 9, was one of customary wintriness in St. Petersburg—cold, gray, and raw. A light snow, driven by a biting wind, was shrouding the accumulated drifts and covering the iciness of the hardpacked snow already deep in the streets. The city was active at an early hour, many of its inhabitants aware of the irregular stirrings at various points. Smoke from open fires drifted here and there in the areas where assembled troops were trying to keep warm as they waited for the word of alert. Units from the city's leading regiments—the Semenovsky Guards, the Horse Grenadier Guards, the Pavlovsky Guards, the Chevalier Guards, the Preobrazhensky Guards, on whose rolls the Tsar was still listed as Commander of the First Battalion—were proceeding to their appointed stations. And from the barracks and rail terminals reinforcements from less illustrious units were moving in, to be deployed where needed to strengthen action against the planned march and to increase the protection that had been set up two days earlier around public buildings and centers of communication. In all, over twenty thousand soldiers, commanded by eight major-generals under Prince Vasilchikov, took their posts to support the police who were detailed for the day's operation.

While all this was taking place, Gapon's followers (the workers now accompanied by their families) were gathering at the various Assembly halls. Their enthusiasm was at a high pitch, though generally restrained,[8] and remained so despite prolonged waiting. It was planned that the groups would form columns and begin to march at different times, depending on the distance of their gathering places from Palace Square. All were expected to reach the square at the same time, about two o'clock in the afternoon. On the way, they were to advance as if in a Procession of the Cross, a dignified progression of devotees following their clergy, carrying icons and singing hymns—a familiar experience to all members of the Russian Orthodox Church.

The column that formed at the Narva hall was accompanied by Gapon; otherwise it was typical. Several thousand men, women, and children, who had gathered by ten o'clock in the morning, were led in devotions and prayer by Gapon and, about noon, having received the order to march, set out on their assigned course. In orderly train, they followed their leader along the Peterhof Chaussée, holding aloft icons, religious standards, the Russian national flag, and portraits of the Tsar and the Tsarina. As they marched they sang such favorite hymns as "Our Father" and "Save, O Lord, Thy People." It was a decorous procession, and police along the route cleared the way for them, as was customary for religious processions, while the crowds who gathered to watch them made the customary signs of respect to religious and national symbols. They moved along thus for about a mile and a half, being given no signal that they were forbidden to march. Then, as they drew near the Narva Triumphal Arch, the familiar monument Alexander I had left to remind them of vic-

---

[8] A few of the workers engaged policemen in a scuffle near the Narva hall when the latter tried to prevent their entering a local chapel for the purpose of removing standards and icons that they wanted to carry in the march.

tories over Napoleon, they saw police and troops drawn up across their route. When they were two hundred paces from the arch, the police ordered them to halt. Despite the order, they continued to move forward[9]—but for only a short distance for, as they advanced, a squadron of the Horse Grenadier Guards galloped into their midst, and they were forced into disorder. Their dispersal was very brief, however; they quickly re-formed their ranks and moved forward again. At that, the squadron fell back; and Captain von Hein, of the 93rd Irkutsk Rifle Regiment, ordered his men to fire into the crowd.[10] The first three volleys did not stop the forward movement, but five additional ones proved unquestionably effective. The terrified crowd broke up, and those who were able fled, Gapon among them. The price of their misplaced trust and determination was left behind: at least ten dead and twenty wounded.

What happened at the Narva Arch was repeated elsewhere: at Alexander Park; in the St. Petersburg Quarter, where two columns—one from that quarter, another from the Vyborg Quarter—converged en route to the Troitsky Bridge; on the Schlüsselburg Chaussée; and on Vasilevsky Island. In each of these places, the final act was about the same: in its first scene, the clamor of confused people running, crawling, or stumbling from the threat of wheeling horses and armed men; in its second, the somber quietness as the dead and wounded

[9] There are many speculations about why the marchers continued to advance after they were ordered to halt (the columns on every route responded in the same manner). But the puzzle remains unsolved. Did they think that the troops would stop short of extreme measures? Were they simplemindedly following instructions to continue the march, whatever the threat or interference? Did they grimly face this obstruction, believing that they could override it and reach the justifying goal, an audience with the Tsar? Were they purposefully urged into this act by some of their more aggressive leaders, marching in the front ranks?

[10] The official report of this event stated that two policemen were struck by shots from the crowd before von Hein gave the order for direct firing (this would explain why he omitted the order for warning shots). Contrary evidence, given by civilian eyewitnesses, indicates that the policemen were struck by shots from the troops.

were carried from where they had fallen in the trampled snow, many of them still clutching icons or imperial portraits. Thus the planned march was stopped. But the day's troubles were not over. Many of the workers and their families, anxious to avoid further consequences of their daring, set off at once toward their homes; some, though awed by the happenings, were reluctant to return, choosing rather to stay near the scene of action, observing but hoping to be unobserved; and small groups—among them, some of the more militant Assembly leaders with followers who had not been intimidated—moved on unobtrusively by various routes toward Palace Square. At the same time, a number of students and other city residents, stirred either to curiosity or indignation by what they had seen or heard of the day's happenings, made their way toward the same place.

Early in the afternoon, when, according to the Gapon plan, the first of the marchers should have been arriving at Palace Square, the troops that Prince Vasilchikov had assigned to that area were waiting in readiness to act as a secondary line for stopping the march if it should have broken through the first cordons at the Narva Arch and elsewhere. They were drawn up in lines of defense before the important government buildings overlooking the square—the Winter Palace, the Imperial Archives, the General Staff Building, the Foreign Office, and the Admiralty. That they were still at their posts after the anticipated threat from the marchers had been forestalled was due largely to faulty communications: their commanding officers lacked complete information as to how successful the outer cordons had been. But, whatever the reason for their still being there, Vasilchikov soon saw a need for them as hundreds of people began to push into the square from Alexander Garden, a small adjoining park. Though it was evident that they were not organized marchers (in addition to students, concerned citizens, and workers from the various parts of the frustrated march, there were many whose sole purpose in coming to the square was to satisfy their curiosity about what was going on), as their number continued to increase—from hundreds to thousands—Vasilchikov anticipated the possibility of mob action and the endangering of property he was commissioned to protect. Therefore he ordered that the area be cleared. At first verbal commands served to scatter the crowds, but soon they were being disregarded by many. There were nuclei of angry men who persisted in returning to the forbidden area, hooting, jeering, whistling in contempt, and suggesting that the troops might be of more service in fighting the Japanese or, better yet, in coming over to the side of the workers. Finally Vasilchikov, determined that his orders be carried out, instructed Colonel Delsal of the Preobrazhensky Guards to have his men open fire. They first fired the usual warning shots. Then, when these were without effect, they fired directly into the defiant groups and continued firing until all dispersed, some dragging with them wounded or dead friends. The scene resulting from the execution of that order was to become etched into the minds of the Russian people as the one, above all others of this tragic Sunday, that represented the brutal injustice under which they lived. It was to be described over and over with many embellishments and much bitter vindictiveness.

After Palace Square had been cleared, Vasilchikov ordered the same procedure for nearby Nevsky Prospekt, the main thoroughfare of the city, which was now more crowded than usual, for the customary Sunday throngs had been joined by many people from the industrial districts. The officers designated for the duty directed their efforts mainly at the points along the street where the largest concentrations of people were to be found—at Police Bridge, at the intersection with Gogol Street, and in the open area before Kazan Cathedral. What followed was a repetition of the other incidents: orders to disperse, warning shots, direct firing, and the grim aftermath.

Such was the easy success of the military and police operations at all points except on Vasilevsky Island, where they encountered some difficulty. Even there, the resistance was not initiated by workers, nor did it amount to anything more than a few hours of harassment. It began with a group of students, mainly from the nearby University and from the more distant Polytechnic Institute, who had made an unsuccessful attempt earlier in the day to infect the Gapon marchers with their spirit of violence and who had thereafter attached themselves to the march. After the general dispersal of the marchers, these students were the core of groups that continued to form and re-form defiantly despite the attempts of police to scatter them. In the afternoon, their contentiousness broke into violence and, dragging together crude barricades—the first in the history of St. Petersburg—they tried to aggravate the annoyance they had provoked. Driven from one area, they would repeat their performance in another, until their spirit and strength began to run low. Though some of them continued to annoy for a while by dodging here and there, pulling down and destroying street lamps, the main action of their miniature revolt had been quashed before the day was over.

By nightfall, a state of general orderliness had been forced from the confusion and consternation of the thousands who had been involved in what was to go down in history as Bloody Sunday. Except for a small number of the more obstinate, the workers had left the scene; and most of the local residents had been glad to retire from the streets as soon as possible. Throughout the city, the prevailing quiet was broken only occasionally—and, even then, briefly. In a few instances, remnants of the irreconcilables caused minor disturbances by whistling or shouting epithets at men in uniform, making clumsy attacks on policemen, or trying to unhorse patrolling officers. But in the main streets, soldiers bivouacked peaceably, their rifles stacked, huddling around fires.

Armed strength had made a considerable showing that day. Official figures, compiled later, showed that 96 had died and 333 had been wounded (34 of these dying afterward), including the government's total loss, two policemen.[11] That the achievement, in retrospect, brought any pride is questionable. True, the disobedient masses had been routed according to

[11] These figures account for only the dead removed by agents of the government and the wounded cared for in hospitals. The number of bodies carried away by friends and relatives, deaths that occurred later in homes, and wounded not taken to hospitals could not, of course, be estimated.

Some time after Bloody Sunday, a group of journalists presented to the Ministry of Interior a list of 4,600 names which, they claimed, represented the dead and wounded for which they could account.

order; but they had represented a very weak challenge. For the most part, the workers had resisted only vocally—with shouted curses and pleas for an explanation of why the Tsar would have his people killed; they had thrown no stones, built no barricades, broken no windows. And when they left the field of contest, they were leaderless.

TERMINATION OF THE GAPONOVSHCHINA

Gapon, having fled the scene of the Narva Arch disorder, was hurried by some of his guardian friends to a safe hiding place. And immediately steps were taken to disguise him, for he was now a marked man, and it was to be expected that all members of the police force and the soldiery would be on the lookout for him. Accordingly, his hair was cut short, his beard shaved off, and his clerical clothes exchanged for those of a layman. Though a fugitive—and now an embittered one—he made a few more attempts to further the cause he had espoused. In the evening after the abortive march, he joined a meeting of aroused liberals in the building that housed the Free Economic Society, a venerable and legally recognized organization that had come to be dominated by liberals. And there, before a most receptive audience, he made an impassioned denunciation of the Tsar, who had just undergone, in his estimation, a mercurial change from the benevolent "Sire" of yesterday to the "soul destroyer of the Russian Empire," and solicited the group's support for action against the regime. Having heard Gapon's speech as well as declarations from a number of leading liberals, the assembled men decided that, though they were not yet ready to support revolution, they would at least declare their position on the day's happenings. They embodied it in a letter with 459 signatures (including those of the ten men who had vainly tried to get a hearing before the Minister of Interior a day earlier) and arranged its dispatch to the "Officers of the Russian Army." It was an open declaration of disaffection:

It is impossible to live thus any longer. The Russian people needs bread, it needs enlightenment, it needs liberty. . . . Russia needs a constitution. The zemstvo representatives, the municipal dumas, the Russian intelligentsia, and the Russian merchant class, the body of students, and the working masses not only recognize this need, they have already formulated it. . . .

Officers of the Russian Army . . . you have a strong sense of honor. Listen to its voice. Where is your place? With him who fears even to accept a petition or with all of honorable and selfless Russia? As men of honor, you will not use arms against the unarmed, you will not take money from the people for its blood, which you have already spilled. Turn your arms against the enemies of the people.[12]

On the same day, Gapon indited a message to the "Workingmen of Russia," in which he exhorted them to carry on the "struggle for national freedom" and promised that he would soon be among them again. Within a few days, however, he found it expedient to flee the country: Once abroad, he asserted himself as a revolutionary irrevocably allied with those who sought "the real emancipation of the proletariat and the whole toiling mass from capitalistic oppression and political slavery." He spent some time in Geneva, where for a while he was quite popular with the Russian revolutionary colony; but his popularity waned, and he had to abandon his fond hope of becoming a leader among the exiles and emigrés. Finally, he returned to Russia and involved himself in a kind of disguised equivocation, trying on the one hand to convince the authorities that he could still serve them and, on the other, attempting to maintain the confidence of the revolutionaries. Inevitably, he failed with both parties. When some of the SR's became convinced that he was serving as a police agent, they delegated one of their number, Pincus Rutenberg, to arrange for his death. He was hanged in a little cottage, across the Finnish border from St. Petersburg, in the spring of 1906. And his name, once familiarly recognized by many (whether in reverence, scorn, or fear), soon faded from memory, not to be restored until the revolution he helped to precipitate had become a matter of history. It was an effacement presaged by the Holy Synod of the Russian Orthodox Church when, re-

[12] Akademiya Nauk, SSSR, *Nachalo Pervoi Russkoi Revolyutsii,* pp. 63-65.

viewing the tragedy in which he had been the central character, it expunged his name from the clerical registry and
reproachfully identified him as a "criminal priest who had
imprudently disdained his sacred vow" while deceiving the
workers and leading them astray.

The Gaponovshchina did not survive its promoter; in fact,
as a political movement, it was over by the end of Bloody
Sunday. Without the leader and his nimbus of government
protection, those of his lieutenants who were not arrested
were disinclined to reactivate his ideas; and they would not
have found sufficient following among the strikers to carry on,
in any case. Not that the spirit of the strike had died; it had
not. The great majority of the workers, however, were tired of
having their problems mixed up with those of political reform; they remained monarchist and, though a bit confused
perhaps, were still hostile to the enemies of the regime—as
they continued to demonstrate by their abuse of students
whose harangues they resented. In a few of them, the treatment they had received on the day of the march had provoked
such disgust that they repudiated their loyalty and went over
to the ranks of the liberals or socialists. But, whether monarchist or socialist, all were strong in their determination to
continue the strike.

The mood of the strikers was just one of the indications
that the government, though it had overridden the Gaponovshchina, had not eliminated the domestic crisis. That fact
was soon to become more widely understood by many individuals in positions of authority who had been giving the
matter only superficial attention. The immediate interpretations of this one brush with a limited phase of the country's
discontent varied widely. The anguished Tsar made this entry
in his diary at the end of Bloody Sunday:

A grim day! As a result of the desire of the workers to go to
the Winter Palace, serious disorders took place in Petersburg. In many parts of the city troops were compelled to
fire; many were killed or wounded. God, how sad and
grim![13]

[13] Nicholas II, *Dnevnik Imperatora Nikolaya II* (Berlin, 1923),
p. 194.

Momentarily an event on the home front had overshadowed for him those on the battle front. General Fullon, frightened and still retreating from responsibility, fled to his quarters and hid there. Svyatopolk-Mirsky saw the broader threat; he prepared to alert all governors on the need to prevent the spread of the strike movement in their areas. The Grand Duke Vladimir, despite his confidence in armed force and his alleged curt summation of the Sunday crisis ("We prevented the assemblage!"), admitted that some improvement in workers' conditions was due. Others felt that, in turning back the marchers, the government had actually repulsed an action of the revolutionaries, whom they accused of promoting the demonstration to further their own aims. And some believed, quite honestly, that behind the strike was an Anglo-Japanese inspired and financed effort to disrupt the Russian war industries. The Ministry of War went so far as to publish in newspapers and announce by placards that "Anglo-Japanese provocateurs" were responsible for the strikes among men employed in the manufacture of naval equipment. Even the Holy Synod accepted this interpretation and, on the 14th, issued a statement deploring the recent disturbances "provoked with bribes from the enemies of Russia."

Understandably, the essential import of the Gaponovshchina was not completely recognized at the time by anyone—that it was the beginning of the Revolution of 1905.

4

Development
of the Revolution: First Phase
January 10–February 18

By means of the events of January 9/22, 1905, Tsar Nicholas has revealed himself as the enemy and butcher of the people. We will say no more about him, nor shall we speak to him henceforth. . . .

Yesterday there were still divisions and parties. Today the Russian liberation movement must have one body and one soul, one unifying thought: retribution and freedom at all costs. . . .

It is impossible to live thus any longer. The annals of the autocratic oppression . . . must be brought to a close.

> —Editorial by Peter Struve (leading member of the Union of Liberation and editor of its organ), *Osvobozhdenie*, January 12/25, 1905.

At present Russia is in a grievous situation, unprecedented in her history, the consequences of which cannot be predicted. Your majesty is the autocratic tsar of the Russian land, and autocracy must be unassailable, resting on a base so firm that no developments can shake it. . . .

> —Report by Alexis Ermolov (Minister of Agriculture) to Nicholas II, January 17, 1905.

AFTER JANUARY 9, the liberation movement could count on far greater support and more favorable conditions for expansion and action than ever before. While shock and repulsion were fresh, the public readily accepted a distorted interpretation of Bloody Sunday which went beyond fact, that the government had been callous and clumsy in dealing with the St. Petersburg strikers, and accused the government of premeditated cruelty. The Tsar, his uncle the Grand Duke Vladimir, the ministers, the police, and the higher army officers were believed to have deliberately enticed a mass of strikers, led by a Judas goat (Father Gapon), into a murderous trap in order to teach them that organized opposition was futile and suicidal. This version, later known to be based on exaggerations and misstatements, was eagerly accepted by the opposition, for it fitted the antigovernment conception of the nature of autocracy and was consistent with the facts then known to the public. It was a version that proved to be a most useful weapon of propaganda, for the government not only failed to discredit it but also unwittingly reinforced it by subsequent actions that seemed to make it more credible.

NATIONWIDE PROTEST

The people of St. Petersburg led the reaction to Bloody Sunday for the quite obvious reason that the events had occurred there and for the less obvious, but more important, reasons that the workers of the capital were more restive than those in other cities and that organized opposition was stronger there.

On Monday, January 10, the city had the appearance of an embattled area where hostile forces were between encounters. Everywhere there were troops and police with orders to prevent demonstrations and to protect government property. On horseback, they patrolled the streets, ready and sometimes eager to use *nagaika* or sword; and on foot, they guarded railway terminals, imperial palaces, and government buildings. The usually busy Nevsky Prospekt appeared desolate, for most of the stores were closed and shuttered. Yet on it, as on other streets, many citizens were in evidence, hurrying to meetings, gathering confederates for some undertaking in response to yesterday's events, or simply exchanging rumors, of which there were scores—e.g., that the Tsar was hiding at Gatchina in fear for his life and that Tsarina Alexandra and her children were preparing to flee to safety. Despite the number of people about, there was little disorder. What there was—jeering at soldiers and police or throwing stones—came mainly from small groups of Putilov men, some mettlesome students, and a scattering of common rowdies.

There were a few instances of alarm caused by sizeable crowds, but no serious trouble developed from them. At the Preobrazhensky Cemetery, where the previous day's dead had been hurriedly buried in a common grave, a hostile crowd of several thousands, attempting to reopen the grave, were driven off by troops. And around the Alexandrovsky Hospital, where the wounded were being treated, a thousand or so persons gathered to wait for bulletins; but this was one crowd that the troops wisely chose to ignore. In the evening, at the Alexandra Theater, a member of the Free Economic Society abetted by two students used the first intermission to remind those present that this was not the time for entertainment, but for mourning. Their sentiments were applauded by the audience who, with little hesitation, donned their wraps and streamed out of the building, leaving the management no alternative but to suspend the performance.

Immediate and spontaneous actions such as these, however, did not indicate the depth to which the people of the capital had been stirred. More truly indicative were the spread of the strike among industrial workers and the simultaneous spread of what may be called a strike among the educated class, both generally peaceful but openly defiant. They represented opposition that was not only increasing but also becoming more receptive to the idea of organized protest.

The original strikers, whose demands were still being stubbornly denied by those in charge of the industrial establishments involved, announced their continued refusal to work after Bloody Sunday. And they were now being joined by workers from many plants and factories that had been operating up to this time—among them, the important gas works and one of the electric power stations.

Soon St. Petersburg was the scene of an unprecedented demonstration of popular protest as thousands of students and members of the professions added strength to the antigovernment forces by declaring their solidarity with the strikers, denouncing the recent official acts, making statements of the incompatibility of their own situations with the existing autocratic regime, and giving united support to demands for change. At the University, some five thousand students, with the support of most of the faculty, went on strike, refusing to participate in any academic work and demanding that the government call a constituent assembly. Students of the Institute of Ways and Communications declared their support of the industrial strikers and collected funds to help them. At both the University and the Polytechnic Institute, professors, hitherto generally aloof from the liberation movement, now spoke up *en masse*, declaring that the continuation of the autocratic regime made normal academic life impossible. Lawyers indicated their cooperation with the opposition by refusing to appear in court and by issuing a formal protest against the "pitiless hand of the government." Medical, legal, pedagogical, and agricultural societies denounced the government and called for a constituent assembly. The Merchants Club barred its doors to guards officers because of the part they had taken in the events of Bloody Sunday. The Manufacturers Association voted to give financial aid to the families of the victims, to refrain from any punitive action against the strikers, and to demand political reforms. An outstanding, and perhaps the most effective, action in stirring the educated to a sense of the urgent need for change was that of sixteen members of the august Academy of Sciences, who made a public declaration of their belief that developments had created the necessity for a change in government. They were joined by 326 eminent university professors and lecturers, and the group circulated the document that came to be called the "Statement of the 342," in which it was affirmed that Russia would enjoy the benefits of education only after "freely elected representatives of the people are given the power to make laws and keep a check on the administration." And that position was immediately endorsed by 1,200 of the country's most noted scholars. By publicizing these activities and declarations of the educated class, the press added to their worth as

MOSCOW IN 1905

PRESNYA DISTRICT

MUNICIPAL DUMA

MOSCOW UNIVERSITY

KREMLIN

MOSCOW RIVER

ZAMOSKVORECHE

propaganda for the opposition. In addition, most of the city's newspapers joined editorially in the growing demand for the convocation of an elected national assembly.

The displays of protest initiated in St. Petersburg were duplicated throughout the country. Moscow was the first to follow; strikes began there on the 10th. On the 11th there were strikes in Warsaw, Kharkov, Vilna, Kovno, and Helsingfors; on the 12th, in Riga, Kiev, Voronezh, Mogilev, Libau, and Saratov; on the 13th, in Lodz, Mitau, Perm, Minsk, and Smorgon; on the 14th, on the Moscow-to-Brest Railroad; on the 16th, in Borisov; on the 17th, in Batum, Ekaterinoslav, Brest, Grodno, and Bialystok; on the 18th, in Tiflis and Samara; on the 19th, in Narva and Czestochowa; on the 20th, in Kazan. And so it went—in all, nearly 500,000 workers were out on strike in January—more than the combined number of strikers for the decade from 1894 to 1904.

More difficult to enumerate were the tens of thousands of students, professors, journalists, lawyers, doctors, merchants, and manufacturers who, in one way or another, expressed their oneness with those who had spoken up in St. Petersburg. At the University of Moscow, a move to strike was supported by 2,635 of the students and opposed by only 102. Students of other Moscow higher schools, among them the Engineering School, the Agricultural Institute, the Teachers Institute, and the Women's Higher Courses, voted to strike. And their example was followed throughout Russia as students of universities and other higher schools went on strike, demanding reforms; often they were joined by the entire student bodies of secondary schools. Faculties also, following the St. Petersburg precedent, promptly and without reserve denounced the autocratic regime as an obstacle to normal academic life.

This collective protest from the educated class was both more inclusive and more defiant than the record-setting one of a month earlier. Now their demands were often supplemented by direct and personal denunciations of officials, regardless of the fact that, in many cases, their own freedom of action and their positions were subject to the discretion of the government. Scholars even dared to repudiate such men as the Grand Duke Constantine, President of the Academy of Sciences, who had reminded them that professors were government employees whose duties did not include the fomenting of unrest. In almost every city, such calculated defiance was flaunted openly and given wide dissemination by the press.

In various parts of the country, strong expressions of disapprobation came also from organizations with legally recognized political status. Assemblies of nobility, zemstvos, and municipal dumas now issued forceful statements of protest and added their demands for reforms more thoroughgoing than those they had felt necessary in November and December of the previous year. They were in general agreement that the bureaucracy had so discredited itself and so subverted the people's confidence in the government that it had become imperative to summon a representative assembly through which the people could participate in reforming Russia. A conspicuous exception to this chorus of disapproval was provided by the Moscow provincial assembly of nobles, which had a strong conservative wing including, among other high officials, nearly half of the governors of Russia. After bitter debate over the position the assembly should take in its address to the Tsar concerning the current situation, on January 22 it brought to vote two statements. One, conservative in tone and expressing continued loyalty to the throne but no wish for reform, was supported by such men as the brothers Alexander and Fedor Samarin; the other, liberal in tone and calling for representative government, was supported by prominent liberal figures—among them, Prince P. D. Dolgorukov, Prince Sergei Trubetskoi, Fedor Kokoshkin, and Vasily Maklakov. The conservative statement was adopted by a vote of 219 to 147. But many who voted for it as an expression of loyalty voted also for the liberal statement as an expression of their opinion. Naturally such equivocal indications of progovernment sentiment made little impression on the public mind. This one was unfavorably received even in the conservative press.

Compared to this swell of response, that which had followed the issuance of the Eleven Theses of the zemstvo congress had been a mere ripple. Yet even this, for all its clamor and vituperation, was far from an armed uprising. The strikes and other manifestations were generally peaceful in the interior provinces because, on the one hand, there was little inclination to violence on the part of the opposition and, on the other, the authorities were under orders to prevent any public mass activity from which violence would be liable to develop.

There were, of course, some exceptions to this rule of non-violence in the interior. One of them occurred in Saratov, where the potentially strong following of the Socialist Revolutionary Party had been held in check by a strong governor, Peter Stolypin. The strike movement which began there on January 12 was at once recognized as being of a more determined and savage temper than was usual elsewhere. Factory workers, joined by railwaymen, government employees, and professionals, went in throngs from place to place, calling out additional workers and displaying their animus against authority by stoning Cossacks whenever they appeared. They marched through the streets shouting demands for a constituent assembly and the end of the war. At the height of their boldness, they attempted to seize the railroad stations and were deterred only by direct threat of armed force. Their tempestuousness reached even the schools and, within three days, the pupils of several secondary schools had quit their classrooms to add to the general disturbance. Some of them clashed with patrolling Cossacks when their attempts to enter and disrupt schools in session were thwarted. The strikers planned to climax their activity by a major march, on the fourth day, to the center of the city. Believing, from Stolypin's record, that he would stop such a demonstration, a deputation from the Saratov municipal duma and the zemstvo of Saratov province entreated him not to take steps that would inflict on the city a repetition of Bloody Sunday. His answer was both brief and direct—he would not permit revolutionary acts, and he would shed blood if necessary. He at once called in additional troops, and that affirmation of intention served him well. The presence of extra force proved sufficient, on the day of the march, to convince the three thousand participating workers and *intelligents* that the alternatives were battle or retreat; and they chose retreat, though some of them had provided themselves with arms and apparently had intended to use them.

Another display of unruly protest was made at the Kiev Polytechnical Institute, where the student body was known to be under Socialist Revolutionary influence. One of their meetings, at which they had voted to suspend studies in order to participate in the "imminent revolution," was interrupted by the arrival of troops and police to arrest their leaders; and, in defiance, they barred the doors, broke up school furnishings and, from the windows, hurled pieces at the forces of authority. Quickly subdued, they would all have been taken into custody but for the intervention of faculty members, who solicited official intervention on their behalf and arranged permission for them to leave the building unpunished.

Violence as a form of protest was much more common in the Russian borderlands than in the interior. In the Baltic provinces, Finland, Congress Poland, and Transcaucasia, where political dissatisfaction was being added to persistent nationalist feelings and economic discontent, outbursts were particularly easy to provoke.

Riga was the trouble center in the Baltic area. The strike movement that began there on January 12 rapidly became a general strike so widely supported that, on the second day, the participants confidently undertook a mass demonstration. Nearly fifteen thousand workers and *intelligents*—Letts, Russians, Jews, Estonians, and Germans—many armed with pistols, marched through the streets in defiance of the forces mustered to oppose them. The results were tragic. A few shots fired by the marchers were answered by concerted fire from the police and soldiers, and some of the demonstrators were killed on the spot. The others, fleeing for their lives, dashed onto the ice-covered Dvina River; and there, as the ordinarily safe ice gave way in places, some died by drowning. In all, according to the official record, seventy civilians were killed, and eight soldiers and policemen were wounded. Thus January 13 became, for the Baltic provinces, the counterpart of Bloody Sunday and the beginning of a period of turbulence and violence unmatched in any other part of the country.

In Congress Poland the strike movement spread from Warsaw and Lodz to virtually every city of its ten provinces, accompanied everywhere by fierce nationalism and violence.

Strikers and their supporters not only stoned soldiers and policemen, but also occasionally fired at them. They made forcible entries into stores and defied authorities in various ways, some of them personally threatening (in Lodz, for example, they held the governor captive in a hotel until he could be rescued by armed forces). In secondary and higher schools, pupils demonstratively demanded the restoration of Polish as the language of instruction and the employment of Polish rather than Russian teachers—often reinforcing their demands with the cry "Down with the *Moskaly!*" (a contemptuous denunciation of Muscovites). Though Congress Poland was not in open revolt, it was so evidently near revolt that the authorities, as a precautionary measure, called for substantial additions to the 250,000 troops already immediately available to them.[1]

Tiflis, the administrative and economic center of Transcaucasia, was the focal point of unrest in that area. The railroadmen were the first to go on strike, on the 18th, and they were followed by workers in other occupations. On the 23rd, thousands of strikers, carrying red flags and shouting "Down with autocracy!" marched through the streets and engaged patrols in desultory fighting. Similar demonstrations occurred in Batum, Sukhum, Baku, Kutais, and other Transcaucasian cities as strikes spread and nationalism flared anew. In Baku, barely recovered from the December strike, the revolutionary mood was particularly threatening, and the local police grew steadily more apprehensive about it. One of the most serious disturbances was in a rural area, Ozurgetsky district of Kutaisk province, where the peasantry had for some time been on the verge of rebellion. Now, led by neighbors who had returned from Batum (exiled from the city to their native homes because of participation in factory strikes), the peasants took to arms, destroying administrative offices of the villages and driving panicky officials to flight. So effective was this outburst

---

[1] It had long been the practice of the Russian military command to maintain a major part of the standing army in Congress Poland for speedy use in the event of war on the western boundary. These troops could, of course, be used also to deal with internal disorders.

that the administration was completely demoralized, and officials did not return to their duties for nearly a year.

Another locality affected by peasant disorder was Eversmuizhskoi volost[2] of Vitebsk province, where there was a distinctly agrarian incident of some note, brief but important as an indication of what concerned the peasantry at this time. It took place at the volost offices, where the entire male peasant population (about five hundred in number) appeared, many of them with weapons, on January 15 to demand 1) the dismissal of the local officials, 2) an auditing of the moneys the officials had handled, and 3) the publication of the real Emancipation Manifesto of 1861 (many peasants believed that the real manifesto had been kept from them), which would prove their right to cut the landlords' timber without payment. They supplemented their demands by the declaration that, whether or not the manifesto were produced, they would begin to cut the timber within two days. The reply of authority to their daring was the usual one—troops arrived to prevent the threatened act and remained until all was quiet again.

These displays of rebelliousness by the peasants in the Kutaisk and Vitebsk provinces were among the very few of their kind during January. Throughout the country, most of the peasantry remained—or seemed to remain—immune to the effects of urban disturbances. Occasionally governors reported that peasants, influenced by rumors, were becoming edgy; but generally they reported nothing untoward in their behavior.

While the movement initiated by the industrial strikers was gaining wide and enthusiastic support from other disaffected groups and even a bit of notice from some of the peasants, the original strikers were finding their personal situations worsening. Industrial management, on the whole, flatly refused to agree to labor's demands. And since the strikers had hardly any funds of their own and had been spreading very thin the amount collected for them by Liberationists and others, they were forced to limit the term of their refusal to work. In St. Petersburg, the return to work began on the 14th and by the

[2] Volost: an administrative unit consisting of a number of villages.

18th was almost complete. Elsewhere the end of the industrial strike came a week or so later. Nevertheless, from the point of view of the opposition, the strikes had not been in vain. The spirit of resentment endured among the workers, and they remained ready to go on strike again when they could afford to do so.

The few revolutionaries who had reacted to Bloody Sunday with the expectation of an immediate armed uprising that would topple the regime were disappointed. But the majority of the Liberationists understood that, in this test of positions, the opposition had gained strength despite the fact that the old regime was still in power (only in Ozurgetsky district was authority broken) and continued to function: the government had not capitulated, but it had been frightened; the revolution had not been realized, but it had undoubtedly begun.

Enduring Effects of Bloody Sunday

Bloody Sunday served as a powerful catalyst that speeded up the tempo of psychological change. It heightened animosity, strengthened faith in the possibility of change, encouraged greater daring in the conception of what could be changed. And the explosion of discontent and anger that it had touched off had a cumulative effect: strikes among workers of one occupation or in one plant encouraged strikes among workers of other occupations or in other plants; mass labor strikes encouraged the liberation movement to greater boldness against the government; and, in time, the knowledge that the government had been challenged and had shown some weakness would encourage peasants to take a strong stand against the landlords. In a country as seriously beset by problems as Russia was in 1905, a loss of faith in the good will of the government and a decline in fear or respect for its authority could not be regarded lightly.

One of the most prominent changes taking place at this time was to be observed among the workers. Russian labor did not become revolutionary overnight; but after January, 1905, it was no longer an unorganized mass, restive but irresolute, and hostile to all ideas of political change. Now it began to organize, to show less reticence about striking, and to move— albeit slowly—toward support of the liberation movement. What happened among the Putilov workers of St. Petersburg after January 9 was, in many ways, typical of what was happening among all workers. Some of them continued to adhere to the Gapon ideal of a kind of Christian monarchist trade-unionism, but their number gradually decreased; some—and their number increased—became receptive to socialist (particularly Social Democratic) propaganda, which placed the revolutionary establishment of a democratic republic ahead of the achievement of economic benefits; and others—by far the largest number—were primarily concerned with continuing the fight for economic betterment, indifferent to the form that the struggle should take but determined that it not be abandoned. Putilov workers were perhaps more militant than other St. Petersburg workers; and the city as a whole was certainly more militant than other cities, with the exception of Warsaw and Lodz. But, generally speaking, developments in the capital were a rough pattern for the rest of the country. Labor was primarily concerned with economic improvement: achievement of the eight-hour day, improvement in sanitary and medical facilities, higher wages, abolition of overtime and the system of fines, recognition of the right to bargain collectively, pensions, and free primary schooling for their children. And to the extent that their aims were economic in nature, they were engaged in a struggle with their employers, not with the government.

The position of management in its relation to labor was one of the peculiar anomalies of 1905: though it resisted as long as possible the workers' economic demands, it supported their political demands. And, as labor manifested increasingly political tendencies, factory owners often found themselves having to oppose one phase of a strike while supporting another. This split-sympathy had developed from the belief common among industrialists that the government too often tried to solve the labor problem and win good will among the workers at the direct expense of management by requiring, on occasion, wage increases and shorter working hours, or at the indirect expense of management by unfortunate experiments in "police socialism"—of which the Gapon Assembly had been the most unfortunate. The industrialists took the position that both they and labor would benefit from expanded political and civil rights: they would have a greater voice in government, and labor would be less given to agitation. Insofar as the workers sought political change, therefore, management wanted to help them. Yet labor, for all its new-found boldness, hesitated to trust the good will of employers in any respect, just as it hesitated to give up all of its hostility toward the intelligentsia.

Among all those to whom Bloody Sunday brought a change in outlook, the educated class was the most outspoken and, hence, apparently the most active. Though deploring the manner in which confirmation had come to their point of view, they could not but be enthusiastic about the improved prospects. Their worst suspicions of government had been sustained, and the imperative need for the political reforms they had urged in the Eleven Theses and in the program of the Union of Liberation had been made clearer than ever. And now their cause was deluged with openly active champions. In January almost every institution of higher learning was on strike or had been closed by the authorities as a precautionary measure. During the remainder of 1905 higher education was almost totally neglected; and, while the majority of professors remained firmly liberal but far from radical in their expressions of opposition, the students threw themselves wholeheartedly into the thick of demonstrative activity for the liberation movement. They prepared illegal political literature and distributed it, and they became the most energetic of agitators—among workers, soldiers, and occasionally peasants.

As might be expected, the atmosphere of the January days was maintained among the national minorities with very little effort. On the whole, they needed less convincing of the need for change than did the people of European Russia, and they reacted eagerly to the opportunity for activity conducive to change. Most of the minority groups were still willing to make common cause with the liberation movement in the belief that the first aim of all should be the achievement of political liberty—without which, they knew, it would be impossible to improve their own positions. Consequently they tended to cooperate among themselves and with their Russian counterparts. In many cities joint action and common tactics were adopted—as in Vilna, where the Social Democrats, the PPS, the Polish Social Democratic Party, and the Bund worked together quite effectively. Not all association, however, either within or among minority parties was agreeable. Internal discord, such as that between the right and left wings of the PPS and that between the so-called "old" and "new" factions of the Armenian Dashnyak Party, expressed itself now and again. Also there were some instances of jurisdictional disputes; for instance, the PPS claimed to represent all the workers of Congress Poland and resented the Bund activities in that area, while the Bund in turn resented the activities of the recently formed Socialist Zionist Party in its sphere. Nevertheless the feeling for a common front was stronger than any divisive feeling.

At the same time there was a steady increase in the number affected by nationalistic sentiments within the minority groups having a traditionally strong national consciousness, notably the Poles, Armenians, Jews, Finns, and Georgians. Though there were still many Russified persons in these groups (particularly among the Jews, Georgians, and Armenians) who were indifferent or antipathetic to nationalistic ideas, their positions were being more frequently challenged than ever before. Those peoples who had hitherto given little evidence of a sense of national identity (Letts, Estonians, Lithuanians, Ukrainians, White Russians, and Moslems of various ethnic groups) now began gradually to become nationality-conscious also, and soon they were establishing separate organizations and using their own language in publications.

Whether or not these various changes in moods, opinions, and attitudes would effect any change in the basic social and political structure of the country had yet to be determined. Much, of course, depended on what the opposition could and would do in order to compel change and on what the government could or would do to stop the further growth of the

opposition. Furthermore, events as yet unforeseeable might tip
the balance: another event like Bloody Sunday might be sufficient to topple the government, and a decisive victory in
Manchuria might disconcert the opposition.

On the face of it, the opposition now had a heaven-sent opportunity to take the initiative. The socialists, in particular,
had been given just what they had sought for years: an
aroused working class. Yet they were not prepared to take the
lead and direct the opposition. They lacked adequate organization, being divided over tactics and goals as in the past, and
they were still far from having the confidence of the masses.
Bloody Sunday and the subsequent strikes found the major
socialist leaders abroad, most of them in Geneva. They were
exhilarated by the news from Russia, feeling that they were
on the eve of the long-awaited revolution. They sang revolutionary songs and talked glowingly of a coming armed rising
against autocracy. Lenin even began an intensive study of
street fighting methods. But, with few exceptions, they remained where they were (Trotsky, with a false passport, was
one of the small number to leave at once for Russia), continuing to argue politics but supplying little leadership. It
was impossible to lead from abroad; yet they understood that,
even if they chose to return to Russia, it was unlikely that
many of them, as well known to the police as they were, could
remain at liberty very long in Russia or that they could even
maintain a well-organized underground organization there.
Moreover, in the final analysis, the heads of the socialist movement did not realize the nearness of the revolution and therefore saw no reason to divert their most serious attention from
internal party problems. Many months passed before either
the SR's or the SD's produced clear statements of their immediate plans.

For these reasons the socialist movement within Russia in
January, 1905 operated, not as a unified army with a defined
strategy, but as a number of isolated guerilla detachments acting in accordance with their own understanding of the program and aims of their parties. Most of them felt that, at this
time, they could function best as part of the liberation movement, dedicating themselves to the overthrow of the regime

and the convocation of a constituent assembly; after that, they would pursue a policy aimed at the development of a socialist society. Recognizing the strike movement as a major weapon, they attempted to organize socialist circles in factories, tried to win over leading workers, and called for more strikes. They quadrupled the output of their illegal printing presses and distributed thousands of leaflets asserting their militancy:

Down with the Tsar-murderer!
Down with autocracy!
Long live social democracy!
Long live the constituent assembly!
Long live the revolution!

They made an extensive effort to propagandize among the armed forces. More often than not their representatives (usually students) among the soldiers would be set upon with cries of "Traitor!" or "Zhidy!" (Kikes, a term of insult to Jews). But here and there—among the personnel of units in Moscow, St. Petersburg, Odessa, and Kiev, on some ships of the Black Sea Fleet, and at various naval bases—they found men who were willing to accept and read their leaflets and, among them, some who could be persuaded to accept their views. They tried also to organize street demonstrations but, during the disturbed January days, the police were usually too alert for them. Some busied themselves with collecting revolvers for the hoped-for armed rising. A few, chiefly among the SR's and the PPS's, planned and committed acts of terror. But at every point, the going was slow, and it was clear that the socialists would not have a commanding status in the opposition until their influence had grown and their present efforts had been given time to bear fruit.

The liberals, on the other hand, were in a good tactical position. They were better organized to take advantage of the growing mood of disaffection, and they were in the midst of a political campaign that was definitely accelerated by recent events. January 9 provided them—as well as others of the opposition—with a gory shirt to wave, a specific indictment of tsarism with which to vivify and dramatize their struggle. They could now argue that they had been proved right in their diagnosis of what ailed Russia, and they could expect therefore greater confidence in their ability to achieve for the country what it needed. The theme of the liberation movement from now on was well expressed in part of the statement issued, shortly before their arrest on January 10, by the ten men who had sought to persuade the government to permit the Sunday march:

> We can no longer be patient with such a state of affairs; We invite all the citizens of Russia to an immediate and relentless and peaceful struggle with autocracy.[3]

This was not a new theme, to be sure. But that fact, in itself, is noteworthy: it is evidence that the liberals were not straying thoughtlessly from previous positions nor being stampeded into revolutionary actions. What was new—and noteworthy—was the mood in which the liberation movement was now working. It was a mood of intransigent defiance that benefited the Liberationists at the expense of the Shipov liberals. It was encouraged by the rapid growth of the liberal following, the growing support for liberal political aims, the mass labor strikes with political implications, and the immediate and bitter international revulsion expressed through antitsarist demonstrations and protests in England, Germany, Austria-Hungary, Sweden, France, Spain, Italy, Belgium, United States, Argentina, and Uruguay. In addition, the strong feeling of camaraderie and unity now evident throughout the opposition strengthened the Liberationists, for they were the most nearly prepared to give the needed leadership.

That this "oneness" of feeling affected so many was of major advantage to the opposition, keeping its forces in line with the theme of the liberation movement when its strength might otherwise have been dissipated. A participant in the events of 1905, the liberal leader Vasily Maklakov, later made this analysis of the general situation:

> Thus there was organized in the year 1905 a common front, from the revolutionary to the conservative strata of our so-

[3] Akademiya Nauk, SSSR, *Nachalo Pervoi Russkoi Revolyutsii*, p. 88.

ciety. There could be no common point of view in this camp. But on one point they all agreed: *that to continue as before was impossible.*[4]

It was this common point of agreement, extending both to the right of the Liberationists (among erstwhile conservatives) and to their left (among revolutionaries) that, at this time, led workers increasingly to support the Liberationist call for a constituent assembly, industrialists to support the workers' political strikes, liberals to support the eight-hour day and collect funds for strikers, socialists to appear on the same platform as liberals and the two groups often to work in the same organization. "Divisions and parties" continued to exist, but Russians in greater numbers than ever before imaginable were admitting comradeship in a common struggle. "Liberty and representative government" was their unifying slogan, the *Marseillaise* their marching song. By the end of January, even the doggedly monarchist and conservative *Novoe Vremya* was impelled to call for a *zemsky sobor* (an elected assembly).

Regardless of their fraternization with groups of basically differing views, the liberals continued to emphasize peaceful struggle—political banquets, petitions, and nonviolent acts of defiance. They approved the methods of lawyers who displayed their contempt for the government by refusing to participate in court proceedings; of professors who made public declarations of their beliefs in the need for political change; of students who protested by refusing to attend lectures or take examinations, even by desisting from "all cultural work" (as did University of Moscow students); of any group that undertook to protest or demonstrate against the regime without intent to injure either persons or property.

OFFICIAL MEASURES OF REACTION

The advantages that could be claimed by the opposition at this time, numerous as they were, stopped short of the ability to compel the government to make any of the demanded changes. Power was still in the hands of the Tsar, and the de-

[4] V. Maklakov, *Vlast i Obshchestvennost* (Paris, 1936), II, 352.

cision about immediately succeeding courses of action would be his. What he decided would depend on his interpretation of the causes and consequences of Bloody Sunday and his judgment of the relative importance of the various steps to be taken in the readjustment now required. It went without saying that he would continue to give priority to the reestablishment and preservation of order, that being the first business of any state and having exceptional importance in the Russian autocracy, the embodiment of absolute power. Concern for order at this time, however, did not imply fear of revolution, only normal sensitivity about the prestige of throne and country. Russian prestige had just been subjected to severe impairment, first by the setbacks at the hands of the Japanese, then by the continuing pressure at the hands of the Tsar's own subjects.

It might have occurred to some rulers, in a situation of this kind, that the most direct method of restoring order could be determined by giving immediate attention to some of the current demands of his people. But Russian tsars were no more accustomed to recognizing impertinent demands for reform than to negotiating with strikers. Nicholas' grandfather, Tsar Alexander II, had imprisoned a group of nobles who had called for a national legislative assembly and directed that they be sentenced to confinement in an insane asylum. Nicholas himself, less than a month before Bloody Sunday, had instructed his subjects (in connection with his ukase) to mind their own affairs. At this time, however, he could not overlook the fact that his instruction had failed to prevent illegal strikes among the workers and verbal abuse from almost every direction. Since he believed that most of these acts of disobedience and all of the violence had been provoked by the revolutionaries, he decided that the first task of the government was to reassert its control with such firmness that the revolutionaries would be warned off. His understanding of the revolutionaries was as fuzzy and distorted as was the opposition's understanding of what went on in his mind.

The regimen of firmness was begun on the day after Bloody Sunday, when General Dmitri Trepov was given the assignment to restore order in St. Petersburg and its environs, using the special power vested in him as governor-general of the city and province of St. Petersburg (a newly created and temporary post). Trepov had been Chief of Police in Moscow for the past nine years, serving under the Grand Duke Sergei, who was then governor-general of the Moscow province. He was known as an uncompromising and exacting man, quite unlike Prefect Fullon, who was now being relegated to an undemanding military command. And he was nowise intimidated by the oppositional abuse heaped upon him when he was given unusual imperial favors, including quarters in the Winter Palace, or when, two days after his selection, the capital was placed under martial law and he was given extraordinary powers. He began promptly his task of restoring order according to the plan approved by the Tsar, putting under arrest those who were known to be agitating for revolution as well as many suspected of connection with such activity. In and about the city, troops and police, by his order, broke up all known attempts to hold public meetings or demonstrations. Within a few days there was no question that his steps had been effective and that the government was in physical control of the city and the surrounding area. Military patrols were removed and, as the strikes came to an end, the local situation seemed to be normal again.

OFFICIAL EFFORTS AT CONCILIATION

The Tsar was aware that police and military action were not enough to remove the effects of January 9. But the public could not know his mind and were predisposed to be suspicious of whatever he did. On January 15, he replaced Svyatopolk-Mirsky, long anxious to escape from his post, by Alexander Bulygin; and the public's interpretation of this appointment agreed with that of the French Ambassador, M. Bompard: "The era of liberalism that had barely opened is already closed."[5] In fact, there was much to support the idea that the inclinations of Bulygin would be directly opposed

[5] Bompard to Delcassé, January 15/28, 1905, French Foreign Office Archives, Russie, Politique Intérieure, I.

to those of Svyatopolk-Mirsky, the harbinger of the political
"spring." He was a conservative nobleman who, like Trepov,
had served in Moscow under the Grand Duke Sergei, and he
had only recently been elevated to the governor-generalship
that Sergei had resigned. Though not given to authoritarian
manners, he was likely to be judged by members of the liberation movement as a representative of inimical authority, for
he had consistently opposed their activities. Politically he represented nothing but blind devotion to the throne. But he was
not another Plehve, nor did he have instructions to follow
Plehve's policies.

What Bulygin's appointment meant was not so much the
end of the "era of liberalism" as the end of efforts to give
"society" a role in making policy. The Tsar had grown weary
of Svyatopolk-Mirsky and his methods and probably felt, as
did many others, that the Gaponovshchina was the ultimate
result of his bungling efforts to establish relations with "society." The appointment of the new minister could be taken
to imply that henceforth reliable bureaucrats were to counsel
among themselves. But it was clear that, even within the highest levels of government, hardly anyone would counsel a return to the days of Plehve. (Pobedonostsev was an exception,
but he was of little consequence at this time—though the public believed that he was still a power behind the throne.) The
majority of the Tsar's ministers were agreed that the effects of
the strikes could not be obliterated and the confidence of the
people could not be regained by police measures alone. It was
necessary, they felt, for the Tsar to make some impressive and
emphatic announcement including certain conciliatory features: his shock at the bloodshed on January 9, his awareness
that workers had some legitimate grievances, his recognition
that there were some imperfections in the political system,
and his intention to improve the state of affairs.

Though the consensus was clear thus far, there remained
the difficulty of deciding what improvements should be made,
how far to go with them, and when to set about them. The
Tsar, as usual, found it difficult to judge any situation more
pressing than the war in the Far East. Just now he had hopes
that the Russian forces under Kuropatkin, readying an offen-

sive south of Mukden, would soon be able to achieve a final victory. Yet he could not ignore the fact that his hopes were not well supported: a number of officers, both at the front and at home, judged Kuropatkin to be no longer capable of effective leadership, and many civilian officials agreed with them. Nor could he overlook the fact that to postpone dealing with the domestic situation would not only weaken military morale in the long run but also invite further trouble among the disaffected.

On one thing the Tsar and his ministers were in accord: whatever the form of official response to the current domestic troubles, it must serve two functions—to placate the workers in the center of unrest, St. Petersburg, and to conciliate the country at large. The first was generally believed to be the more urgent.

Kokovtsev, reporting to the Tsar two days after Bloody Sunday, argued that since the turn of events had not only impaired morale at home but also lowered Russia's financial credit abroad, it was imperative that something be done at once to regain public confidence. He suggested that a few simple, direct words from the Tsar to the St. Petersburg workers, assuring them that he had their best interests at heart, would serve the purpose. The majority of the workers, he believed, had not wanted to strike, had been misled into the act, and would welcome any show of understanding and assurance that he might give them. Witte wanted the Tsar to go further. He feared that the "aureole of the ruler would be destroyed" if he did not somehow publicly dissociate himself from Bloody Sunday—perhaps by declaring that the troops had acted without his orders. This suggestion, made at a meeting of the Committee of Ministers, died there when Count Solsky declared the suggested cure to be worse than the disease: to assert that troops could act without orders from the Tsar was tantamount to repudiating autocracy. Nicholas did not think the troops had been at fault, nor would he have deigned, in any case, to evade responsibility for what had happened.

It was the Kokovtsev suggestion that was finally accepted and turned over to Trepov for development and implementation. The latter arranged for the election of thirty-four loyal workers from St. Petersburg factories and sent them by special train to Tsarskoe Selo, on January 19, to meet the Tsar. This was Nicholas' first extended face-to-face encounter with factory workers. What he said to them, guided by the text of a prepared speech, indicated his limited conception of the problems facing the government. He explained to them, as a patient father to children, that the workers had been deceived by wicked men, who treacherously led them into taking part in "sedition" and quitting their "honest toil" at a time when they should have been working relentlessly to do their part in conquering the foreign enemy. He pointed out that, in consequence of what they had done, it had been necessary to use force against the evildoers and thus sacrifice the lives of innocent people. But, he assured them, he forgave these unfortunate mistakes and still trusted the workers as true supporters of the Russian Orthodox faith, the Tsar, and the fatherland. Moreover, understanding their plight as he did, he intended to do everything possible to make conditions better for them. He asked that the thirty-four return with "God's blessing" to their places of work and report to their comrades what he had said.[6]

The speech was remarkably ineffective. If the workers of the capital were moved by it, they failed to give any confirming evidence in their subsequent activities. The public was apparently unimpressed by it. The newspapers barely mentioned it. All told, the Tsar's effort proved worthless as an antidote to the impression created by Bloody Sunday. Trepov, however, was convinced that it was a great success; and Nicholas, flattered by his ministers, continued to believe that his words were cherished by the simple Russian with his innate sense of loyalty to the throne.

Ten days later, the Tsar took another step expected to ease the local tension. He appointed Nicholas V. Shidlovsky, a member of the State Council and the Senate, to the chairmanship of a commission that was to investigate the causes of unrest in the capital. The commission would include not only

[6] The text of the speech will be found in *Pravitelstvennyi Vestnik,* January 20, 1905. For an English translation, *see* R. W. Postgate, *Revolution from 1789-1906* (New York, 1962), pp. 368-69.

representatives of government and industrial management but also elected representatives of the workers. The results were not what had been expected. The workers' representatives on the commission were to be chosen by nine groups of electors, whom the workers designated by vote on February 13. Twenty percent of them were aligned with the SD's; 40 percent were radicals not identified with any party; the rest represented no particular position or were interested only in supporting economic goals for labor. The advantage was clearly with the SD's and radicals, who quickly assumed leadership and declared that they would not participate in the election of deputies unless the government agreed in advance to grant civil liberties and to throw the proceedings of the commission open to the public. Some of them went further and privately agreed to call new strikes as a prelude to armed uprising if their demands were not met. When convened to elect deputies, on February 18, they were informed that their demands would not be met, and seven of the groups refused to go on with the election. That day a new wave of strikes began in the city. Confronted thus by the perseverance of willfulness, the Tsar agreed to Shidlovsky's recommendation that the commission be dissolved. It had become clearly evident that the government was making no progress toward mollifying the labor force in St. Petersburg.

PREPARATION OF REFORMS

Meanwhile, work on the second part of the official program, aimed at bringing about a reconciliation between the government and the general public, had been going ahead—but very slowly. The Committee of Ministers was continuing its efforts to work out means of putting into effect the reforms promised in the ukase of December 12, by which the government hoped to eradicate some of the deep-seated causes of discontent. And, the Tsar having agreed to issue a manifesto informing the people of the government's position with respect to the recent happenings and explaining what it proposed to do, much attention was being devoted to the preparation of that document. Though the Tsar had approved the idea of it just after

Bloody Sunday, he had acquiesced to the advice that the details of its contents should be carefully considered before being made final and publicly proclaimed. Now the Committee of Ministers was undertaking to devise the overall plan for it, and the Tsar himself was carrying on private discussions about it, having summoned Pobedonostsev—whom he often employed for editorial work, but for little else—to help on the text. Unfortunately this multiform consideration proved excessively slow, and no individual minister or group of ministers seemed willing to advise greater speed. Kokovtsev was at first too occupied with the question of Russia's financial credit abroad and his quarrels with the Ministry of Interior. Witte, the ablest of them all, was busily mending political fences, making himself seen and felt in government circles and the diplomatic corps, taking care to sustain the impression that he was so indispensable that sooner or later the Tsar would have to call him to a position of authority. There were some officials in the government who interpreted the situation as immediately dangerous to the regime and grew daily more impatient with this temporizing by the ministers, but it behooved them to respect the ministerial priority in the matter.

The first to point out to the Tsar the seriousness of procrastination was Alexis Ermolov, Minister of Agriculture, hitherto noted for his inaction and apparent insignificance. When he delivered his regular report to the Tsar on January 17, he took what some would have considered a desperate chance, speaking openly and at length about conditions in Russia and making suggestions that reflected his somewhat liberal viewpoint.

The burden of his words was indeed a *cri de coeur*: much was amiss in Russia; though much had been promised in the ukase of December 12, the Committee of Ministers was not only working too slowly on means of activating the projected program but also neglecting to keep the people informed of what it was doing; the country had no real government, only a collection of ministers pursuing separate and often disparate ends; the clergy was without influence on the people; the nobility was split between liberals and conservatives; Bloody Sunday was a disaster, a blot on the honor of the government;

the army had obeyed orders on January 9, but there was no
assurance of how it would respond if disorder should spread
to the countryside and the men, most of them peasants, were
required to shoot other peasants; even if the army remained
loyal, there was a question as to whether or not it would be
large enough to deal with an uprising in the countryside. His
summation was equally specific, pointing out that the strength
of the throne was dependent on the support of the people;
that the people must therefore be told what the government
was planning; that there must be forged a direct link between
people and government; and that the government must act in
a coordinated and energetic fashion.[7]

Though Ermolov's words were rather strong, even intem-
perate, the Tsar did not take them unkindly. He had, in fact,
already thought of doing some of the things suggested, and he
was willing to accept others that had not occurred to him
before. But he could not feel the urgency that the minister
indicated. Considering what was already under way, it seemed
to him that the government was acting with unusual energy
(as indeed it was—for his government). Apparently he did
not recognize the fact that, with the recent digressions from
routine, lines of authority had become thoroughly confused,
most ministers were far from informed about all that was
going on, and only delay and ineptness of procedure were to
be expected.

Moreover, he and his ministers were now accepting or having thrust upon them conceptions and duties completely foreign to their customary thinking and acting. Just after the
Ermolov report, he himself acceded to a suggestion that he
had stubbornly refused before, that there be created a body
of elected representatives to advise him. It was understood
among officials that the announcement of this important concession would either be included in the manifesto or made
public simultaneously with the manifesto. The alternatives
were debated at length. Meanwhile, some of the protracted
considerations were gradually being speeded up, new under-
takings were being proposed, and different approaches were

[7] A. S. Ermolov, "Zapiski A. S. Ermolova," *Krasnyi Arkhiv,* VIII
(1925), 49-69.

being tried. The Committee of Ministers increased the frequency of its meetings under Witte to deal with the promises made in the ukase of December 12. Nicholas empowered the seventy-two-year-old Count Dmitri Solsky, now Chairman of the State Council (the ailing Grand Duke Michael having retired), to convene and preside over the Council of Ministers— the prerogative of the Tsar, regularly exercised in the past— while it dealt with broad questions that he would present. He appointed Dmitri Kobeko, Director of the Imperial Library, to head a new commission to review legislation on censorship. He authorized Witte to publish the current minutes of the Committee of Ministers in order that the public might be thereby informed about some of the reforms under consideration. The last was an unprecedented act for a Russian autocrat, but unfortunately it served little purpose since the minutes suggested only that piddling bureaucrats were employed in discussing less than major changes. Though the Tsar worked with rare vigor on these operations, the results, being poorly coordinated and on the whole inadequately publicized, were as ineffectual in dealing with the general unrest as his speech to the St. Petersburg workers and Shidlovsky's commission had been in dealing with local unrest.

On February 3, the Tsar presided over an all-day discussion of the proposed manifesto by the Council of Ministers. Ermolov argued earnestly for the inclusion in the manifesto of the Tsar's promise to allow the election of an advisory assembly, but he received only limited support from his colleagues. No agreement was reached on the point, but Nicholas directed that a rescript be drafted, instructing the Minister of Interior to make the legal provisions for such an assembly and that the draft be submitted to the Council at a later date.

The next day, the SR's in Moscow, who had made repeated attempts to assassinate the Grand Duke Sergei, found their target open to attack; and Ivan Kalyaev, a former student and a member of the SR's Fighting Organization, threw a bomb that killed him instantly. This was the first assassination of a member of the imperial family since 1881 and the SR's first major act of terrorism since its murder of Plehve.

For the Tsar the death of his uncle was a double shock. It

not only meant that he had lost a friend and confidant, but also indicated that he and other members of his family might be in personal danger. Officials responsible for the protection of his person, chief of whom was Palace Commandant P. P. Hesse, advised against the risk of his attending the funeral; and with that instance of restraint, he began a period of what amounted to voluntary imprisonment at Tsarskoe Selo, able to travel with a feeling of safety only between Tsarskoe Selo and Peterhof or on short, well guarded trips on the imperial yacht. Even the capital of his empire was now outside the bounds of safety for him.

The death of the unpopular Sergei was both a victory for the opposition and a setback to governmental efforts at winning good will. As at the time of Plehve's death, the people were now reminded afresh of their hatred for officialdom and given the chance to acclaim an assassin as a public champion. The Fighting Organization[8] received little disapproval when it announced that it had executed Sergei "for a crime against the people." And the death was followed at once by renewed demands from the opposition for civil and political liberty. Small wonder that Nicholas wrote to the Kaiser on the day of Sergei's funeral that what was happening in Russia was a "downright shame and disgrace before the whole world."[9]

On the same day, attention was drawn again to a critical situation in the Far East, where the main forces of the Russian and Japanese armies were engaged at Mukden. Although it was general knowledge that, among men of respected judgment, there was a lack of confidence in Kuropatkin's ability as a commander, his popularity in the country was so great that it had seemed politically unwise to remove him. Now, as many

[8] The Fighting Organization was headed by Evno Azef, an agent of the Ministry of Interior (a fact unknown to the Tsar at that time), loyal to neither the SR's nor the government. Since this agent bore the ultimate responsibility for the killing of both Plehve and Sergei, and since another one (Gapon) bore at least some responsibility for Bloody Sunday, the Ministry of Interior might properly be held liable for three incidents of the utmost importance at this time.

[9] Nicholas II to William II, February 10 (OS), 1905, German Foreign Office Archives, Russland No. 82.1, V-VI (Geheim).

government officials were beginning to see it, Russia was indeed beset: faced by domestic violence, renewed alarums, and the imminence of defeat by Japan. They felt that conditions called for some kind of immediate action or grand gesture by the Tsar—perhaps, some suggested, a public announcement of broad political reforms and the Tsar's assuming personal command of the forces in Manchuria. Soon the spirit of urgency began to spread and, in view of the buildup of emotional pressure, many observers felt that the regime was breaking down. French Ambassador Bompard wrote to his foreign minister, "It looks as if the bureaucracy . . . has capitulated in the face of general reprobation."[10]

In the belief that only the Dowager Empress Maria Feodorovna could persuade Nicholas to take the necessary steps quickly enough to save the country, a complicated stratagem was devised. Apparently within hours after the news of Sergei's death, Baron Osten-Sacken, the Russian Ambassador to Berlin, saw the Kaiser and enlisted his aid in persuading the Dowager Empress to urge the Tsar into action. Vain though he was, the Kaiser did not overestimate his influence on Maria Feodorovna and therefore attempted to increase his chance of success by writing nearly identical letters, some twenty-two pages long, to both mother and son. In the one he sent to Nicholas, he affected to be passing on information, not offering advice, while he made a good summary of the case as it had been presented to him: there was a common feeling that the Tsar had lost a certain amount of public support by omitting the traditional pilgrimage to the Kremlin cathedrals at the beginning of the war and by failing to address his people from the Winter Palace on January 9; he could regain popular support and, in fact, fire public enthusiasm by going now to Manchuria as warlord (but keeping Kuropatkin as chief of staff), stopping en route at the Moscow Kremlin to proclaim the establishment of habeas corpus and the expansion of the State Council and, standing with the clergy, to address the assembled crowds; then, with the Russian people firmly behind him, he would be easily able to inspire

[10] Bompard to Delcassé, February 12/25, 1905. French Foreign Office Archives, Russie, Politique Intérieure, I.

the troops to victory and restore strength and dignity to his government.[11]

Nicholas shared his cousin's faith in the psycholgoical influence of the Russian autocrat, but he disdained what he considered theatrical gestures, particularly when directed by William. His reply took up less than a line: "Your long letter interested me greatly."[12] Maria Feodorovna answered in the same vein. And that was that.

Imperial Acts of February 18

Nicholas had set his course and meant to follow it. He was going to issue a manifesto that should pacify the country; but, in the light of Sergei's death and the reactions to it, he felt more keenly than ever before that precedence should be given to a strong admonition to his people regarding their conduct. Without keeping his ministers properly informed, he hurried forward the work on the three documents that he had decided were now called for: the long-gestating manifesto, a ukase, and the rescript to the Minister of Interior. And on February 18, he issued the manifesto and the ukase without having asked for a final discussion of them by his ministers. The manifesto was the Tsar's reproof to those who had participated in the disturbances that had been afflicting the country for more than a month and a reaffirmation of the principle of autocracy. The ukase was his decree that his Russian subjects had the right to send him proposals "for improving the public well being," which he would turn over to the Council of Ministers for consideration (in short, the right of petition). It was an extreme measure for a ruler whose ukase of two months earlier had charged the people to mind their own affairs and not to presume to petition the government for change. The rescript was issued later on the same day, after it had been discussed and approved by the ministers. It ordered that Min-

[11] William II to Nicholas II, February 21 (NS), 1905, German Foreign Office Archives, Russland, No. 82.1, V-VI (Geheim). A reprint of this letter will be found in *Letters from the Kaiser to the Tsar* (New York, 1920), pp. 156-70.

[12] Nicholas II to William II, February 12 (OS), 1905, German Foreign Office Archives, Russland, No. 82.1, V-VI (Geheim).

ister of Interior Bulygin prepare legislation that would put into effect the Tsar's resolve "to assemble the most trustworthy men, having the confidence of the people and elected by them, to undertake the preliminary examination and consideration of legislative measures." This also was an extreme measure for a ruler who, on his accession a decade earlier, had labeled the hope for such a thing (a consultative legislative body) "a senseless dream."

The ukase and the rescript indicated a major retreat from policies stubbornly adhered to by Nicholas II and his father, Alexander III, in whose footsteps he had vowed to walk. What would be their effect at this time of crisis? The Tsar hoped that, without infringing upon the principles expressed in the manifesto, they would bring Russia both benefit and calm—as expressed in his diary, *polza i preusplenie*.

❦ 5 ❦

Development

of the Revolution: Second Phase

February–August

Disturbances have broken out in Our country, to the grati-
fication of Our enemies and Our own profound sorrow.
Blinded by arrogance, the ill-intentioned leaders of this insurgence are brazenly attacking the foundations of the Russian Empire, sanctioned by the Orthodox Church and based
on law. They are seeking to sever Our bonds with the past,
to break down the present state structure, and to replace it
by another form of government, alien to Our country.
—Imperial manifesto, February 18, 1905.

Russia is passing through a crisis: she is sick; and her sickness is so grave as to demand immediate and radical cure.
Palliatives can be of no use; rather, they but increase the
gravity of the situation. To pretend that all is right in
Russia, except for a few "ill-intentioned" persons who are
making all the fuss, is no longer ridiculous, it is criminal.
—Paul Milyukov, *Russia and Its Crisis*, 1905.

THE RESULTS of the Tsar's declarations and proposals of February did not sustain his hopes. What he had intended as
evidence of magnaminity was taken—to use the words of *Liberation*—as "a white flag . . . a symbol of cowardice and weakness." Instead of calming the populace, he seemed to have
spurred them to greater boldness and more ambitious counteraction.

Miscarriage of the
February Acts

The ukase permitting petitions was interpreted as an invitation to legalized mobilization of dissent, and the words of the manifesto regarding the proper attitude toward the war-burdened government were almost wholly disregarded. The manifesto proved to be, in fact, yet another of the Tsar's ill-timed efforts, coming as it did only four days before the end of the battle of Mukden, when the Russian ranks were broken and forced into retreat after ninety thousand of their men had been killed, wounded, or taken prisoner. Antiwar sentiment, which flared up again after the news from Mukden, continued to spread, unaffected by the official assurance that the defeat had not been a rout and that, with the additional reservists being rushed to Kuropatkin, the Russians would have numerical superiority by summer.

Emboldened and stimulated by the public recalcitrance, the antigovernment groups stepped up their activities, encouraging unrest wherever it was to be found; and after the news from Mukden had been added to that from the capital, their field of operation was wide indeed. Not only was there unrest among the educated class, labor, and the national minorities but also, to a perceptible degree, among the clergy, the peasants, and the armed forces.

Zemstvos, municipal dumas, organizations of the nobility, university faculty councils, and professional organizations—groups that had not always been willing to pull together—were now coming to fairly close agreement on at least one aim: to work for either a constituent assembly or a *zemsky sobor*. And they were expanding their efforts in every part of the country, meeting more openly and more frequently than they had in the past. Often, without government authorization, they used school buildings for meeting places as public interest grew. Many men of wealth threw open their homes to political gatherings. In the space of a few months, the Russian mentality had undergone a decided change: to be against the government was now more nearly an act of conformity than of daring. And gradually both prestige and range were added to oppositional efforts as elements of society hitherto withdrawn from politics or excluded from participation began to take part.

The Academy of Sciences was one of them—a very prominent one. While some of its members had helped to initiate the "Statement of the 342," the body as a whole had remained aloof from political matters. But it broke tradition on February 18, when in answer to a request from the Committee of Ministers for an opinion concerning existing restrictions on the printed use of the Ukrainian language,[1] it declared its opposition to such restrictions (thus, inadvertently perhaps, helping to promote the cause of Ukrainian nationalism). Even more important was the Academy's reaction to a request made by the Committee of Ministers a few weeks later, that it help to revise the existing censorship laws in such a way as to permit the Academy to cooperate in their application; the academicians declared that they favored freedom of the press and were more interested in removing censorship than in acting as censors.

Further support came to the opposition with the growing popularity of a sympathetic attitude toward equality of rights for women. There had been no specifically feminist movement in Russia before this time, but there were obvious feminist implications in the idea of four-tail suffrage, universal suffrage being understood to include the right of women to vote. And they had encouraged the faint beginnings of a movement that now began to pick up a following.

The unrelieved restiveness among workers was quickened when it became evident, after the collapse of the Shidlovsky Commission, that the government had no further plans for dealing with their needs. Thereafter they showed little hesitancy in using their only weapon—the strike. There was no pattern to their strikes, usually spontaneous and unorganized as before, but each one helped to impress the "strike habit" more firmly on Russian workers. And the habit was spreading. By the last week of February, strikes were commonplace.

[1] Minister of Interior Peter Valuev had asserted in 1863 that "there never was, is not, and never will be a Ukrainian language." This opinion had long been held the official one in Russia.

Within one work week, streetcar workers in Astrakhan went on a one-day strike; workers in the factories of the country's richest industrialists, the Morozovs, stopped work, defied and attacked infantry patrols; strikers in Ekaterinoslav province became so disorderly that troops were called to quell them; the railroad shops of Tashkent and other Central Asian cities were beset by strikes; work was stopped in the South Russian Machine-Construction factory in Kiev; in Perm, Minsk, Baku, Poltava, St. Petersburg, Revel, Rostov-on-Don, and numerous smaller cities, there were strikes by factory workers, railroad-men, bakers, salesmen, and streetcar conductors, all demanding improvements in working conditions and wages. In some instances, their demands brought results; in the South railroad workers were granted the nine-hour day, and others were allowed some of the less important changes they sought.

But the most outstanding feature of these strikes was that, as they continued, the idea of trade-unionism began to receive some attention among the groups involved. It was a relatively novel idea to Russian workers, who lacked not only the tradition of trade-unionism but also any real knowledge of developments along this line in Western Europe. Before 1905 there had been rudimentary efforts to organize trade unions in Moscow, Kharkov, Vilna, and a few other industrial cities, but they had not led to permanent organizations; so in 1905 it was necessary to make an essentially new beginning. The printers of St. Petersburg led the way. Having participated in the Gaponovshchina, they continued to strike after it had run its course, but in the end they won no concessions beyond the willingness of their employers to negotiate with their representatives. In another strike, at the end of February, some of them won wage increases, others did not; and from those results grew the notion that all would have a better chance of success if they organized and consolidated their strength. But it was not until April, following a lecture on typographical unions in the West, that the first organizational efforts were made. What happened in St. Petersburg was repeated in other trades and other cities—but somewhat later in most cases. In the first months of 1905, Russian trade-unionism was just being born, but mass strikes were already an ever-present and powerful force.

Other areas where the opposition could always look for support, the borderlands, were responding according to form and adding some features to their programs of disaffection. In Congress Poland, the Baltic provinces, Transcaucasia, Lithuania, Little Russia, and Finland, the concessions of February 18 fanned rather than quenched antipathy toward the government and stimulated nationalistic aspirations. Evidence of governmental weakening on the one hand and the opening of legal opportunity to petition on the other encouraged demands for restoration of suspended rights and privileges and for the complete removal of disabilities imposed on national and religious minorities. And usually the efforts aimed at the removal of disabilities was accompanied by demands for the concurrent recognition of legal equality among peoples. The urge toward improved status was particularly strong among the Jews. Only a few days after the right of petition was granted, Jewish religious congregations of thirty-two cities sent to the government a petition for "freedom and equality" with the rest of Russia's peoples.[2] The sentiment of that petition, taken up by other congregations, led to the establishment, at the end of March, of a full-fledged political organization, the Union for the Attainment of Full Rights for the Jewish People of Russia. Among the Transcaucasian Moslems a similar movement began, and on March 25 they submitted to the government a petition asking that they be given equal treatment in government service, that no more Russians be permitted to settle among them (it was imperial policy to encourage Russian settlement), and that the organization of zemstvos be allowed in Transcaucasia. And another voice was added to the dissonant response when the Buryat Mongols in Siberia, hitherto hardly vocal in political affairs, began to demand the right to use their own language in their schools.

Supplementing the intensified dissidence from the usual sources of widely shared discontent, some stirrings were be-

[2] *Voskhod,* March 4, 1905.

coming evident elsewhere. In March the Holy Synod of the
Russian Orthodox Church made a cautious but significant
move. Established as the governing body of the Church by
Peter the Great in 1721, after he had abolished the office of
patriarch, it had functioned during all the intervening years
as little more than a branch of the government, for few
churchmen had dared to ask for autonomy—and they had
been denied. Now the thought of impending reforms encouraged the members of the Synod to frame and send to the
Tsar a resolution favoring the reestablishment of the office of
patriarch and the calling of a Church Council, no meeting of
which had been called since the seventeenth century, to select
a man to assume patriarchal duties. To be sure, it was a small
voice in which the Church spoke, implying no disloyalty to
the state, and having no immediate effect. But that it spoke at
all was an indication of the depth to which the movement
against the *status quo* was reaching.

It was reaching peasants very slowly in the late spring and
early summer of 1905, but there was unrest among them that
would in time be turned to advantage by the opposition.
There had been practically no interruption in the disorders
that had begun in the Kutaisk province of Georgia in January. And now sporadic troubles broke out among the peasants
in several provinces of European Russia—chiefly in Vitebsk,
Kursk, Orlov, Chernigov, and Voronezh—as well as in Tiflis,
Warsaw, and the Baltic provinces. The peasants involved in
these outbursts, however, rarely had any direct ties with organized opposition in the cities. Among the exceptions were
the several SR-organized brotherhoods in the provinces of
Saratov and Penza. Membership in them ranged from 20 to
100, and they were reinforced by auxiliary armed detachments
of 8 to 12 peasants. In these brotherhoods there was a tendency toward violence (not entirely welcome to the revolutionaries, who were not yet ready to call for agrarian revolution)
and much talk of "black partition," the forcible seizure and
distribution of landlord estates. In other provinces there was
occasional reference to "black partition," but more often the
rebellious peasants sought only reforms to meet their more

immediate needs: lower rents, the right to cut timber freely in the landlords' forests, and an increase in agricultural wages.

The peasants, of course, soon became aware of what was happening in the cities, and thereafter it was up to the organizers to heighten their unrest and to utilize their response, if possible, on behalf of the opposition. Though there was at first little contact between the peasants (the "dark people") and urban dwellers, the conditions prevailing in 1904 and 1905 opened important channels of communication and began to build up a common sentiment among them. Peasants who worked in urban factories returned home with news of the strikes and often brought with them antigovernment leaflets for their literate comrades, some of whom read them, ignoring instructions to turn over such papers to the police. Others who had worked in the city and acquired a bit of education might come back indoctrinated as socialists and become leaders of influence among their neighbors. The village teachers or the zemstvo statisticians might help their peasant charges to bridge the gap between city and village. And the continued call-up of reservists and the news of repeated defeats in Manchuria built up an antiwar sentiment closely akin to that found in the cities.

An intimation of how such things, added to routine grievances, could accumulate and transform a commonly peaceful peasant group occurred in Orlov province on the Dolbenkino estate of the Grand Duke Sergei. The estate manager, the notoriously severe Filatev, was able to rent most of the land to local peasants at prices much higher than the market warranted because of their desperate need for land. And their burdens were multiplied by the fact that Filatev, who retained the preemancipation outlook common among contemporary estate managers, laid numerous fines on them—for such offenses as failing to remove their hats in his presence, picking berries or smoking on seignorial land, and letting their cattle stray. About two weeks after the death of Sergei, it was rumored that the local peasants were planning an attack on the estate; but responsible officials, knowing how the peasants had endured their lot in the past, refused to credit the rumors.

Provinces of
EUROPEAN
RUSSIA
in 1905

KEY TO CITIES

① St Petersburg
② Kronstadt
③ Moscow
④ Ivanovo-Voznesensk
⑤ Vladikavkaz
⑥ Baku
⑦ Tiflis
⑧ Kutais
⑨ Novorossiisk
⑩ Rostov-on-Don
⑪ Kharkov
⑫ Sevastopol
⑬ Odessa
⑭ Kiev
⑮ Lodz
⑯ Warsaw
⑰ Riga

NORWAY
SWEDEN
GRAND DUCHY OF FINLAND
ESTLAND
Baltic Sea
LIVONJA
COURLAND
ST. PETERSBU
PSKOV
KOVNO
VITEBSK
GERMANY
VILNA
MOGILEV
GRODNO
MINSK
CONGRESS POLAND
CHEF
VOLHYNIA
KIEV
AUSTRIA-HUNGARY
PODOLIA
BESSARABIA
KHERSON
RUMANIA
BULGARIA
Black
T U R

0   Miles   300

palacios

ARCHANGEL

OLONETS

VOLOGDA

PERM

VGOROD

YAROSLAVL

KOSTROMA

VYATKA

VER

MOSCOW •

④

VLADIMIR

NIZHNY
NOVGOROD

KAZAN

UFAL

ORENBURG

③

URAL MOUNTAINS

URAL MOUNTAINS

UGA

RYAZAN

SIMBIRSK

TULA

PENZA

EL

TAMBOV

SARATOV

SAMARA

KURSK

VORONEZH

⑪

KHARKOV

TERINOSLAV

DON

ASTRAKHAN

RIDA

⑩ •

⑨ KUBAN

STAVROPOL

Caspian Sea

ea

TEREK

⑤ •

CAUCASUS MOUNTAINS

DAGHESTAN

⑧

⑦

E   Y

TRANS-CAUCASIA

⑥ •

S   I   B   E   R   I   A

And when the peasants sent their representatives to require concessions of Filatev, he was confident that his soft words and hard liquor had mollified them. On the following day, however, peasants from nearby villages arrived at the estate to join the local ones, their manner so disorderly and belligerent that neither the manager nor local police could handle them; and, having struck down Filatev and routed the police, they turned to looting and burning the estate buildings. The damage they did before troops could arrive and put an end to their outburst, amounted to about a quarter of a million rubles. Similar peasant raids, on a smaller scale, occurred on a number of estates. Usually there was a long history of tension and distress in the area where trouble broke out—as in the Voronezh province, where the estate of the multimillionaire Yusupov family in the village of Veseloi was subjected to pillage and torch. The course of the outbreaks became almost routine: peasants would meet quietly at night to make plans, a pole to which was fastened a bundle of straw would be put up near the estate designated for attack, and when the time for action came, entire villages of peasants would take part. These agrarian disorders, though increasing in number, were not extensive enough or well enough organized and led to produce any serious alarm in the first half of the year. But their threat was recognized. In Voronezh, the news of the attack on the Yusupov estate led landlords to ask the governor to station more troops and rural police near the trouble spots, and here and there others were following their example.

One of the chief reasons authority could be maintained with such relative ease in the face of the aggressive discontent in the country was that the armed forces were, so far, little affected by civil unrest. Ermolov's fears that the peasants in uniform would refuse to fire on peasants in mufti were not realized for many years. Though the soldiers were earnestly urged by both liberals and socialists to refrain from acts of "fratricide," they continued to obey whatever orders were given them—except, sometimes, orders that they restrain themselves when taunted or attacked by civilians. In fact, they usually interpreted attacks by civilians as acts of hostility toward themselves, not toward the regime. This was especially true of the Cossacks; more than any other part of the armed forces, they dissociated themselves contemptuously from the mass of the population. It was quite common for Cossack patrols, acting against orders, to ride down civilians who whistled, jeered, or threw stones at them.

While all members of the armed forces remained submissive to military discipline, some were being reached individually and influenced by subversive propaganda. That fact was recognized by the government, and cautionary steps were taken to prevent untoward results from it. Enlisted men were ordered not to read any leaflets handed to them, but to turn them over at once to their officers. Nevertheless, spot-checks of barracks showed many a leaflet hidden in enlisted men's belongings. And the officers themselves were not always beyond suspicion: some guards officers, even, were known to have accepted and read forbidden literature. These preliminary gains, though small, were cherished by the opposition, and the socialists made special plans to increase them through military committees organized and trained for concentrated work among soldiers and sailors.

LIBERATION MOVEMENT STRENGTHENED

All these new or renewed stirrings among educated Russians, the national minorities, and labor—and becoming recognizable now also among the clergy, the peasantry, and the armed forces—were, of course, reinforcing the liberation movement. The liberals saw in them the awakening of the "real Russia" to the defects of "official Russia," a situation that would ultimately bring about the capitulation of the latter. But they all recognized that the tendencies toward opposition had to be encouraged and that the pressure against the government had to be organized in order to achieve that end. The Liberationists were particularly hopeful that what had been done and was being done would serve the purpose. They thought of the Paris conference of the previous year as the guarantee of a common front against autocracy. And they depended upon a nationwide organization of professional unions, now in the planning stage, to serve as the organizational hub for it. When achieved, the common front they foresaw would be an alliance of all groups—liberal or socialist, Russian or non-Russian—that opposed autocracy.

During the spring months, there was much activity in political organization and negotiation among all opposition groups. The liberals, operating virtually in the open, were the most vocal and the most prominent. They became widely known through the speeches, writings, and organizational work of men such as Fedor Rodichev, Vasily Maklakov, the Princes Peter and Paul Dolgorukov, Fedor Kokoshkin, Fedor Golovin, Ivan Petrunkevich, and (on his return from the United States in April) Paul Milyukov. In Moscow the zemstvo office and the homes of many wealthy nobles became the liberal assembly centers, and in St. Petersburg the premises of the Free Economic Society and the offices of *Pravo* and other newspapers served. Inevitably the general acceleration led to much waste motion and unproductive talk, but in it all there was a persistent consciousness of urgency and purpose.

The liberals—particularly the Liberationists—pushed energetically for an agreement on common aims: those of the Liberationists. At its Third Congress, in March, the Union of Liberation adopted a program based, as usual, on the demand for a constituent assembly. And the program specified what the Union intended to require of that assembly: a government both democratic and decentralized, founded on universal suffrage (defined so as to include women as well as men) and recognizing the separation of church and state; the restoration of Finnish autonomy; the granting of limited autonomous rights to Poland, Lithuania, Little Russia (Ukraine), and Transcaucasia; the transfer of state, crown, and some noble lands to the peasants; and the concession to labor of the right to strike, the eight-hour day, and government-provided insurance (health, old-age, and life). It was a broad program, offering something for almost every dissident group. It was also far more radical than the program represented by the Eleven Theses of the November Zemstvo Congress—and it would surely have been rejected by that congress.

But the Second Zemstvo Congress, held in April, displaying

a more radical bent than the first, accepted the Liberationist position in part. It did not adopt the slogan calling for a "constituent assembly elected by four-tail suffrage" in that exact phrasing; but by the use of somewhat roundabout terms, it adopted the substance, calling on the government to permit the election of a "representative assembly" chosen by universal, equal, secret, and direct suffrage to "establish the political law and order of the Russian Empire"—a euphemistic phrasing of "imperial constitution." This was too much for Shipov, who led his followers, a minority, from the congress in protest (though he later agreed to a temporary truce with his opponents). This incident revealed two significant aspects of the zemstvo movement at this time: the extent to which many of the formerly moderate zemstvo leaders had moved to the left and into closer ties with the Liberationists, and the serious rift that had developed among its supporters.

Another step toward cooperation among oppositional groups was taken in April, when some Liberationists and other liberals came to an agreement with a gathering of Polish nationalist liberals whereby the Russians would support autonomy for Congress Poland within the Russian empire, and the Poles would support the common aim to establish a constitutional order. As for the Jewish liberals, their participation was practically assured, for Maxim Vinaver, highly influential in the Union for the Achievement of Full Rights for the Jews, and many of his associates were closely connected with the Liberationists. And still further support was anticipated after an April agrarian congress attended by zemstvo leaders, agronomists, and economists; for the program adopted by that body, under the leadership of such liberals as Ivan Petrunkevich, Michael Herzenstein, and Alexander Manuilov, was highly acceptable to those in the liberation movement.

Important as all these activities were for the opposition, they were soon overshadowed by one that had been in process since January: the organization, throughout the country, of political unions with the hope of their eventual unification into a "union of unions," strong enough to achieve results. Work on the project had begun slowly but quickened after the publication of the ukase of February 18, which the liberals interpreted as giving the populace the right to hold meetings for formulating petitions. This interpretation, which the police reluctantly accepted, provided the organizers of political unions with a degree of legal protection, and they used it to the full. The organizers were for the most part Liberationists, but there were among them some liberals a bit to the right of the Liberationists—yet sympathetic to their aims—and a few SR's and Mensheviks. The original intention, to organize only professions, was at first respected as unions were formed by lawyers, engineers, primary and secondary school teachers, professors, doctors, pharmacists, veterinarians, journalists, and agronomists. But the planners soon agreed that any union, professional or not, accepting the proposed aims and methods should be included in the scheme. The organizing groups, usually holding their meetings with some semblance of secrecy (an unnecessary precaution, since the police were generally neither deceived by their ruses nor particularly responsive to their doings), found that people were anxious to pledge themselves to the achievement of a "democratic constitution" by peaceful means and liked the idea of joining others in a union dedicated to that end.

By May, fourteen of these unions had been organized and were considered stable enough to constitute the foundation of the proposed larger body. Accordingly their representatives met in Moscow and entered them upon the next phase of the plan by forming the Union of Unions, devoted to the liberation of Russia by means of a constituent assembly, for which all were pledged to work. The new organization selected as its president Paul Milyukov, now the leading figure in the Union of Liberation. It was to operate through its Central Bureau, which was to consist of two representatives from each union.

Among the fourteen unions represented at the founding meeting were nine political unions of professionals; two—the Union of Clerks and Bookkeepers and the Union of Railroad Employees and Workers—combining political and economic aims; the Union for the Achievement of Full Rights for the Jews; the Union of Equal Rights for Women; and the Union of Zemstvo-Constitutionalists (close in position to the Union of Liberation), a small group organized in 1903 to exert liberal influences on zemstvo leaders. The Union of Unions invited others to join whenever they were ready. And many others were being planned or were in process of organization. Among them was one that could add great strength to the Union: a politically oriented peasants union, for the formation of which preparations were being made by some liberal *intelligents* connected with the zemstvo movement.

In the late spring and the summer of 1905, the Union of Unions was the embodiment of the liberation movement and, in a sense, provided the much-talked-of common front. In addition, it was the support, either directly or indirectly, of the current program of the Union of Liberation.

The Liberationists, telling themselves that there were "no enemies to the left," were now confident that they could count on peaceful partnership with the socialists as they continued the drive toward a constituent assembly. The socialists, however, were beginning to get out of step with the Liberationists at some points. Though they were still agreeable so far as aspirations for the immediate future were concerned and admired some of the leading Liberationists personally (Milyukov had been invited to become a member of the SR Central Committee), they were, in final analysis, only friendly opponents. There were real and ultimately significant differences between them and the liberals with whom they were currently cooperating.

Socialists agreed that a constituent assembly was the immediate essential, but they disagreed sharply with the liberals as to the means to be used in achieving it. Moreover, they were quite far from the liberals in their interpretations of the historical process they were witnessing and would witness as events proceeded. In the spring of 1905 most of them felt that they were experiencing the first stages of the expected "bourgeois" revolution that would overthrow the autocracy; and most of them believed that the revolution would be completed only through an armed uprising. The liberal program of peaceful pressure was clearly not enough in their view. On these issues, most socialists were in agreement among themselves. But on many others they disagreed.

By April the differences among socialists were becoming

quite evident. In the Russian Social Democratic Labor Party, the Bolsheviks and Mensheviks were openly demonstrating their rivalry. The Bolsheviks had summoned a congress of the whole RSDLP, announcing that the "revolution had already begun," but the Mensheviks had denied the authority of the Bolsheviks to call the congress and had chosen to meet separately. Gathering in London, the Bolsheviks declared that, since they represented the larger portion of the party, their meeting was officially the party's third congress; in Geneva, the Mensheviks modestly called their meeting a conference. The two factions agreed on basic questions but disagreed materially on tactics. The Bolsheviks, led by Lenin, saw an armed uprising as the only means of overthrowing autocracy, while the Mensheviks, led by Julius Martov, recognized alternative means—for instance, a revolutionary assumption of power by some popular representative body. The latter expressed less apprehension than the Bolsheviks about cooperation with the liberals, being inclined toward the belief that, after the overthrow of autocracy, the bourgeoisie could safely be permitted to dominate the new democratic state while the proletariat would struggle for its own interests and prepare for the inevitable, but somewhat distant, decisive conflict with the bourgeoisie. The Bolsheviks, on the other hand, while recognizing that the revolution would put the bourgeoisie into power, intended that, upon the overthrow of the tsarist regime, a provisional revolutionary government dominated by the proletariat should act as a check on the bourgeoisie.

The Socialist Revolutionary Party was not yet ready to call a congress, but its position had become fairly well defined and publicly understood. Its members placed more emphasis on preparation for an armed uprising than did the Mensheviks; and, in contrast to both factions of the SD's, they continued to believe in political assassinations, terror, as a useful tactic. Though in theory as suspicious of the liberals as the Bolsheviks were, in practice the SR's were more cooperative than they were. Perhaps the most significant position of the SR's was that taken on the agrarian question. They favored the transfer of all land—that of the landlords, the church, and the government—to the peasant village communes. But they expected the transfer to follow the overthrow of the regime and therefore did not seek an immediate agrarian revolution aiming at "black partition."

Among them, the Mensheviks, Bolsheviks, and SR's represented all the major positions held by Russian socialists in the spring of 1905. But most of their controversy was, for the moment, factitious because they were not yet prepared to implement policies of any kind. Many of their leaders recognized the fact that their problem at this time was not to make a definite decision about the means by which to bring about the ultimate overthrow of the regime, which might or might not come in the near future, but how to deal with the current reality of growing antigovernment sentiment, which might be harnessed to their program. Therefore the immediate need was to give more energy to organizing, propagandizing, and training for action. And they set about it as if determined to make up for lost time. They recruited members. They operated their illegal presses without letup. They held meetings and gave lectures wherever they could: in theaters they were sometimes able to convert audiences into political meetings; in the Jewish Pale, Bundists often interrupted religious rites to harangue the captive assemblage on politics; and in Moscow and other large cities, they used the homes of wealthy men such as the Morozovs (who themselves were frequently under attack as employers) as meeting places. They organized students. They held secret meetings with sympathetic soldiers and sailors. And they gave especial attention to workers, organizing the sympathetic ones into study groups (sometimes placing socialists at their head), urging them to consider political demands as important as economic demands, and always urging them toward short political strikes—which, in socialist opinion, were the most effective of immediate weapons to be used against the regime.

Looking toward a future aspect of their program, the socialists joined in an accelerated effort to provide sufficient arms and training for their military action. Wherever there was a sizeable socialist group there was some kind of quasi-military preparation or planning, much of it more nearly in the manner of comic opera than of serious undertaking. For many,

especially students, this part of socialist activity was romanti-
cally appealing and they were zealous in its pursuit, collecting
funds for arms at almost every meeting. But the actual accumulation of arms seemed quite incommensurate with the effort and time spent. Most of the arms were purchased abroad
and smuggled in, but within Russia there were a few illegal
sources from which pistols and revolvers might be bought. To
supplement these, workers in metallurgical plants—the Putilov
Ironworks, for example—sometimes made "cold arms" (knives,
bludgeons, and the like) with company materials and on company time. To use these assorted weapons when they were
available, almost every socialist group had its "fighting detachment" of a dozen or so, which practiced marksmanship and
engaged in some form of training for street fighting. In keeping with this part of the program, the Bund, which had begun
organizing "self-defense units" for use against anti-Semitic attacks before 1905, now increased their number. All together,
the armed and trained socialists in Russia would have made
up no more than a regiment or two, a rather inadequate nu-
cleus for a successful insurrection. Yet they had their value:
they served to promote the state of mind conducive to violence and armed rising, and they provided cadres capable of
leading and organizing local revolutionary efforts.

Whereas the socialist factions were fairly agreeable in organizational and preparatory operations, they took differing
stands on other activities. Some SR's, while admitting the importance of mass agitation and organization, contended that
individual acts of terror should not be neglected, and they
continued such acts, particularly the assassination of odious
officials. And some of them—a much smaller number—believed in "agrarian terror," and encouraged peasant violence.
Though the SR's worked among the peasantry more than did
any other party, their influence was quite limited (largely
confined to the Volga region), and the violence they stirred
up was generally insignificant. Social Democrats gave only
little attention to the peasantry—and that, not to the landholding peasants, but to the agricultural laborers in a few
places close to such urban centers as Moscow. On the evaluation of the Union of Unions there was wide diversity. The

Mensheviks and SR's usually cooperated with the liberals in it, while the Bundists and the Bolsheviks opposed it. The Bolsheviks tried, with limited success, to form organizations to rival it or, failing at that, to work within some of its components—the Union of Pharmacists, for one—in an effort to convert them to the idea of a general political strike and armed rising.

Though socialist activities differed sharply in many respects from those of the liberals, they were on the whole condoned by the latter since they were directed at the regime. Some liberals—among them, Milyukov and other Liberationists—welcomed them; others—those of the right wing—were censorious of the Milyukov attitude and actually fearful that the socialist emphasis on armed action might lead to civil war. But as long as the possibility of peaceful political change remained in sight, as long as it seemed possible to defer the threat of revolution, the weakly united front of liberals and socialists continued.

So numerous, prominent, and articulate were the liberals that, for a time, interest was concentrated on them both in Russia and abroad, where the liberation movement was being followed closely. But their center-stage position should not be allowed to detract from two significant developments, neither of which fitted directly into the framework of the liberation movement. The government, of its own accord, though thoroughly discredited, was still seriously struggling with problems and plans, trying to activate important reforms. In addition, among the masses throughout the country, there were beginning new or newly enlarged movements not led by liberals, and their forms and proportions indicated that important changes might be in the making.

MAY DAY, 1905

One new aspect of unrest was introduced on the first day of May, a labor holiday (having been designated as such by the Second Socialist International in 1889), which fell on a Sunday. The socialists had let it be widely known that, unlike past celebrations of the day, which had been indoor and secret, this year's would be held openly and complemented by political strikes. Forewarned, the authorities reinforced military and police units in the cities and arrested numerous socialist leaders who had been under surveillance. But the plans were carried out, with somewhat irregular success, in scores of places throughout the country. In St. Petersburg only a few hundred demonstrators gathered and quickly dispersed. In Moscow some street meetings were held; and outside the city, in Sokolniki Park, popular for Sunday outings, thousands who gathered to hear socialist speakers were scattered by mounted troops. As for the strikes that were called, they were variously scheduled (since May 1 was a nonworking day) and variously handled. In a number of Baltic cities, they started on April 30 and continued until the beginning of June. In most places the workers responded by striking on the first working day after the holiday. In St. Petersburg, the men of the Neva Ship-building Works reported to work on that day but immediately marched out singing revolutionary songs. In Saratov, Samara, and Ekaterinburg, on the same day, the strikes were virtually general ones. And in Kharkov and a number of other cities, the demonstrators clashed with soldiers. The chief importance of all this activity lay in the fact that these demonstrations and strikes, though geographically separated, were relatively concerted operations, each with frankly political overtones, each responsive to socialist leadership.

EMERGENCE OF THE BLACK HUNDREDS

Another display of feelings roused by events—this, a form of counteraction not new but appearing for the first time with appreciable strength—came from militant supporters of the regime who engaged in or encouraged physical reprisals against non-Russians and nonmonarchists. Though now most active in the Pale of Settlement and in Transcaucasia, they were increasing in number and aggressiveness in central Russia as well. Generally known by the loose designation "Black Hundreds," they were members of various groups with ideas planted deep in Russian tradition and reflecting two sentiments common to many Great Russians: opposition to those who made open attacks on the monarchy (especially in the time of war), and bitter resentment of all members of despised minorities who "insolently" displayed their antipathy for the government. As their popularity grew, they received aid and abetment from the police in some places and indirect encouragement from the Russian Orthodox Church. The former sometimes organized and promoted "patriotic" attacks or demonstrations against the *kramolniki* (seditionists), as the opposition was officially known. And since the Church denounced *kramola* (sedition) as treason, it was not unusual for priests to add their voices to those of laymen who, claiming to have the endorsement of the Church, spread hatred in the guise of patriotism. Those who suffered the consequences were any who might be charged by the Black Hundreds with offense, according to their interpretation, against the fatherland —particularly the intelligentsia, Poles, Jews, Finns, and Armenians. Economic considerations also led to provocation in some instances; workers or storekeepers, for example, who were unsympathetic to the opposition often reacted to the economic burden of strikes by attacking those who fomented them or were responsible for unrest in general. Thus supported, this movement growing freely among the masses was to affect thousands and lead to violent acts that, in some instances, would make changes necessary in well-laid plans.

THE TSUSHIMA STRAITS DISASTER

The opposition had barely remarked this growing counter-activity when Russia received news of the greatest naval disaster in her history, the destruction of her fleet at Tsushima Straits, on May 14. The succeeding wave of antigovernment feeling was grist to the opposition's mill; criticism of the regime mounted once more, and the demand for peace became more insistent. The Tsar and his advisers faced a dilemma; to make peace now would lower the government's prestige; to continue building up the land forces (War Minister Sakharov anticipated that Russia could have five hundred thousand men to Japan's three hundred thousand in Manchuria by

July) might give Russia a chance for one more major victory to redeem her honor—but troop morale was reportedly so low that the result might instead be defeat, which would both increase domestic unrest and decrease Russian bargaining power in peace negotiations. After a meeting on the 24th with Sakharov, the Grand Dukes Vladimir and Alexis, and several ranking generals, who gave their evaluations of the situation, the Tsar chose an indeterminate course. He would continue to build up Russian strength in Manchuria, meanwhile entering upon secret negotiations for peace, the United States' President Theodore Roosevelt acting as intermediary.

THE BURGEONING STRIKE MOVEMENT

The public, unaware of the secret conferences or negotiations, knew only that reservists were still being dispatched at the behest of what appeared to be incompetent and blundering leadership. The result was hostility and unease, which, though not producing strikes, affected the general temper in such a way that workers were responsive when it was suggested that strikes be begun or continued. The number of strikers grew from eighty thousand in April to two hundred and twenty thousand in May.[3]

Of these, the one in Ivanovo-Voznesensk was outstanding, being the one of longest duration in 1905 as well as the one most nearly revolutionary in nature. Begun two days before the news of the Tsushima Straits defeat was received and lasting ten weeks, it involved seventy thousand men and women, virtually the whole labor force of the "twin cities." Ivanovo-Voznesensk, a major textile center of Vladimir province, lo-

[3] These figures are based on reports made by members of the government's factory inspection service. A study made by A. S. Amalrik ("K Voprosu o Chislennost i Geograficheskom Razmeshchenii Stachechnikov v Evropeiskoi Rossii v 1905 Godu," *Istoricheskie Zapiski*, LII [1955], 142-85) argues that official figures are too low because the inspection service did not report on establishments with less than fifteen employees, those under the Ministry of War, those in the Northern Caucasus, or those in Transcaucasia. He would, by estimation, raise the official figures by 50 percent.

cated some two hundred miles northeast of Moscow and known as the "cotton kingdom," had experienced strikes in the past but had no history of political disaffection. Unlike the workers of Moscow or St. Petersburg, the workers here had been little affected by the liberal or socialist movements and, in the four months following the Gaponovshchina, had taken no active part in the general turbulence except for staging a small strike in protest against Bloody Sunday. There was, however, a tradition of tension in the area, understandable in view of the difficult labor conditions—of which an average work day of fourteen hours, including overtime, was the most aggravating. In the early spring of 1905, when SD agitators (among them the future Soviet War Commissar Michael Frunze) tried to explain to the workers the need to end autocracy, they were rebuffed with cries of "No politics!" By May, however, a strike sentiment was developing in Ivanovo-Voznesensk and being taken up with enthusiasm by these same workers—just why, it was difficult to determine. Perhaps economic distress had made them susceptible to political propaganda; perhaps growing awareness of the regime's weakening had encouraged them to take action for economic improvement. Their first demands of the factory managers were for concessions to improve their general conditions as workers: an eight-hour day, a minium monthly wage of twenty rubles, factory nurseries, the right to sit while working, the right to read newspapers during free periods, old-age pensions, abolition of factory police, freedom of assembly to discuss labor conditions, and full pay for the period of the strike. As the strike went on, certain of the demands they added were definitely political in nature: holidays on February 19 (anniversary of the liberation of the serfs) and on May Day, as well as the calling of a constituent assembly.

When the strike began, the troops available were insufficient to prevent the workers from meeting openly in Ivanovo-Voznesensk, where their number and temper induced such fear that most of the factory owners and managers hurriedly left the area. But soon, provincial governor I. M. Leontiev sent additional troops, and the strikers were forced to move their meetings to the banks of the nearby Talka River. There they worked out a rudimentary organization for bargaining collectively and directing the strike. Their strike committee of 150 (a quarter of whom were SD's) began, about the middle of May, to call itself a *soviet* (council) of deputies. And gradually the soviet began to assume political powers in local affairs, prohibiting storekeepers from raising prices, even organizing a workers' militia. This was the first Russian soviet of the type that was later to become a powerful revolutionary institution: a body of workers', peasants', or soldiers' deputies that arrogated political power. It was a spontaneous phenomenon, but it corresponded to the Menshevik notion of the revolutionary body ultimately to take over power from the autocracy.

As their activities continued, the strikers' sympathy for political ideas increased. They listened with interest to lectures on the history of the *Marseillaise*, on Saint-Simon, and on the works of Nekrasov, a favorite poet of the intelligentsia. Their attitudes were by no means completely changed, nor was the partial change enduring in all individuals. The fact that they showed any political interest, however, was significant. It was a kind of interest that was now becoming widespread among workers in other industrial centers.

Because the nature and duration of the Ivanovo-Voznesensk strike suggested the danger of violence and its possible spread to other parts of the province, Governor Leontiev urged the employers to deal with the soviet and meet some of its demands. At the same time, he put pressure on the strikers by increasing the number of troops in the area. The soviet was willing to compromise, for it was evident that morale could not be sustained much longer among the workers: they were near starvation after weeks of unemployment, and some had begun to loot food stores. So, when the employers reluctantly offered slight wage increases, the soviet declared the strike at an end and dissolved itself.

The extent of this great strike's influence would be difficult to assess; but many strikes in many parts of the country were displaying the same characteristics at the same time or soon thereafter, and some of them were certainly influenced by it. There was a growing tendency toward radicalism and the use of force among strikers, more sympathy for the notion of a constituent assembly, and an increasing—but by no means uniform—willingness to accept socialists as leaders.

In Lodz, where the workers had not lost the fiery spirit built up during the January days, fighting between workers and government forces began in May and continued sporadically until June 5, when it settled down to serious conflict. On that day soldiers fired on a socialist-led demonstration, killing ten of the participants, and thereby touched off a general strike in the city. Led by the PPS, the Polish SD, and the Bund, the workers built barricades and challenged the government troops. The fighting lasted three days, and fair estimates indicate that during that time about three hundred men were killed and a thousand wounded. The "June Days of Lodz," as they were called, affected industrial centers throughout the country, and the revolutionary threat reached such proportions in Warsaw and other cities of Congress Poland that the government increased the number of troops in the area from two hundred fifty thousand to three hundred thousand.

In the troubled spring and summer of 1905, railroad workers added complications with a rash of strikes, some stopping train movements, others limited to work in railroad shops. The most ominous of them were the several on the Trans-Siberian line, over which thousands of troops were being moved to the front. The railroad strikers often included with their demands for increased wages and better working conditions two additional ones: cessation of the war and the calling of a constituent assembly. And, as further evidence of their sympathy with the mood now becoming common among workers, they sometimes resorted to violence. An instance of this type of response developed in the course of their strike in Novorossiisk, where, having stopped all but mail trains, they were joined by all other workers in the city. When the government attempted to restore railroad operations under troop protection, the combined forces of the strikers protested with violence, overturning a coach, throwing stones, and firing some shots. The troops responded, and the skirmish resulted in the death of thirteen workers.

Among other centers marked by violence at this time were

Kharkov, the industrial center of Little Russia; Baku, where, despite the fact that martial law had been in effect for months, fighting erupted repeatedly between troops and workers as well as between Moslems and Armenians; and Odessa, where the current wave of turbulence reached its peak.

Strikes had first become serious in Odessa in April, affecting butchers, bakers, tailors, shoemakers, printers, and textile workers. And they continued (under close watch by military detachments) without any untoward incidents into the middle of June, by which time tempers on both sides were keyed for trouble. It came quickly when one of a group of demonstrating workers outside a plow factory fired at a Cossack officer and retaliation followed. For two days the city was the scene of nightmarish street fighting: on one side the police, soldiers, and Black Hundreds; on the other, strikers and sympathizers, led by SR's, Bundists, Mensheviks, and Bolsheviks. There were scores of deaths on each side, and dozens of buildings were fired before the governor, in desperation, asked the Tsar to place the city under martial law. The Tsar's order was published on June 15.

THE *Potemkin* MUTINY

On that day Odessa's disquiet was aggravated by the arrival in her harbor of the mutinous battleship *Potemkin*. Its crew, under orders to test gun linings at a distance from the other ships of the Black Sea Fleet, had risen against their officers after an incident involving a meat ration that they believed to be tainted, and had shot, thrown overboard, or imprisoned all of them. Now, a group of maverick sailors with the fleet's finest battleship in their power, they might have been quite a threat. But since their mutiny lacked the support of other sailors in the fleet (among some of whom mutinous plans were in the making nevertheless), since most of them had no personal revolutionary feelings, and since only a pitifully small number of them could qualify in any respect as leaders, their presence at Odessa was more of a problem than a threat. Their foremost spokesman, a twenty-five-year-old Ukrainian, Panas Matyushenko, and some of the other leading mutineers thought of themselves as SD's and soon therefore were in consultation with local socialists. Among them, they set up two plans: to give the support of the *Potemkin*'s guns and crew to the antigovernment forces in the city and to call the rest of the Black Sea Fleet into mutiny. A few indulged in the bold hope that the fusion of the *Potemkin* mutiny with the Odessa street fighting would mark the beginning of the longed-for armed uprising that would spread through all of Russia.

At first, it appeared that the presence of the *Potemkin* in the harbor had raised the temperature in the city both literally and figuratively. What happened on the night of June 15/16 marked it as perhaps the bloodiest of the 1905 revolution: by morning much of the city was ablaze, and nearly two thousand persons had died. The *Potemkin* sailors, however, had been only spectators. Their first shore venture came on the following day, when they were given authorization to bury in a local cemetery one of their number who had been killed during the fighting with the ship's officers. The funeral procession was fired upon by troops, and in retaliation the ship's gunners opened fire on a theater where a meeting of military authorities was in session. Their aim was defective, the damage small; and the plan to bombard the city was thereafter abandoned. But there remained the second plan, to call the other ships of the fleet into mutiny. And when, on the second day after their defection, the fleet arrived, under command of Vice-Admiral Krieger, the *Potemkin* refused the order to surrender and signaled the call for fleet-wide mutiny. One ship, the *Georgy Pobedonostsev*, came over to the *Potemkin*; and Admiral Krieger, uncertain of the morale of the remaining crews and aware that the guns of the *Potemkin* outranged any that he had at his command, withdrew the others. The crew of the *Georgy Pobedonostsev*, lacking the courage to sustain their temerity, started back to the fleet, ran their vessel aground, and had to be rescued. Meanwhile the *Potemkin* fled to Constanza, in Rumania, where her crew, after sinking the ship by opening the seacocks, sought refuge inland.

Though it ended thus ignobly and futilely, the *Potemkin* mutiny, worst so far in Russian naval history, aroused some apprehension in the government—and, of course, hopefulness in the opposition. The whole Black Sea Fleet was temporarily inactivated as a result of it; the commander, now distrustful of his men's loyalty, sent about five thousand of them on extended leave, hoping to replace them with more reliable sailors. The prestige of the Russian navy could hardly have been lower. And, even with strict screening of those who were brought in to man the ships again, it was years before the fleet was considered worthy of renewed confidence.

While the government recognized the condition of the Black Sea Fleet as a serious state of protest, underlined by the general turbulence in the industrial centers and the intimations of unrest elsewhere, it still assumed that it had the advantage in both time and strength. And it continued to move with caution and deliberation in the matter of fulfilling the promises made on December 12 and February 18.

FURTHER CONCESSIONS BY THE GOVERNMENT

Some of the December promises had been met in March and April, when the Tsar, acting on the recommendations of the Committee of Ministers and other governmental bodies, had approved a series of measures lifting certain restrictions on national and religious bodies. These measures affected the Finns, Poles, Armenians, Ukrainians, Old Believers,[4] and Uniats.[5] But while representing serious concessions from the government's viewpoint, they removed only some of the disabilities under which these groups lived, and none of those under which the Jews lived. Moreover, some of the important

[4] Old Believers, a religious group (numbering at least 15 million in 1905), had refused to accept the slight modifications in the rites of the Orthodox Church as imposed by the Council of 1666–67, had been anathematized, and thereafter subjected to persecution.

[5] Uniats, adhering to the agreement (Union of Brest, 1596) of certain Orthodox bishops to unite with the Roman Catholic Church in Eastern Europe on the condition that they be allowed to retain the Byzantine rite (instead of accepting the Latin rite), had been under compulsion by the government to worship as regular communicants of the established Church or to suffer penalties as heretics.

concessions promised in December—for example, the mitigation of censorship rules and of the exceptional laws—were still lacking because of the inability of the Tsar's responsible advisers to reach agreement on how to effect them.

The project on which the Tsar placed greatest hope as a means of conciliation—the consultative assembly (Duma, in official parlance), arrangements for which had been ordered in the February rescript to Minister of Interior Bulygin—was developing very slowly. Bulygin, Solsky, and others conferring on the problem of drafting the legislation necessary for its establishment were giving more attention to insuring that the projected body be in harmony with established tradition than to hurrying the work on it. One of the snags in their deliberations was the question of what basis to use in providing representation in the body. And they finally overcame it by deciding to follow the example of zemstvo elections—that is, to provide for a type of indirect election in which voting would be by class, with preference given to the peasants and landed nobility. Then there was the question of whether or not Jews should be allowed to vote, since they were legally barred from voting in zemstvo and municipal duma elections; it was answered by the decision to continue their disability.

While the government was following its time-consuming course, the populace had only hearsay for consolation—or disturbance. There were rumors that the government had given no consideration to the provision of four-tail suffrage, that traditional and unfairly representative schemes were being considered, even that the whole idea of a national Duma had been abandoned. It was under the impact of such rumors as well as the disagreeable news of the defeat at Tsushima Straits that the Third Zemstvo Congress met in Moscow for a three-day session beginning on May 24. What the assembled zemstvo leaders wanted was what had been made clear by the majority vote of the April congress, and that was obviously more than could be expected from the Bulygin Duma (as the projected representative body was now commonly called). Unlike the Union of Unions, just getting under way on a program of denunciation of the government, the Zemstvo Congress wanted to follow the path of persuasion and conciliation. Accordingly the delegates adopted the text of an address to the Tsar, in which they stated their views, and selected from among themselves a number of distinguished men to present it. To their representatives several members of the St. Petersburg municipal duma were later added, making a total of fourteen men; among them were such leaders as Dmitri Shipov, Ivan Petrunkevich, Prince George Lvov, Count Peter Heyden, and Prince Sergei Trubetskoi.

On June 6, the Tsar received the delegation at Peterhof and, in so doing, made history: this was the first time that he had ever agreed to meet such a group. Prince Trubetskoi read the address. Its theme was that Russia had been brought close to an abyss by the irresponsible actions of bureaucrats that had forced her into disastrous war and dangerous domestic turmoil; and the only chance of saving her was through the Tsar's granting the promised assembly, which would present the true voice of the people and help in deciding questions of war and peace. And it added a poignant plea:

> [It is] necessary that your subjects feel themselves to be Russian citizens, equal and without differences . . . , that all your subjects, even though they be of a different faith or race from you, see in Russia their fatherland, and in you, their sovereign. Just as the Russian Tsar is not a tsar of the nobility, nor of the peasantry, nor of the merchants, nor of classes, but the Tsar of All the Russias, so the persons elected by the entire population should serve the interests of the entire polity and not of classes. Sire, return to the formula of Svyatopolk-Mirsky, that the renewal of Russia must be based on confidence.[6]

Though the occasion was historic, the results were trivial. The Tsar was polite and attentive, he assured the delegation that he would summon a Duma, but he was not moved from the course he had been following. This was the last time that the zemstvos spoke with one voice. The address in the name of all zemstvos, however, received wide currency despite the attempts of the government to deprecate it and those of the leftist leaders in the opposition to solicit public disapproval of its conciliatory tone. And Prince Trubetskoi himself was pop-

[6] *Pravitelstvennyi Vestnik*, June 8, 1905.

ularly acclaimed as a spokesman for the conscience of Russia—an indication that public opinion was still liberal in temper.

Attempts by political groups to counteract the spirit of the zemstvo address came not only from the left but from the right also. The Patriotic Union and the Union of Russian Men—small rightist groups of nobles organized in the spring of 1905, the former in St. Petersburg and the latter in Moscow—sent a combined delegation of their own to the Tsar with an address designed to neutralize that of the zemstvos. The Tsar received them on June 21 and heard their appeal to maintain the class principle in the organization of the new Duma. In contrast to the zemstvo address, this one received little public notice; but its delivery marked the coming into prominence of such men as Count Alexis Bobrinsky and Senator A. A. Naryshkin, leaders of the delegation, who were to become out-standing and effective leaders of the right wing of the nobility.

Neither the zemstvo address nor the counteraddress had any direct effect on the shaping of the Bulygin Duma. Its development proceeded as planned, except that the decision to deny the franchise to the Jews was rescinded, not as a direct result of the liberal pleas but of the insistence by several bureaucrats that exclusion would be unwise. This matter and others that had been left for a final review were settled at a secret conference held at Peterhof near the end of July. The personnel and tenor of this conference, at which the Tsar himself presided, was almost wholly bureaucratic: in attendance were five grand dukes, all the ministers, and many other high officials. Only one outsider was present, the conservative historian Vasily Klyuchevsky, and he was a man quite close to the imperial family.[7] In short, this was not an instance of society's talking to the government, but of the government's talking to itself, attempting to decide how the opposition could be placated without the sacrifice of any autocratic power.

Finally, on August 6, the Tsar issued the long-awaited legislation establishing a State Duma; he did not then set the

[7] Apparently without intending to be disloyal, Klyuchevsky privately acquainted his former pupil Paul Milyukov with the happenings at the conference, thus enabling him to publish some rather severe attacks on the Bulygin Duma.

election date, but ordered that elections be held in time to permit the new body to meet before January 15, 1906. Since it followed the instructions given to Bulygin in the rescript of February 18, the legislation contained no surprises; to most of the opposition groups it was an entirely inadequate measure, a bitter disappointment. They had asked for a legislature: the law specified a Duma "to provide preliminary consideration and discussion of legislative proposals, to be transmitted through the State Council up to the supreme autocratic authority. . . ."[8] They had asked for universal suffrage: it was strictly limited by the law; most of non-European Russia was excluded from representation, the franchise being denied to all the inhabitants of Congress Poland, Siberia, Transcaucasia, and Central Asia except for those in the cities of Baku, Warsaw, Irkutsk, Lodz, Tashkent, and Tiflis; and in all areas to be represented, the franchise was to be restricted to males twenty-five years of age and older who could meet stipulated property qualifications, which were so much higher for the cities than for the rural areas that they disfranchised not only most wage earners but also most urban property owners of limited means. They had asked for direct elections: the law provided instead that Duma deputies were to be elected by provincial or city electoral assemblies, which were to be chosen by a cumbersome method similar to that followed in zemstvo elections. They had asked for equal suffrage: the law assigned electors to each class of voters—peasants, landlords, and city property owners—according to a complex formula that weighted votes on the basis of class and, occasionally, nationality.

The intention of the Tsar was clear: to have a Duma with the right to speak but not to act, a Duma that would be predominantly Russian and rural. He did not believe that it would have anything worthwhile to say; but if such a public forum would placate the opposition, he was resigned to it—providing that it spoke in Russian (the law restricted membership in the Duma to those who spoke that language) and that it spoke softly.

[8] Russia, *Polnoe Sobranie Zakonov*, 3rd series, Vol. XXV, Sect. 1, No. 26661.

6

Development

of the Revolution: Third Phase

August–October

[In the fall of 1905] liberalism had no independent power. Power still belonged to the established regime, which was then ready to make concessions. Through agreement with the regime, it would be possible to follow the evolutionary path; and in alliance with it, to continue and complete the Great Reforms [begun in the 1860's]. If the regime continued the struggle against "liberal tendencies," then "liberalism" would find itself compelled to rely on the only real power, that of *Acheron* [as interpreted, violence]. This path would inevitably lead to revolution—either to its success or to its defeat; but in either case, liberalism would only lose.
—Vasily Maklakov (moderate liberal), *Iz Vospominanii*, 1954.

Taking note of all that has been done in recent times in the struggle of the people against its oppressors, we see the joyous day of the people's judgment against the barbarous regime drawing nigh and note that the class-conscious revolutionary part of the working class is taking its place as the leader of the struggle. . . . On the basis of the general policy of autocracy toward the people, it is evident that this shameful and damnable regime can be destroyed only by a nation-wide armed uprising.
—From a resolution adopted on August 3, 1905, by the Social Democratic workers of Saratov.

ON AUGUST 6, after he had issued the Law on the Bulygin Duma, Nicholas II was anticipating for the third time during the ten years of his reign, a return of domestic harmony. He had been over-credulous about the effectiveness of his acts of December, 1904 and February, 1905, but that fact apparently did not temper his reliance on this last one, which he considered the ultimate concession possible from an autocrat. On this occasion he anticipated also a favorable readjustment in foreign affairs. A month earlier he had sent Sergei Witte (chosen after preferred men had proved unavailable or unwilling to serve) to the United States, where he would negotiate terms of peace with Japan at a conference to be held in Portsmouth, New Hampshire. And when the Treaty of Portsmouth was signed, on August 23, though the terms were adverse from the Russian viewpoint, he derived some comfort from the fact that he had required Witte to take such a firm stand that, even while granting unexpected concessions to Japan, Russia retained some semblance of strength in negotiations and the enemy did not receive all the rewards expected. An important secondary benefit from the war's end would be added strength for the government on the home front; it was expected that, as they were released from the Far East, the troops could be deployed with advantage to the various trouble spots reported by provincial governors. Believing the situation to be thus well in hand, Nicholas left Peterhof at the beginning of September for a two-weeks' cruise with his family in the Finnish waters.

ASSESSMENT OF THE PROJECTED BULYGIN DUMA

The Tsar's mood was not matched by that of the opposition. For most of the liberals the announcement of the Law on the Bulygin Duma raised questions rather than hopes. To be sure, it was a major concession on the part of autocracy, granting nationwide elections and promising free speech on the floor of the new assembly. Yet they were uncomfortably aware of certain disturbing aspects of the gain. Not only had they not been consulted on any details of the new law, but

they well knew (from Milyukov's reports based on Klyuchevsky's inside information concerning the final conference on
the law) [1] that it had been prepared in a bureaucratic atmosphere altogether unfavorable to them. Moreover, they were
disappointed that no accompanying provision had been made
for general civil rights, which they regarded as essential con-
comitants of representative government: the inviolability of
person and the freedom of press, speech, and assembly. From
these conditions arose difficult and disquieting questions for
many liberals. Should the Bulygin Duma be accepted despite
its shortcomings? Was there a chance that the tsarist government could be compelled to make concessions greater than
those represented by the Bulygin Duma? What would be the
best means of testing the government's disposition regarding
further concessions—political strikes, armed uprising? Would
the cost of making such tests justify the possible returns?

It was imperative for the oppositional parties and groups, if
their influence was to be continued, to take a definite stand
on the coming election of deputies to the Duma: to declare
themselves either willing to participate or committed to non-
participation. To boycott would signify a resolution to continue the struggle for further concession from the government
—that being, for most of them, a constituent assembly. That
position, of course, was a hazardous one because, if it proved
ineffectual, it would detract from the influence of those supporting the boycott. The alternative, participation in the elections, had its drawback also: though it would not necessarily
indicate satisfaction with the Duma, it would mean that the
liberation movement should thereafter expect to confine its
campaigning for additional change to action within the Duma
rather than continue its operation through public organizations.

The question of whether or not to boycott stimulated much
debate among the liberals during the last weeks of August and
the first part of September. The result was the first open and
large-scale schism in the liberation movement. The line of

[1] The complete stenographic report of the conference was later
obtained by the liberals, reprinted abroad, and disseminated in
Russia.

division was, as might have been predicted, between moderates and extremists, the former generally favoring participation and the latter generally favoring boycott. This definite taking of sides brought back to the ranks of the moderates many who had, before August, moved over to extremist positions. An instance of such sober second-thinking occurred in a September congress of zemstvo and municipal duma delegates, when a majority of them took the moderate position and voted to support the Duma. The Union of Unions, on the other hand, voted for boycott. But even that body was not of one mind: some of its members—the Union for the Attainment of Full Rights for the Jews, for example—declared their support of the Duma and their intention of participating in the elections.

For the socialists there were no divisive questions. They were unequivocally opposed to the Duma and intended therefore to work against it. They began in many cities by calling strikes in protest against it. Then they set to work on plans to use the boycott of the Duma elections as a political weapon. For action on such plans an early-September conference of Social Democratic organizations was called and held secretly in Riga. It was attended by representatives of the Menshevik and Bolshevik factions of the RSDLP, the Lettish SD Party, the Bund, the Polish SD Party, and the recently organized Ukrainian Revolutionary Party. They agreed (all except the Mensheviks, who planned to take a somewhat divergent course toward the same goal) [2] to an active boycott, which would culminate, at the time set for the elections, in a general political strike making it impossible to hold the elections. And, as a final gesture, the conference reaffirmed the Social Democratic position that only an armed uprising could bring about their immediate objective, the creation of a democratic republic.

The problem of what to do about the Duma engaged the

[2] The Mensheviks had the notion of creating some kind of "revolutionary self-administration" in the form of elected assemblies of workers' and peasants' deputies, which would establish a national assembly to rival the forthcoming Duma and force the government to convoke a constituent assembly. This idea was never implemented.

students of the higher schools just as it did their elders; but their consideration of it, though similar in many ways, was soon complicated by a feature peculiar to their status. By a ukase of August 27, the Tsar restored to the universities the autonomy of which they had been deprived in 1884, hoping that the act would pacify the students and faculty (who had been urging the repeal of the law of 1884 for many years) and make it possible to reopen the universities and other higher schools under peaceful conditions. And this concession presented an immediate dilemma to the students. If they continued to strike, they would be subject to the same restrictions and prohibitions under which they had been working as supporters of the liberation movement. On the other hand, if they should return to their classrooms, they could use to revolutionary advantage some very attractive opportunities legally provided as elements of the restored autonomy—among them, the immunity of university and other higher school premises from police interference, the right of students to hold meetings, and faculty (instead of government) responsibility for student discipline. To decide which course to take, they convened a September congress of student representatives in Vyborg, located eighty miles from St. Petersburg, in Finland (where police interference was less likely than in European Russia). The SR and Bolshevik students argued earnestly for a plan to carry on the revolutionary struggle for a constituent assembly and a democratic republic by a continuation of the student strike, but the congress finally voted in favor of the plan supported by the Mensheviks: that students should resume their academic roles, without forfeiting any of their aims, in order to profit from the immunities.

Thus the liberation movement seemed to be split three ways, one wing favoring acceptance of the Bulygin Duma, a second favoring boycott of the Duma elections while continuing a peaceful political campaign for a constituent assembly, and a third preparing for an armed uprising as a prerequisite to the establishment of a democratic republic and the convening of a constituent assembly.

The aspirations of the third, though more ambitious than those of the first two, were not founded on any real strength.

As late as October 3, Lenin, writing from Geneva to the fighting committee of the St. Petersburg Bolsheviks, upbraided
them for the slowness of their preparations for an armed uprising. He pointed out that, though the committee had been
talking for months about bombs, as yet it had not a single
bomb; that it lacked revolvers and incendiary devices; and
that if it did not increase the number of its fighting squads[3] by
two to three hundred within a month—or two, at most—it
should consider itself out of business. It was clear that the
socialists did not expect an armed uprising in the near future.
An illustration of their lack of immediate concern with such
action was the Bund's turning of its attention in October to
the business of its convention in Switzerland with no indication that it expected anything critical on the home front for
some time. The socialists as well as the extreme liberals in the
late summer of 1905 talked much about general strike and
armed uprising but continued the tactics they had used before, singling out as their present target the new Duma. Final
plans were still in the uncharted future.

TIGHTENING OF AUTHORITY

While the forces of the opposition were working through
the possibilities newly opened to them and assessing their
changed positions, the government was moving ahead with un-
wonted determination toward the restoration of order. At the
head of this operation was General Trepov who, while retaining his post as governor-general of St. Petersburg, had been
appointed Assistant Minister of Interior and charged with the
administration of the country's entire police system. Now he
was tightening the controls at many points, employing somewhat the same tactics he had used in the capital after Bloody
Sunday. While not showing any intention of pushing pacification to the degree that Plehve had, he was providing forces
sufficient to improve and expedite the handling of disorder
and to limit antigovernment activities. Into many cities where
the police had shown laxness in dealing with the opposition,

[3] The size of these squads varied from three to thirty men, the
average being between five and ten.

extra detachments of troops were sent. The use of workers' bourses (open areas where workers were accustomed to gather, often to seek employment) for political agitation was brought to an end, the process involving many instances of bloodshed. The spate of accompanying arrests included those of many persons highly placed in the opposition; leaders of the Union of Unions, for instance, were arrested in August and held in prison for a month. Since the government seemed more sure of itself now than in the months recently past and since it was moving more systematically to reinforce its authority, most uninvolved observers concluded that the outlook was entirely favorable. The British ambassador, Sir Charles Hardinge, expressed the general feeling thus in a report at the end of September:

> The unhealthy season here is just beginning [the St. Petersburg climate was notoriously bad except during the brief summer], most of my colleagues have already left, and as I do not foresee any urgent questions arising that would require my presence here, I should be glad of a rest.[4]

New Wave of Unrest

At the time no one could have recognized all the potential trouble spots in the country or foreseen that sporadic disorders, often with no visible relation to one another, could coalesce and produce a nationwide upheaval. But the troublesome elements were there. In some cases their menace was overlooked or misinterpreted because the authorities were overly confident of their ability to dissipate unrest or contain it at the place of its origin.

During the summer, occurrences in the agricultural areas of the borderlands might have suggested that the situation was serious enough to merit concern. Unrest erupted in violence in the Baltic provinces, where the percentage of agricultural proletariat was higher than in most of Russia. In Courland—and to a lesser degree in the two other Baltic provinces, Livonia and Estland—economic and political tensions interacted to

[4] Hardinge to Sanderson, October 8 (NS), 1905, British Public Records Office, Foreign Office, 65/1703.

heighten a rebelliousness of many years' standing. In that province, the property owners in both city and countryside were, for the most part, Baltic Germans, generally hated by the laborers, who were Letts. Early in the summer, the landless agricultural laborers of Zemgale, the most important farming area of Courland, united and began paying off old scores against the German landholding nobility, burning both estate and government property and beating—occasionally killing—landlords and police officials. Before long they were joined by the Lettish peasants of the region, and the united forces turned the general apprehension into definite alarm. Not even the churches were exempt from their excesses. During July many Lutheran churches attended by both Germans and Letts were scenes of revolutionary rioting as the Letts began to use them as forums from which to denounce the government and the landlords. The German nobles organized self-defense units and, supported by Russian troops, started counterresistance, but the violence continued and began to spread. Finally, in August, the Tsar declared Courland under martial law. But the laborers and peasants were not easily pacified and, instead of subsiding before armed force, the trouble spread to Livonia and ultimately to Estland.

Of other areas where insurgence among agrarian elements defied efforts at pacification, the Georgian provinces were the most resistant. A punitive force of ten thousand could effect only temporary calm there, and in some places—Kutaisk province, for example—estate disorders continued with little change. In Congress Poland there was some agrarian violence, though it was less extensive than in other border areas, Polish unrest being more often expressed in strikes of agrarian laborers for higher wages.

Even in European Russia, which the Tsar considered the heart of the empire and the stronghold of true Russian peasant conservatism, agrarian turmoil was demanding attention. The incidence of strikes by agricultural laborers and of the illegal cutting of landlord-owned timber, hay, and grain was on the increase in the provinces of Kiev, Volhynia, Podolia, Kharkov, Poltava, Chernigov, Saratov, Samara, Orlov, Kursk, Tambov, Moscow, Nizhny Novgorod, and Penza as well as in the Don Cossack region. The burning and looting of estates were still uncommon, but those acts of defiance also were becoming more frequent.

The noticeable changes in agrarian areas were qualitative as well as quantitative: the peasantry was finally being reached by the idea of political opposition. Dramatic evidence of this fact was to be seen in the formation of the Peasants Union, the first real link between the peasants and the liberation movement. It was initiated by views emanating from the zemstvos—in particular from the Third Element (as professionals employed by these local organizations were collectively called), men closely connected with the formation of the Union of Unions. And it was given predicative consideration in May, when some fifty persons, meeting in Moscow, made plans to proceed with the organization of a union—to be called the All Russian (i.e., including the whole empire) Peasants Union. Branches were then formed in the Don Cossack region and in the Kursk, Tula, and Saratov provinces, soon to be followed by others; and a founding congress opened in Moscow at the end of July. Composed of one hundred peasant delegates and twenty-five delegates classified as *intelligents* (self-appointed or sent by zemstvos and party organizations), it met for two days and formally established the new organization, the delegates coming to agreement on tactics as well as long-range goals.

It was clear from the beginning that the Peasants Union would be pulled in two directions on the matter of priorities: one leading to participation in the Union of Unions in order to promote the liberation movement, the other leading to efforts for the immediate solution of the agrarian question. As the pressures from the two directions were reflected in the adopted program, the political was stronger than the agrarian: first place was given to the call for a constituent assembly, and the second to the agrarian question. The delegates declared themselves in favor of the nationalization of land owned by landlords, with partial compensation to them, but left the details to be worked out by the anticipated assembly.

During the following two months, further organizational work of the Peasants Union gave it a membership sufficient to insure the range and strength of cooperation necessary for an active agrarian movement. Local branches were organized in villages and volosts throughout most of the provinces of European Russia—from Moscow south to the Don River, and from the Volga west to the Dnieper. The growth in the number of branches indicated a large following for the movement, but by no means did it indicate that the union idea had swept all, or even the major part of, the peasants into accepting a place in the cooperative effort. The union leadership, dominated by Liberationists and usually connected with zemstvo work while receiving some support from SR's and Mensheviks, emphasized political aims and methods. They promoted campaigns urging the peasants to adopt petitions for political reform and, by the right of petition granted in February, to send these to the Tsar. By late summer, peasant meetings in various provinces had adopted petitions calling for the by-now-familiar political reforms, to which they often added items of more pressing importance to the peasantry—such as calls for measures to make land available for purchase and to eliminate onerous taxes. This was the first time that the peasantry had ever shown a readiness to act as an organized political force.

In some areas, the Peasants Union developed an ominous corollary—revolutionary stirring. Although the central leadership did not see the organization as a revolutionary weapon, there were local leaders who did. In addition, there was a degree of peasant sentiment for action more forceful than that called for by the union. It was present, for instance, in the Don Cossack region, where Ukrainian and Russian settlers were in a position inferior to that of the Cossacks and consequently responsive to oppositional ideas. The large union membership in that region was led by two Ukrainian socialists, the brothers Mazurenko, who, while not in favor of immediate agrarian revolt, thought of it as a proper long-range goal. A similar notion of the union's ultimate aim prevailed in Saratov province, where SR's were prominent in the local leadership and, like their counterparts in the Don Cossack region, not particularly responsive to directions from the Central Bureau in Moscow. In areas such as these the peasants of the union were often eager to follow local leaders into immediate action against landlords and officials. And their attitude could be expected to become more defiant at times when their situation showed any signs of worsening. Such a time came in more than twenty provinces during the fall following the organization of the union. The harvests were exceptionally meager, and the prospects of famine kept the peasants in a mood of desperation that was easily turned to any action promising improvement.

Being more removed from the domestic scene, the men of the armed forces were exposed to direct antigovernment propaganda later than most other groups sought out by the opposition. But their potential contribution to it was not to be evaluated by that fact alone. When the war ended, responsible officials in the government faced with some misgiving the prospect of nearly a million men returning to their homes from the Manchurian front. The Caucasian Cavalry Brigade and the Cossack divisions that had been serving in the East were considered sources of dependable strength, and their return would be welcomed. But many reserve units were not trusted, the state of their morale being generally uncertain. One minister suggested keeping a large number of them in eastern Siberia by offering them land for settlement (the idea was not pursued). The concern about the reservists—not only those who saw service in Manchuria, but others as well—was warranted. Once the fighting ended, they were anxious, as civilians in uniform, to be demobilized; and they were ready to translate what they had heard of the popular opposition into their own terms—opposition to the authority of their officers. But the problem of assimilating returning troops, trustworthy or otherwise, remained for a time a relatively distant one. Preparations for bringing them from Manchuria went slowly, the War Ministry working with military leaders to devise some scheme for handling their grouping and transportation; and it was more than a month after the signing of the Portsmouth treaty before the first trainloads began to move westward, toward home.

What was going on in the countryside and among the soldiers was, for a time, merely backstage activity in comparison with what was taking place in the larger cities, where the

labor movement was daily making itself more prominent. Encouraged by small successes gained through strikes in the first
part of the year, those involved in the movement were now
devoting themselves to keeping it vigorous. And the trade-
union movement, though still in its infancy, was thriving. By
late summer, several trade unions—of printers, salesclerks,
pharmacists, jewellers, and bakers—were functioning openly,
regardless of legal prohibitions, in St. Petersburg, Moscow,
Kharkov, and other cities.

The union of greatest potential power, the All-Russian
Union of Railroad Employees and Workers (commonly shortened to Union of Railroad Workers), was as yet an anoma-
lous kind of organization—part political union, part trade
union. Its Central Bureau was committed to supporting the
tactics of the Union of Unions and, consequently, favored political petitioning and the boycotting of the Bulygin Duma.
But the union did not include all of the country's railroad
employees and workers by any means, nor did it in fact control all its members. Among them various, and often con-
tending, forces were exerting their influence—Liberationist,
Menshevik, Bolshevik, SR, or purely trade-union influence.
Moreover, attitudes and reactions were likely to be peculiar to
one region or one occupation. That was to be expected in
such a complex industry with such a variety of personnel: certainly the civil service employees in the administrative headquarters of the railroads were unlike the machinists; and each
group differed from the maintenance men, usually local peasants, who worked on the tracks. In this situation, the union's
Central Board had to face the fact that its competitors were
often the winners. In the Moscow workshops of the Moscow-
Brest line, the Mensheviks were the chief political influence;
on some of the Siberian lines, the Bolsheviks were the leaders;
and in many railroad centers the leaders were those who continued the agitation for more strikes of an economic nature as
proper accompaniments of political strikes.

The government, extremely sensitive to the potential power
of the railroadmen, had attempted both to coerce them—by
making them liable to mobilization earlier in the year—and to
placate them—by agreeing, after a number of strikes, to a de-

crease in their working hours. And as a part of a continuing effort to placate them, the Minister of Ways and Communications, Prince Michael Khilkov, planned a railroad employees' congress. It was intended, according to his announcement, to give their elected delegates an opportunity to come to St. Petersburg and review the rules governing their pension funds. The Central Bureau of the Union of Railroad Workers, declaring the congress to be a government effort to divert the workers from their immediate political struggle, called on union members to boycott the election of delegates. The boycott failed; but oddly enough, a large number of the delegates chosen were politically more radical than the central leadership and had no intention of avoiding politics at the congress but planned to use it as an arena for conflict with the government.

As the date set for the congress (September 20) approached, there was much talk about the need for a general political strike. The topic was current among railroadmen, in several of the trade unions, and in the left-wing factions of some political unions. But the talk, on the whole, was vague and with little direction. In one instance a bit of anticipatory action was taken: near the end of summer, several left-wing lawyers and representatives from some political and trade unions organized a strike committee in Moscow. And the September decision of the Social Democrats to call a general political strike to disrupt the coming Duma elections lent support to the idea that action was to be expected.

The fact that rumors were now being passed around freely, that suggestions were getting ample circulation, and that ideas were being more widely disseminated was due largely to an unwitting concession of the government itself: the reestablishment of immunity rights on the premises of universities and other higher schools. Student leaders, most of them revolutionary in their views, began during the first days of September, in cooperation with socialists and liberals not connected with the institutions, to turn their buildings into political meeting places. This was a special boon to the socialists and labor groups (shared also by the liberals), who had hitherto lacked the means of communicating their views to large crowds. They had been limited to small surreptitious meetings in private homes and suburban woods or hasty and frequently interrupted meetings at factory gates or in workers' exchanges. Now as many as ten thousand persons could meet—and often did—in a single evening in auditoriums, lecture halls, and laboratories of the universities in St. Petersburg and Moscow, while similar groups of smaller number met in other cities. This access to meeting places made possible for the first time the free intermingling of workers, students, and older *intelligents*. And though certain individuals and groups continued to hold aloof, such meetings were narrowing still further the gap between workers and *intelligents*, raising the sense of excitement among the radical opposition, and making more tangible than ever the notion of "two Russias."

INCREASING STRIKE ACTIVITY

On the eve of the St. Petersburg congress of railroad employees, representing one of the government's rare invitations to the discussion of a problem by those involved, the idea of a general strike remained a subject for random discussion, and these oppositional meetings were still treating it as something to be given detailed consideration at some future date when it would be possible to execute plans for it. But they were behind time: the great strike began in Moscow, without benefit of detailed planning, on September 19. It was initiated—unintentionally—by the printers of the Sypin press, who went out on strike in support of their demands for a slight wage increase, which the press management had disregarded, though agreeable to their requested reduction in working hours. On the following day the Moscow Printers Union called out all other printers in the city. And within ten days they were joined by the city's bakers, wood workers, machine tool workers, textile workers, tobacco workers, and workers from the railroad shops. Making political and economic demands, the strikers held frequent and boisterous meetings in the halls of the university and the Surveying Institute, marched through the streets singing the *Marseillaise*, and occasionally threw stones or fired at police and troops. The Central University

Organization, formed among the students of the University of Moscow a few days before the beginning of the strike, took an active and vociferous part in the activities.

Both the government and the faculties were shocked at the use to which the educational institutions were being put. And Prince Sergei Trubetskoi, just elected rector of the university under the new rules, appealed vainly to the students for moderation. He then turned to the faculty council, the governing body, asking them to suspend classes and close the buildings in order to prevent the continuation of the rebellious meetings. They declared the buildings closed, but that made no apparent impression on either students or strikers.

What may be called the first period of the Moscow strike came to a climax on October 2, when a soviet of representatives from five trades was formed to direct the operation of strike activities. By the time the soviet started functioning, most of the strikers had reached the limit of their means and were beginning to lose their enthusiasm. Gradually they resumed work. No immediate advantage could be claimed for either side: the skirmishes left the strikers with 110 dead or wounded men, the government authorities with 30; and the action, having brought neither success nor defeat for strikers or established authority, left the former unreconciled, the latter, uneasy.

As the fever of opposition subsided in Moscow, it began to rise in St. Petersburg, displaying itself—as usual with indications of suppressed mood in unstable times—in situations apparently unrelated to the underlying impulse. One such situation developed after the sudden death of Prince Trubetskoi, who had come to the capital on university business. Although he had been known as a moderate liberal, rather than an extremist, he had been popular among most opposition groups, particularly since he led the delegation that presented the zemstvo address to the Tsar in June. Now his death was used by them to stir up a great manifestation of feeling. The Social Democrats organized a demonstration of some six hundred students and workers to follow his body, accompanied by relatives and professional deputations, when it was taken to the railroad station to be sent to Moscow for burial. As the

cortege passed along Nevsky Prospekt, the demonstrators, carrying red signal flags they had seized from streetcars, dispersed
when police approached, re-formed when they were at a distance. From the station, they marched back, heading for the
university but pausing briefly in Palace Square, the most publicized scene of Bloody Sunday events, to remove their hats
and kneel silently, as if in respect to those who had died there
for the cause they represented. Back at the university, they
were forced by mounted police to disperse and abandon their
demonstration.

But there were to be further activities in which they could
join. On that very day a group of printers in the capital
planned a three-day strike to show sympathy for the Moscow
printers and, on the following morning, set it in operation.
Within twenty-four hours they had the support of practically
all of the city's presses, including that of the government
organ *Pravitelstvennyi Vestnik*. They were unsuccessful, however, in their attempts to call out the printers of the General
Staff press and those employed in the chief government printing office. And when two thousand of the strikers attempted
to bar the nonstriking men from the printing office the next
day, the Izmailovsky Guards were called upon to drive them
back. Though they lost that encounter and suffered several
casualties, they were by no means discouraged. The men of the
Neva Shipbuilding Works, in the Schlüsselburg district, joined
them, and soon workers from other parts of the district
swelled the striking ranks. For most of them, the strike was
clearly a political demonstration and they did not bother
even to present economic demands. They denounced the
Bulygin Duma and displayed an openly bellicose attitude.
Resorting to violence, which included the erection of barricades, they were checked only when armed force was used
against them. On the evening of the second strike day twelve
thousand workers, *intelligents,* and students crowded into the
university buildings and, among them, worked up a great
deal of enthusiasm for a major political strike. As the strike
reached its crest, on the following day, it was joined by the
men of the important Obukhovsky Steel Plant, operated by
the Naval Ministry, who marched from their work to the ca-

dence of the *Marseillaise* and the chanted call for four-tail suffrage (later their foremen joined the strike also).

Meanwhile the tempo of disturbances in Moscow was picking up once more. The upswing began at the time of the Trubetskoi funeral. It was transformed into a great political demonstration when the official delegations invited to accompany the procession to the burial place, within the walls of the Donskoi Monastery, were joined by thousands of workers, white-collar employees, students, and *intelligents*. Though the assembling of the procession might be seen as symbolic of unity within the liberation movement, what ensued at the monastery underlined the differences: while the liberals at the graveside spoke in terms that Trubetskoi would have approved, revolutionary students harangued the crowds outside the monastery walls in quite dissimilar terms.[5]

The extremist point of view was, for the time being, ascendant in Moscow, where the Central Bureau of the Union of Railroad Workers was caught up by the currently growing desire for action and encouraged by the fact that some of the Moscow railroad workers were already out on strike. Its call for all railroadmen in Moscow to stop work on October 4 was respected only half-heartedly. But two days later, when rumors reached them that several delegates to the railroad employees congress then meeting in the capital had been arrested (a rumor that proved later to be false), the men began to respond with vigor. The results quickly became a matter of wide concern. Moscow was the railroad hub of the empire: the major lines originated there and the administrative offices were located there, as were also the chief workshops. A mass strike would be a serious matter indeed. The men of the Moscow-Kazan line were the first to stop work, and their example brought out those of other lines until, by the 8th, all the Moscow lines had been idled. The strikers included employees from the administrative offices, terminal employees, machinists, telegraph operators, train conductors, and engineers. All movement was suspended on the lines out of Mos-

[5] This type of memorial service was arranged by dissidents in many cities for the sole purpose of declaring political positions and arousing antigovernment feelings.

cow except for a train to St. Petersburg; trains already en route to or from the city at the strike's beginning were stopped when their crews received the news, and passengers were left to seek some other means of reaching their destinations.

THE OCTOBER GENERAL STRIKE

The tie-up of the Moscow lines soon became the heart and center of Russia's first general strike, known popularly as the "Great October Strike"—an unplanned but roughly concerted movement that reached into and involved every part of the country. Though without specific plan or national leadership, its development was made possible by years of political preparation and propaganda, the recent ten months of constantly aggravated unrest that had begun with Bloody Sunday, and the readiness of established oppositional organizations to join in its promotion.

Once begun, the Moscow strike, unlike many others of past months, was not allowed gradually to lose momentum. The Central Bureau of the Union of Railroad Workers called on all railroadmen not only to strike but to persevere until the government was ready to bargain with representatives of the entire railroad system. To bargain for what? To the usual demands for economic betterment, the strikers were now being urged to add political demands. The Moscow committee of the union reminded them that economic freedom depended upon political freedom and that, to achieve either, they must combine forces with the rest of "laboring Russia." The radical delegates to the Khilkov congress appealed from their meeting in St. Petersburg for a rail strike throughout the national system. Then, on October 9, on behalf of those they represented, they submitted to the government a list of demands including economic betterment for railroad workers, a constituent assembly for all of Russia, and amnesty for all political prisoners (this last, a demand to which many groups were now beginning to subscribe).

With the vigorous beginning of the railroad strike, the still uncoordinated aspirations for a general political strike were revived and strengthened; and here again Moscow became the leader of the moment. As the railroad strike progressed, there were daily additions to the number of factories idled by striking workers; and enthusiasm for a general strike mounted as meetings went on day and night at the university, the Surveying Institute, the Technical Institute, and the Engineering Institute. Strike inspired strike, the movement spreading farther and farther through the life of the city; for example, when the Union of Pharmacists went on strike, on October 9, it was able to close almost all of the variously located local pharmacies by the next day. Within a week, Moscow was virtually isolated, and most of her important public activities were at a standstill. All train connections were severed. All telegraphic connections along the lines emanating from the city were silent. Only the central General Telegraph Office remained in operation in the city to provide communication with the outside, and the railroadmen were planning to close it.

The contagion of the strike, in both its economic and its political aspects, quickly became apparent elsewhere. As soon as the trains from Moscow to Kharkov were halted, the Kharkov railroadmen began stopping all branch-line traffic into and out of that city; and, by the 10th, they had not only cut off rail communications but had also spearheaded an outbreak that became revolutionary in nature and serious in proportions. As they called for collaborators, they were joined by throngs of striking factory workers, students, and sometimes older *intelligents,* whose mood soon led beyond the shouting of slogans and general unruliness to the looting of arms stores and attacks on soldiers and police. The governor of the province, K. S. Starynkevich, was caught in a most difficult position, limited as he was in means of communication with General Trepov or others to whom he might have appealed for assistance. The forces at his command were clearly unable to cope with the disorder, which grew more threatening by the hour. The SD's and SR's formed the joint Fighting Committee to give general direction to the strike, oversee the operations of their local fighting detachments, and guide the newly formed units of workers' militia. As a countermeasure,

the liberals of the city established the Committee of Public
Defense to help maintain order and try to serve as intermediary between the rebellious strikers and the faltering civil
authorities. This committee in turn, with the consent of the
governor, organized small militia detachments of armed workers and soldiers to prevent looting.

The strike leaders and their followers established their
headquarters in the University of Kharkov and used its property freely. On October 11, a group of strikers on the way to
the university met a patriotic counterdemonstration, which
they broke up with gunfire, thereby finally exhausting the
patience of the government. The city was immediately thereafter placed under martial law, and legal authority over the
city was transferred from the governor to a military man,
General N. I. Mau. His first act was to send troops to surround the university. There, during the night of October
11/12, students and workers prepared to resist his authority,
barring doors and windows and throwing up barricades.
Bloodshed was avoided only because the Committee of Public
Defense was able the next morning to persuade the general to
grant free and safe exit to the besieged on the condition that
they give up their arms and agree to leave quietly. The city
itself was not so easily subdued, however, and the troops had
to be held at the ready for some time to come.

Whereas the disturbances in Kharkov were influenced by
disturbances in Moscow, St. Petersburg was influenced by
both: the news of the Moscow railroad strike helped to re-
juvenate the declining strike movement in the capital, and
news of the Kharkov disorders helped to fire the imagination
of those with revolutionary leanings. Excitement was mounting by the 10th, and it grew with a readiness easily predictable in the light of the city's recent experiences. On the
night of the 11th, some ten thousand workers and students
congregated in the halls and laboratories of the university—
railroad workers in one place, salesclerks in another, and so
on. As each group occupied itself with discussions and planning, students made the rounds to collect money for arms,
and SR's urged the consideration of terroristic methods.
There was no collaboration among the groups and no com-

mon decision, but there was an obvious community of feeling, a conviction that the hour of crisis was near. The most noteworthy decision of the night was that made by the railroadmen—to strike on the following day.

The railroad strike, which began on the 12th, affected all lines connected with the city, and by the end of the day no trains were being dispatched, not even to Peterhof, where the Tsar was in residence. And though neither the railroadmen nor any other group had planned a general strike at this time, one was soon in the making. Several factories were shut down simultaneously with the railroads. On the following day St. Petersburg witnessed a recurrence, in vastly amplified form, of the events of January 7-8. The strike spread from district to district; factories, retail stores, and offices closed as if on prescribed schedule. Secondary school boys left their classrooms and set out in search of any delinquents whom they might bring into line with the strike. Almost no street transportation, either electric or horse-drawn, was functioning. And that night the number of factory workers, railroadmen, teachers, clerks, and students who pushed into and out of the university buildings, listening to speeches and advocating the extension of the strike, was increased to some thirty thousand. On the following day pharmacists, secondary school girls, insurance company employees, and chocolate factory workers joined the strike; and a day later, the movement reached government personnel—the printers in the Ministry of the Navy, the employees of the local branch of the State Bank, the actors of the imperial theaters, and the employees of the port and customs service. When some of the staid members of official establishments came out in support of the "liquidation of the old regime" and the convocation of a constituent assembly, it seemed that the zenith had been reached, that the most unpromising had succumbed. By the evening of the 14th, the halls and courtyards of the university and the nearby Academy of Arts were crowded with an estimated fifty thousand, and higher schools elsewhere in the city were likewise overflowing with excited strikers and their vociferous supporters. Anarchists vied with socialists for attention, and socialists with liberals. The general strike was under way with undeniably strong backing from socialists and liberals, from trade unions, from the Union of Unions, and from large groups of civil servants.

Beginning in the big cities of the central areas, the railroad strike fanned out to the far reaches of the empire. In Congress Poland most of the rail service stopped on the 12th. On the 13th Warsaw checked in its last train from St. Petersburg; and on the same day, most of the lines in Transcaucasia and western Siberia were idled. On the next, movement was halted on those east of Lake Baikal, where trains carrying the first troops from Manchuria were tied up. Then, when the Finnish railroads joined the strike, on the 16th, the entire imperial railroad system, comprising 43,000 miles of line, was shut down.

The strike movement followed a general pattern in most cities: the railroadmen would strike first; other workers would join them; then socialists, branches of the Union of Unions, and other such groups would formalize the call to general strike. Thus Odessa, Kiev, Warsaw, Lodz, Riga, Libau, Poltava, Tiflis, Baku, Minsk, Homel, Vilna, Rostov-on-Don, Helsingfors, Ivanovo-Voznesensk, and most other cities with any degree of industrial life or even one higher school, were caught up in the Great October Strike. In the major cities, when the strike had claimed the factory workers, printers, clerks, teachers, students, civil servants, retail store employees, doctors, and lawyers, almost all activity stopped except for the movement in support of the strike, on the one hand, and that of the police and troops on the other.

Some hitherto quiet cities were affected, in varying degrees, as the strike progressed. In Tashkent striking railroadmen made a march on the governor-general's home—without untoward effect on either side, troops turning them back without bloodshed. In Tyumen, an out-of-the-way city in western Siberia, schoolboys thronged the streets, waving red flags. Novocherkassk, the capital of the Don Cossack region, experienced a number of strikes and political demonstrations. Tsarskoe Selo, a small city almost completely dominated by the imperial residence, had its day also: local secondary school boys went out on strike and were joined by the pupils of the girls' secondary school; and the primary school children registered their feelings by refusing to say their morning prayers and, when the prayers were read to them, responding with the favored Russian form of disrespect, whistling.

Even in the places that subscribed to the strike in a generally wholehearted manner, there was usually a minority that expressed private disapproval of both the strike and its leaders by the simple expedient of remaining aloof. And, here and there, some individuals and groups held themselves openly and stubbornly apart despite urgings and, in some cases, attempted coercion from the majority. The streetcar employees in Warsaw, for example, held out for several days, agreeing to strike only after incidents that made operation impossible: strikers overturning cars, throwing stones through windows, and resorting to bodily harm when regular cars were replaced with windowless ones. Another such instance of obstinance, among the employees of the General Telegraph Office in Moscow, resulted in an uneasy victory for the non-strikers. Armed guards were able to insure their safety while they kept the office functioning, but only after force was used to drive off two waves of strikers (about three thousand, mostly *intelligents,* in the first; and a larger number in the second, mostly of the working class), who gathered around the office, on the 11th, in an attempt to bring out the employees. Even so, the settlement was far from peaceful; the crowds continued to shout and keep up a din sufficient to make work difficult for those inside.

The strike agitators made little effort to solicit the support of the rural populace and, with rare exceptions, only those already caught up in disorders added anything to the spreading disturbance. Among the exceptions were the agricultural "fighting detachments" of Saratov, which made a number of destructive forays against the properties of prominent estate holders of that province—among them, Musin-Pushkin, Volkonsky, Vorontsov-Dashkov, and Shuvalov. But their rebelliousness was soon quelled and routine restored in that area.

Of the urban classes, however, though some were not in-

volved in the strike and though some who joined it did so out
of fear or momentary excitement, an impressive number became active participants: about one million factory workers,
over seven hundred thousand railroadmen, fifty thousand government employees, and tens of thousands of clerks in offices
and retail stores, professionals, and students. Municipal dumas,
in most cities, took a position either of neutrality or of support. The result was what seemed to be a union of forces in a
general display of contempt for the regime. Yet, actually, the
concerted action of the various groups in the general strike
did not constitute union. The fact that this oppositional movement was in the form of a strike gave organized labor and the
socialists a place of importance in it, but credit for its effectiveness had to be distributed—among liberals, socialists, and
those with no specific political identity. Among all of them,
there was support for basic elements of the liberation movement's program: demands for a constituent assembly, political
amnesty, the eight-hour day, and the end of legal disabilities
imposed upon national and religious minorities. But that fact
did not insure practical unity.

Nature of Strike Leadership

Had the various groups involved in the strike been inclined
to yield to expediency and form a practical union for the
promotion of the movement, they would have faced some
quite unsurmountable obstacles. No organization or committee among them had the power or the influence to take over
national leadership. The organization with the greatest national scope was the Union of Railroad Workers but, as has
been seen, its General Bureau lacked the ability to lead its
own members. Even if any group could have produced an
ably functioning leadership, it would have lacked the means
of communicating readily with its potential following. At the
height of the strike activity, the whole Russian empire was
without newspapers except for the reactionary Kiev newspaper *Kievlanin*, whose printers had refused to strike; most
telegraphic communication was cut or was being operated under government protection; travel was generally limited to

private conveyance or the individual's stamina as a walker; and the movement of the post was now almost halted.

Consequently whatever the strike leadership, it was necessarily local, each city's leaders being in virtual isolation from the others and involved almost exclusively with the immediate problems of its vicinity. And strike committees varied from city to city: in some, they were composed of all oppositional groups; in some, they included only labor and socialist elements; in some, the socialists dominated but formed rival committees—Menshevik and Bolshevik. Under such conditions, the committees could not be expected to follow a common plan. Most of them called for the strike to continue until the government gave in. The socialist Fighting Committee of Kharkov, among the exceptions, limited the general strike to three days, stipulating that only the railroadmen should remain out indefinitely. Some found that the length of the strike had to be adjusted to accord with the strikers' means of support while idle, or to changes in public mood as the strike progressed. And everywhere, the strike leaders were forced to improvise, not only in the matter of tactics for the immediate future, but also in the handling of immediate problems facing them. Maintaining order was one of their pressing duties. In many cities, local authorities were inadequately prepared to handle the violence that accompanied the strike: looting, street clashes between strike supporters and so-called Black Hundreds, damaging use of public property, and the like. In some, the beginning of the strike had set off panic buying and hoarding of food, with the result that some necessities of life were in short supply even before the strike began their further reduction; and it was necessary therefore to arrange for the opening of some bakeries and stores. As the problems accumulated, it was not unusual for strike committees to take on quasi-governmental functions. In Odessa, Vilna, and other large cities, student and workers' militia units were quickly organized to help keep down disorder, and almost everywhere their efforts were reinforced by fighting detachments of the socialist parties.

The quasi-governmental functions were carried further in St. Petersburg than elsewhere. The strike committee here, un-

like that in most cities—where members were appointed by
whatever oppositional organizations were prominently involved in the strike—was elected under the direction of certain influential leaders (among them Mensheviks, Socialist
Revolutionaries, and liberals) on the basis of proportional
representation, one deputy for each five hundred workers.
And these leaders, before the first meeting of the elected
deputies, decided to call the group, not a committee, but a
soviet. Though the change in name was not intentionally
revolutionary, it suggested, as had the Ivanovo-Voznesensk soviet five months earlier, the Menshevik desire to insure the
developing of extra-legal organs of "revolutionary self-administration." In the beginning this soviet was no more than a
strike committee with a different name, but as the strike continued it became evident that several of its leading members
—notably the elected chairman, George Khrustalev-Nosar, a
lawyer with Menshevik ties, and its vice-chairmen, the Menshevik Leon Trotsky (then using the pseudonym Yanovsky)
and the Socialist Revolutionary Nicholas Avksentev—hoped
that it would develop into something more. In its composition, the soviet was a mixed labor and socialist group, with a
slight liberal tinge. Though not a part of the Union of Unions, it maintained connections with it and was sympathetic
to its aims. It represented a major part of the factory labor
force of the capital, a substantial number of white-collar
workers, and a small number of professionals, mostly pharmacists. The great majority of those it represented were not
socialists, but simply antigovernment and antimanagement
dissidents who, for the time being, were willing to follow a
leadership in which socialists and *intelligents* happened to
predominate.

While attending to its duties of conducting and extending
the strike, the St. Petersburg Soviet found time for some
other, and quite ambitious, activities also—again reflecting the
nature of the earlier soviet. It sent a delegation of workers
and *intelligents* to the municipal duma to make an extraor-
dinarily bold, but unsuccessful, request for funds to aid the
strikers and buy arms, and it began to issue orders for which

it had no legal authority (for example, that retail stores open for certain hours each day to meet the basic needs of the population). St. Petersburg was witnessing a demonstration, in miniature, of the "two Russias" in simultaneous operation.

Government Efforts to Halt the Strike

Just as the leaders and supporters of the strike movement were having to become acquainted with their own strength and to meet unexpected problems, so the government was having to become acquainted with the new force and form of the opposition and to meet unexpected problems. During the first days of the strike, the government seemed paralyzed; and in many ways it was. General Trepov, proceeding as the Tsar expected, used the forces and measures he deemed necessary to stop the strikes and prevent meetings; and, assisted by regular authorities throughout the country, he succeeded in some instances in dispersing crowds and protecting government property. But, short of using armed force in open warfare against the civilian population, he could not keep the strike from spreading. Responsible officials tried every plan they could devise, and none worked. In an effort to stop the railroad strike, Prince Khilkov tried to reason with the Moscow railroadmen, but to no avail. They knew that, as long as they held the country's lines of communication inactive, their immunity from punishment was assured. The strength of their position and the evidence of their intention to hold it were important factors in creating faith in the possibilities of the strike and encouraging others to join it.

The central administration of the government was practically immobilized: officials could not travel between Moscow and St. Petersburg; and between the latter and Peterhof, where the Tsar and his family were in residence, movement was limited to a tenuous steamer connection. To consider means of restoring railroad operations, Nicholas called a conference of ministers on the 12th; but, all things considered, they could recommend nothing except to leave the task to the railroad administration. Such was the stalemate when the Tsar reported the situation to the Dowager Empress, then in Copenhagen, in these words:

> God knows what happened to the universities. *Every kind* of riff-raff walked in from the streets, riot was loudly proclaimed, nobody seemed to care. . . .
>
> It makes me sick to read the news! Nothing but new strikes in schools and factories, murdered policemen, Cossacks and soldiers, riots, disorders, and mutinies. But the ministers, instead of acting with quick decision, only assemble in council like a lot of frightened hens and cackle about providing united ministerial action.[6]

Believing that current happenings were developing toward armed rebellion, the government made two efforts to prevent the mass meetings, which seemed to be the principal means by which enthusiasm was stimulated, supporters were rallied, and demonstrations provoked. The first of the efforts came from the Tsar, who ordered Trepov to restore order in St. Petersburg, enforcing dispersal commands by the use of armed troops—using live ammunition if necessary. But this imperial order was not carried out, and no record shows whether it was rescinded or simply ignored. It became known among the people, however, and actually served to strengthen the appeal of those instigating armed uprising, rather than to lessen attendance at meetings. On the 15th, the day following the order to Trepov, the government published an order forbidding the higher schools to allow the presence of outsiders at meetings on school premises and warning that, if the faculty councils could not enforce the order, the schools would be closed. In Odessa and Warsaw the order was enforced, with police help, and outsiders who challenged it were ejected. But in St. Petersburg, where the students were aroused by news of clashes between students and troops in Kharkov and other cities, it was emphatically repudiated. In preparation for fighting to defend what they considered their rights, groups of students took their stand in various buildings and set up de-

6 Nicholas II to Maria Feodorovna, October 19, 1905, *The Secret Letters*, pp. 186-87.

fenses; some five hundred young women of the Women's Higher Courses organized medical units to serve the "embattled" men; and at the Academy of Arts, students seized medicines and bandages from their infirmary and began to lay in a stock of food in anticipation of siege. They might have spared themselves the trouble. This second order, like the first, was never enforced; and the students found that they could continue in their roles as hosts to the local supporters of the general strike.

RELUCTANT FINAL CONCESSION: THE OCTOBER MANIFESTO

Though the Tsar was inclined to use the authority of the government to compel the cessation of activities that seemed to be leading directly to revolution, neither he nor the responsible members of his government could see any way of using that authority effectively. To subject this great mass of Russian subjects to physical chastisement, to resort to force with the so-recent tragedy of Bloody Sunday fresh in every mind, to try to compel a resumption of loyalty—such measures would be rash indeed. Yet day by day the government was watching the approach of a condition reminiscent of that faced by the French government in 1789. The majority of officials remained calm but helpless, able only to ask questions or make suggestions that proved to be either impractical or impossible of execution. Should efforts be concentrated first on regaining control in St. Petersburg, the seat of the imperial government, in the hope of thus restoring some prestige and respect for authority? If an uprising started in the capital, would the troops be able to handle it? Was Peterhof a safe place for the Tsar's family, or should they be removed to Copenhagen? Perhaps troops should be used to man the railroads and get some normal and essential activities going, suggested some; but the new Minister of War Roediger doubted that he had a sufficient number of reliable troops for the task. Others thought that perhaps the Tsar's uncle the Grand Duke Nicholas Nicholaievich might be able to restore order if given dictatorial authority; but all knew that any authority would have to depend upon an element as yet un-determined—the degree of loyalty that might be expected from the troops in such a situation.

Only one man connected with the government stood out at this time as a likely "man of the hour"—Sergei Witte. On his return from Portsmouth, he had received recognition for his work at the peace conference, where he had shown his nim-bleness as a negotiator (not to mention his artfulness with newspapermen) ; and, in the intervening two months, he had applied himself diligently to parlaying that recognition into something of greater importance. He believed, and made oth-ers believe, that if the Tsar had followed his advice in foreign and domestic affairs, Russia would have been spared both the disastrous war with Japan and the current disturbance. Even now, he let it be known, he could retrieve some of the re-gime's losses and bring tranquility back to the country if given the necessary authority. His analysis of the country's situation was contained in a report handed to the Tsar on October 9.[7] Its argument in brief: the prevailing turbulence was caused by the disparity between that to which the educated class aspired (representative government) and Russian reality; to restore serenity, the Tsar should take the initiative and, even before the elections to the proposed Duma, announce the granting of a constitution and civil liberties and the establish-ment of a unified body of ministers to direct the work of government. He predicated this analysis, he stated, on his be-lief in "the political sense of Russian society" and his unwill-ingness to concede that Russian society wanted anarchy. There was one unpleasant alternative to these measures, he admitted—to appoint a military man with full power to stamp out disorder; but to let things drift was to invite dis-aster.

As hopes for improvement waned and other suggestions proved unacceptable for one reason or another, Witte's report took on more significance for the Tsar. Though he disliked the man who wrote it and abhorred the idea of further politi-cal concessions, he saw the growing need to respect the almost

[7] For text of the report, see Appendix, p. 289.

unanimous opinion of those close around him (his Minister of Court, Baron Fredericks, was a notable exception) that to take Witte's advice was his last resort. His advisers were as averse to representative government as the Tsar himself, but they believed it a necessary indulgence under the circumstances. These words in a letter from the Dowager Empress— which, by the way, came too late to influence his decision—are typical of those the Tsar was receiving from many sources:

> I am sure that the only man who can help you now and be useful is Witte, because he should be well disposed again *now* [implying perhaps a change in attitude due to the Tsar's having just given Witte the title of Count], and besides he is a man of genius, energetic, and clear sighted.[8]

Slowly, painfully, Nicholas began trying to bring himself to the acceptance of Witte's views and of the suggestion that Witte himself was the man to carry them out. But he could not surrender his personal belief, that authoritarian firmness was the most desirable weapon, before he had made one more effort to determine the feasibility of trying it. Accordingly he called into consultation at Peterhof, on the 15th, a group of three whom he considered among the wisest military men in the empire, in order to get their opinions on the problem basic to his final decision: whether or not he could count on adequate military power to stop disorder. They were the Grand Duke Nicholas Nicholaievich, a professional soldier; Baron Fredericks, a veteran guards officer; and General Otton Richter, who had enjoyed the confidence and affection of Russia's rulers since 1858. Witte was invited to the meeting also, so that he might present his views to the experts. The ensuing discussion was thorough and long, consuming a whole day. When Richter and the Grand Duke finally came around to the view that Witte's proposals were safer than dependence on available military strength, the Tsar was very nearly convinced. Yet, since General Roediger had assured him that St. Petersburg could be held by the troops in case of an uprising, he was reluctant to give up the idea of relying wholly on the

[8] Maria Feodorovna to Nicholas II, October 16, 1905, *The Secret Letters,* p. 184.

armed power of the regime to hold throughout the country.
So he decided to consult still another man, Trepov, whose
knowledge of handling disorder was the most direct of any
man in the country. He at once sent to Trepov a copy of the
Witte proposals and requested of him two opinions: one, on
the advisability of the proposals; another, on the length of
time St. Petersburg could be held against an uprising without
the shedding of blood.

Trepov's position was a difficult one. He opposed political
concessions on principle, but he could not be sure that this
was the time to stand on principle. When he reviewed the
current situation in Moscow and observed that the situation
in the capital was approaching the same state, he could
understand easily the importance of an immediate decision.
In Moscow the strike had affected municipal services as well
as industry. By the 15th, most municipal offices were closed;
the water works, gas works, and power stations had abandoned service; lawyers were demanding that the courts suspend their sessions; doctors and other employees of the city
hospitals were supporting the liberation movement and undertaking to give 20 percent of their salaries to the strike
committee. The center of the city, heavily patrolled by troops,
was quiet; but there was imminent danger of civic strife and
the breakdown of order. In the industrial outskirts, strikers—
many of them armed—were marching freely through the
streets; and in every part of the city, higher schools were seeth-
ing with meetings of strikers and political groups. The municipal duma had tried to work out some kind of group-control,
soliciting the cooperation of the strike committee and others
prominent in the liberation movement. But after a night of
futile argument with their representatives over alternative
proposals, the duma had created its own Committee of Social
Order—whose ineffectiveness was quickly proven. The duma
itself was at times operating in the midst of disorder: near its
headquarters, during one session a band of students were attacked by soldiers and merchants from the nearby Okhotny
Ryad (an open-air market where students and merchants were
enemies of long standing) —a prologue to serious defiance.

The students retreated a short distance, to the university buildings, where workers helped them to throw up barricades and prepare for a battle—fortunately avoided, thanks to the leniency of a military unit that offered the students safe conduct off the premises. Such incidents kept Moscow in constant fear of serious insurgence. And in St. Petersburg, though it was still less disorderly, the general strike was growing steadily; the discontinuance of public services was creating both hardships and health hazards; the Soviet was expanding in pretentiousness; and a unity committee of Mensheviks and Bolsheviks was busily collecting funds for the purchase of arms.

Only a feeling that he was bound by exigency could have compelled Trepov to answer the Tsar as he did. He believed that if the government took the offensive at once—and timing would be an essential factor—with troops using live ammunition to clear streets and break up meetings, the cost in blood would be enormous. And that fact was darkly overshadowed by the possibility that even such action might end in failure. Therefore he counseled agreement on Witte's terms.

The Tsar had reached the end of his wavering. He turned at once to the carrying out of the plan he had so reluctantly accepted, having the necessary documents prepared and seeing that the involved personnel were advised of the new program. Then at six o'clock on the evening of October 17, before witnesses of varying sympathies—Count Witte at one extreme, Baron Fredericks at the other, and the Grand Duke Nicholas Nicholaievich between—he signed the imperial manifesto announcing his decision.

The shortness and conciseness of the document, which came to be known as the October Manifesto, were not commensurate with its import:

> By the grace of God, We, Nicholas II, Emperor and Autocrat of All the Russias, Tsar of Poland, Grand Duke of Finland, etc., etc., etc., declare to all Our loyal subjects:
> Disturbances and unrest in the capitals and in many places of Our Empire fill Our heart with a great and painful grief. The welfare of the Russian Sovereign is indissolubly bound to the welfare of the people, and their grief

is His grief. Out of the present disturbances there may grow a serious popular disorder and a threat to the integrity and unity of Our Empire.

The great oath of Imperial service requires that, with all the force of Our intelligence and authority, and as quickly as possible, We bring to an end disturbances perilous to the state. Having ordered the appropriate authorities to take steps against open acts of disorder, riot, and violence, so as to protect peaceful persons who seek quietly to perform their duty, We, in order to carry out the general policies outlined by Us for quieting the life of the nation, have found it necessary to unify the activities of the central government.

We make it the duty of the government to execute Our firm will:

1) to grant the people the unshakable foundations of civic freedom on the basis of genuine personal inviolability, freedom of conscience, speech, assembly, and association;

2) to admit immediately to participation in the State Duma, without suspending the scheduled elections and in so far as it is feasible in the brief period remaining before the convening of the Duma, those classes of the population that are now completely deprived of electoral rights, leaving the further development of the principle of universal suffrage to the new legislative order;

and 3) to establish as an inviolable rule that no law may go into force without the consent of the State Duma and that the representatives of the people must be guaranteed the opportunity of effective participation in the supervision of the legality of the actions performed by Our appointed officials.

We call on all faithful sons of Russia to remember their duty to their Fatherland, to assist in putting an end to these unprecedented disturbances, and to exert with Us all their power to restore quiet and peace to Our native land.

Issued at Peterhof on October 17th, in the year of Our Lord 1905, and in the eleventh year of Our Reign.

The original text signed in His Imperial Majesty's own hand.

Nicholas[9]

[9] Russia, *Polnoe Sobranie Zakonov*, 3rd series, Vol. XXV, Sect. 1, No. 26805.

With the issuance of this manifesto, the Tsar violated principles that he had sworn never to change. His first reaction was one of despair, a feeling that he had lost everything. But gradually he became resigned to the new era. He still felt keenly that he had abandoned what were to him articles of faith, but he recognized that the only other choices, possible loss of the throne or civil war among his people, were more objectionable than the one he had made. He had chosen as best he could: as Paris had been worth a mass to Henry IV, St. Petersburg was worth a legislature to Nicholas II.

7

Development
of the Revolution: Fourth Phase
October–December

[The November strike movement in St. Petersburg] included many other classes of people besides the factory
workers. One day the barbers would strike; another day it
would be the restaurant and hotel employees. No sooner
would these strikes end than the newsboys would strike;
then it would be the salesmen in stores. This unprovoked
and senseless cessation of work became a sort of sport in
which everyone indulged regardless of his position or age.
Lectures and studies in the universities and colleges were
supplanted by meetings where socialists and anarchists conducted fiery debates. High-school students and even small
children followed suit. They presented demands and ulti-
matums to their principals and left their classrooms in a
body. The strike movement also provided some amusement;
some conservative newspapers announced that patients in
maternity wards had gone on strike and refused to bear children until universal suffrage was granted. Another anecdote
concerning the universities had it that a madame of an establishment, the activities of which did *not* include the
study of ancient languages, had told her turbulent charges:
"This is not a university, thank heaven; this is an establishment."

—Vladimir Gurko (conservative bureaucrat),
Features and Figures of the Past, 1939.

History provided only a short period—a month and a half—
in which to exploit the newly found opportunities of organizing the proletariat so as to consolidate the power that the

revolutionaries had already won and to prepare systematically for a new and decisive attack on the tottering but still powerful fortress of autocracy. The "breathing space" turned out to be too short. Autocracy decided to finish with the proletarian vanguard before the one-hundred-million-strong peasantry could shake itself into motion and join the ranks of the "fighting army" of the revolution.

—Peter Garvy (Menshevik leader), *Vospominaniya Sotsial-Demokrata*, 1946.

THE REVOLUTION OF 1905, the first dramatic act of which took place on January 9, might have ended with the dramatic act of October 17 if the issuance of the manifesto had served its intended purpose. Had society accepted the October Manifesto for what it represented to the government, a liberal treaty of peace, all the hoped-for results might have been achieved: the end of the general strike, the lessening of popular political antagonism, and the avoidance of armed revolt. Society's response, however, could hardly be called acceptance. There was immediate evidence, as the news of the manifesto began to spread, that it was to have a mighty impact on the country. Quite clearly it was to mark the beginning of a new era. But unfortunately there were soon indications that the era would not be one of good will.

PUBLIC REACTIONS TO THE OCTOBER MANIFESTO

For about three days, it appeared that all of urban Russia was holding jubilee, not just relieved by the turn of events, but irrepressibly elated by them. Some of the liberals actually felt the thrill of accomplishment after long years of struggle, satisfied that they were now witnessing the introduction to a future in which the people, with confidence restored, were to receive the recognition and opportunities they deserved from an understanding and benevolent government. And certainly, whatever the spirit behind the response, it was gripping the people as no other had ever done. City officials made stirring announcements of the news. The text of the manifesto was read in churches, synagogues, and mosques to receptive audiences. Civilians embraced one another as they met and discussed the changed prospects. Crowds cheered soldiers in the streets, as if now proud of the country's "strong arm." It was soon apparent, however, that the elation prompting most of these demonstrations was caused, not by the end of hostilities between Tsar and people, but by what the majority considered a preliminary victory over the enemy, an advantage to be followed by a final assault on autocracy.

All over the country, crowds milled and marched, waving red banners, singing the *Marseillaise*, shouting their triumph, and generally acting the part of conquerors. They were particularly arrogant in St. Petersburg, Moscow, Kiev, Odessa, Tiflis, Warsaw, Helsingfors, Vilna, Baku, Minsk, and some of the smaller cities deeply affected by recent occurrences. In many places they organized processions to the residence of the governor or to a session of the municipal duma, there to exult and make demands, the first usually being the demand that political prisoners be released. Often the demonstrators skirmished with the police or progovernment groups; and, if any of their number were killed in the encounters, elaborate funerals would be arranged to honor them as martyrs. One of the most spectacular of such funerals was that of Nicholas Bauman, in Moscow. He had been one of the men released, as a compromise, by Governor-General Durnovo when threatened by an overwhelming crowd demanding the release of all political prisoners in the city's jails, and he had been killed by a member of the Black Hundreds shortly after his release. Durnovo agreed to permit a public funeral and promised that it would not be obstructed in any way by the police. And, on October 20, over one hundred thousand workers, students, *intelligents,* and even soldiers in uniform followed the cortege for nearly eight hours through the Moscow streets in what was clearly an antigovernment demonstration.[1] On their return from the cemetery, some of the students were attacked by Cossacks; and a student fighting detachment responded by seizing and holding a university building.

[1] Bauman, a Bolshevik, has been treated by the USSR as a major revolutionary martyr. His name has been given to streets and schools and, in Moscow, to a city district. The Soviet estimate of the number attending his funeral is two hundred thousand.

This spirit of defiance flourished and spread, nowise weakened when the end of the general strike was called; and radical leaders, with deliberation and foresight, made the most of it. As they directed the strikers back to their occupations during the week following the manifesto, the St. Petersburg Soviet, the Moscow Strike Committee, the Central Bureau of the Union of Unions, the Central Bureau of the Union of Railroad Workers, and lesser administrative groups—all indicated that they were employing only an interim measure. They accompanied their directions with explicit announcements that they were calling off the strike, not because satisfactory results had been achieved, but because it was not feasible to continue striking at the time. Milyukov's often quoted evaluation of the situation, "Nothing has changed, the struggle goes on,"[2] was that of much of the opposition. Yet all must have recognized that the continuation of the struggle depended, not on the will of the organized opposition alone, but on that of the masses as well—whether born of programmed, oppositional intent or of variously aroused revolutionary ardor.

For the time being, there seemed to be every assurance that the mass support was forthcoming, almost unlimited in scope and representative of all elements in the empire. As cities with large non-Russian populations began responding to the manifesto, the minority-conscious and nationalistic groups were seen to be inspired by their own interpretations of it. Jewish students and workers were particularly prominent in the crowds that swarmed around—and sometimes took over temporarily—government offices in Odessa, Kiev, Minsk, and Vilna. In Kiev, demonstrators invaded the municipal duma, and dozens of revolutionary orators harangued the outside crowd from balconies of the duma building. There was no overt anti-Russian feeling in such actions, only a reckless display of the belief that a downtrodden minority was coming into its own. Even in Congress Poland, where it appeared that the whole population came out to demonstrate, little hostility against Russians as such was revealed; most of the animus was

[2] P. Milyukov, *Vospominaniya* (2 vols., New York, 1955), I, 329, states that he may not have used these exact words but that they certainly represent what he thought at the time.

directed at the Russian yoke over Poland. In the cities, thousands cheered the Polish national colors and took up the cry
"Long live the Polish Tsar!" (the slogan of their struggle for
the restoration of an autonomous Kingdom of Poland). A
type of gesture they relished was made by some young Poles in
the province of Radom: by way of venting their anger at
being called to military service, they broke into a school building and threw the Tsar's portrait as well as all the Russian
books from the windows, thus debasing the symbols of Russification, despised by all. In Finland, the spirit was much the
same as in Poland, but more violent in expression. Governor-
General Obolensky, unable to counter it and fearful for his
own safety, fled, leaving the turmoil to result as it would.

As the public displays of animation continued, most of
them openly hostile to the government, there was speculation
as to whether or not the government's failure to do anything
about them was due to unwillingness or inability. But there
was to be no answer during the first three days, while the excitement spread and caught up additional thousands. On the
whole, governors and other officials used their own discretion
about handling the demonstrations, deciding on the basis of
local circumstances whether to fold their arms and watch or to
use their authority. Those who acted as did Governor Kurlov,
of Minsk, who ordered troops to fire on demonstrators, were
exceptions. Generally all effort was concentrated on safeguarding government property. Prefect Neidhardt, of Odessa, went
to the limit in inaction: on the 18th, he ordered all police and
troops into their quarters and for four days left the streets in
charge of the throngs, among whom a semblance of order was
maintained during the first day by armed members of the
student militia and a Jewish self-defense unit.

Even in the armed forces authority faltered. In some cities
soldiers, and occasionally officers, in uniform joined celebrat-
ing crowds. And in many units, enlisted men, despite their
officers' specific explanations to the contrary, interpreted the
October Manifesto as conferring on them the same rights as
on civilians and began to demand the ones that they felt all
were now entitled to enjoy: the right to organize, to attend
meetings, and to present grievances. In Vladivostok, soldiers

and sailors asking the garrison commandant for permission to attend meetings, accompanied their request with attacks on officers' quarters. And units of the Eighth Eastern Siberian Infantry, ordered to subdue the troublemakers, refused to do so. The result was that the commandant had to make concessions that weakened his own position and strengthened that of the insubordinates.

In Sevastopol, the base of the Black Sea Fleet, military intransigence became something of a melodramatic display. It reached its height when, on October 18, soldiers and sailors joined civilians in demanding the release from the local prison of men who had been arrested for their part in the *Potemkin* mutiny. Opposed by troops, the crowd, under the leadership of Lieutenant Peter Schmidt, succeeded in freeing the prisoners, a number of whom were killed immediately after their release. Two days later, at their funeral Lieutenant Schmidt exhorted a large and responsive crowd:

> Let us take our oath to them [the dead] that among us there shall be neither Jews nor Armenians nor Poles nor Tartars, but henceforth only free and equal brothers in a great and free Russia.
> Let us swear to them that if we are not given universal suffrage, we shall once more proclaim the great all-Russian strike.[3]

"We swear it," was the solemn reply. The next day Schmidt was arrested, but not before he had defiantly proclaimed that the real guilt was upon the government, not himself. As the first officer to come out openly against the government, he at once became a hero. And when the public demanded his release, it was granted by authorities uncertain of their ability to defend a refusal just then. That Schmidt received a dishonorable discharge from the service simply added to his heroic dimensions in the minds of his defenders.

All told, the events of October 18-21 made a pitiful spectacle of Russian autocracy, apparently helpless before its opponents. But by the 20th—in a few cities by the 19th—a monarchist, patriotic counteraction was in the making as de-

[3] *Pravovaya Zhizn*, No. 1, 1906.

fenders of the regime rose to meet its opponents, to match their denouncements with displays of loyalty. Many of the patriotic demonstrations in which they participated were organized or encouraged by local officials and led by Russian Orthodox clergy. Some of them began simply as parades led by the clergy, usually displaying icons, the national colors, and portraits of the Tsar as they passed the antigovernment demonstrations and proceeded to church or cathedral to take part in religious services and expressions of loyalty to the sovereign. Dwarfed in size by the other paradings of public feeling, such displays made little impression if they went off without incident. But many incidents were provoked, usually by some limited act of violence from one side or the other, and they rarely ended without carnage.

Probably the worst of such incidents took place in Odessa, where the vivid and bitter recollections of the June days kept the population primed for trouble. It broke out when a patriotic demonstration was fired on by revolutionaries, many of them Jews. The marchers raised the cry, familiar in Russia, "*Bei zhidov!*" (Beat the kikes!) and turned on their attackers, setting off a three-day anti-Jewish pogrom. Reinforced by other groups, mainly Russian, they ranged through the Jewish quarter of the city on an uninhibited course of looting, burning, and killing. This incident began just after Prefect Neidhardt had ordered the police and troops away from their duty posts; but he refused—and was supported by the commander of the Odessa Military District, Baron A. V. Kaulbars—to order them back, declaring that the Jews had brought the trouble on themselves. The pogrom continued until the 22nd, by which time it had burned itself out—and five hundred had died. Bitter outbursts against the Jews, somewhat less extensive, occurred also in Kiev and other places. In Tiflis and Baku, pogroms were instigated by Russians and Moslems against Armenians. And in Tomsk, Russian Christians were among the victims when a Black Hundreds crowd killed some two hundred of an antigovernment group by setting fire to the building in which they were assembled.

More common than the mass pogroms were the smaller incidents provoked by the Black Hundreds. Their groups moved freely about the streets of St. Petersburg, Moscow, and other cities, frequently forcing those of whom they disapproved into physical conflict or some demonstration of unfelt loyalty to the regime. In Moscow, they liked to compel students and Jews to kneel before a picture of the Tsar. And in Nezhin, where the monarchists were chiefly peasants, they drove students of the Philological Institute as well as Jews to the local cathedral behind an imperial portrait, then ordered them to kneel and swear allegiance to the Tsar. Happenings of this nature, though minor, were numerous and often marked by such bitterness as to be quite ugly aspects of the general ferment.

The conflicting elements of the population were evaluated according to the point of view of the observer, of course. The Tsar saw them thus:

> In the first days after the Manifesto the subversive elements raised their heads, but a strong reaction set in quickly, and a whole mass of loyal people suddenly made their power felt. The result was obvious, and what one would expect in our country. The impertinence of the Socialists and revolutionaries had angered the people once more; and, because nine-tenths of the trouble makers are Jews, the people's anger turned against them. That's how the pogroms happened. It is amazing how they took place *simultaneously* in all the towns of Russia and Siberia. In England, of course, the press says that those disorders were organized by the police; they still go on repeating the worn-out fable. But not only Jews suffered; some of the Russian agitators, engineers, lawyers, and such-like bad people suffered as well.[4]

The opposition interpreted the counteraction as the work of an unrepentant and dishonest government that did not intend to live up to the promises of the October Manifesto. Lenin, for example, wrote:

> The proclamation of "liberties" which adorn the scrap of paper called the manifesto of October 17 is only an attempt to prepare the moral condition for a struggle against the revolution—while Trepov at the head of the All-Russian

[4] Nicholas II to Maria Feodorovna, October 27, 1905, *The Secret Letters*, pp. 191-92.

Black Hundreds is preparing the material conditions for this struggle.[5]

But neither Nicholas II nor Lenin was expressing a considered view. Nor were the many who declared the Black Hundreds to have been drawn only from among hotheaded hooligans. Although there are insufficient records on these counteractionary groups, it can be established that their intentions were not always simply to protect the regime, that they were not called into being by the central government, and that they were not, on the whole, hooligans. Steeped in Russian tradition, accustomed to the manners and judgments of the bureaucracy, and united in the Orthodox Church, thousands responded readily, and in a conventional way, to the leadership and inspiration of local officials, local clergy, and occasionally local army officers. Undoubtedly many of the rank and file of Black Hundreds groups were hooligans bent on taking advantage of what appeared to be officially sanctioned rowdyism, but there were many who had a rationale for their participation. A large part of the Orthodox clergy saw oppositional activity as an attack on the church; and many of them, like the Metropolitan Vladimir of Moscow, denounced it publicly, often indicating that it was largely the work of Jews and other non-Russians. Civil authorities and officers also tended to interpret attacks on the regime as attacks on themselves, and they did not need to be prodded into what they considered self-defense. Even among the workers, now so deeply involved in the disturbances, some of the Russians, still stubbornly monarchist and devoutly Orthodox, despised the radicals. And Russian peasants, when confronted with oppositional ideas, were likely to interpret them as attacks on their own basic beliefs: in Volsk, in Saratov province, peasants in town for market day fell upon antigovernment demonstrators—mostly *intelligents* and students, some from the local seminary—as upon wicked enemies. Sometimes the conflict was born of a long-standing feud—as in the case of some Black Hundreds action against students in Moscow. In that city, for years, there had been town-and-gown tension, break-

<hr>

[5] V. I. Lenin, *Selected Works* (New York, n.d.), III, 329.

ing sporadically into fights between students on one hand and, on the other, the Okhotny Ryad merchants and the *dvorniki* (concierges). Now the latter groups were only too happy to join the Black Hundreds against the students.

The emergence of the Black Hundreds, from whatever source, made a harmonious settlement between the opposition and the government more difficult than it might have been otherwise. Many among the opposition forces accepted and used as effective propaganda the interpretation of the patriotic gangs as the true face of autocracy, and the October Manifesto as but a mask. Some of the odium was dispelled by such governmental and church action as the removal of Neidhardt from the prefecture of Odessa after the tragic pogrom, and a statement of censure from the Holy Synod against Metropolitan Vladimir. And it was lessened by the stand that many governors as well as high churchmen took, opposing the Black Hundreds. But the fact remained that, in both the government and the church, approval of these counteractive groups was considerable and undisguised.[6] Their continued activity, repeated armed clashes with gangs of the opposition, and their appearance of *locum tenens* for the government created an atmosphere of tension and illegality most unpropitious for the development of a regime based on the rule of law.

WITTE'S FAILURE TO CONCILIATE "SOCIETY"

These immediate public reactions to the October Manifesto, however troublesome and sometimes serious, were not the basic difficulties standing in the way of the projected new dis-

[6] On December 26, 1905, the Tsar himself received a delegation from the Union of the Russian People, the largest group of the Black Hundreds, and listened to the reading of a statement urging him not to trust the non-Russian elements of the population, least of all the Jews. He responded to the statement noncommittally, then urged the delegation to "unite the Russian people," and accepted an organization badge for himself and one for his son. This gesture did not indicate that the Tsar accepted or meant to carry out the program of the Union (subsequently, in many cases, he followed policies to which it was opposed), but this open display of sympathy for it was charged against him by the opposition.

pensation. The first step toward the reestablishment of domestic harmony was going to depend on the carrying-out of the plan for forming a unified Council of Ministers; and therein irreconcilables were to be encountered. Neither the Tsar nor Witte intended this to be a council with ministerial responsibility in the Western sense of the word; rather, it was to be a body enjoying the respect and confidence of society but responsible to the Tsar, not to the Duma. As conceived, it was to be established through the transformation of the existing Council of Ministers, which included all ministry heads and was convened at infrequent sessions, presided over by the Tsar, to consider policy matters. The new body would retain the same name and membership, but would meet under the chairmanship of an appointed official and exercise the broad power of a cabinet—that is, the power to coordinate and direct the executive branch of the government. In this arrangement, the existing Committee of Ministers would, of course, become redundant as its functions were absorbed by the Council of Ministers. In agreeing to the transformation, the Tsar was not relinquishing his executive power: his assent would be necessary before any decision of the council could be put into force, and his would be the last word on most appointments in the executive branch.

Witte's confidence in the feasibility of such a plan was based on his belief that, once the liberal opposition was satisfied, as he felt it would be when a parliamentary form of government was being provided, all would be well. He apparently failed to appreciate two other aspects of the situation: 1) the necessity of convincing the liberal opposition that the government was acting in good faith and 2) the necessity of taking into consideration the nature and strength of the revolutionary forces in the country. He saw Russia's fundamental problem as one growing out of a squabble within a family of educated men, and he entertained no misgivings about the result of the practical settlement he had in mind.

The first real test of Witte's position came just after his formal appointment, on the 18th, to the post of Chairman of the Council of Ministers. He was now empowered to seek out and recommend such men as he deemed proper to replace the heads of all the government ministries except four—those of Foreign Affairs, War, Navy, and the Court, appointments for which remained the prerogative of the Tsar. He expected to be able, as soon as the Tsar had removed the reactionary ministers and other department heads from their posts, to present a strong list of "public figures," men outside the established bureaucracy, suitable to succeed them. And he was confident that he could find these men among the moderate liberals.

The removal of the old bureaucrats went rapidly enough: within a few days Over-Procurator Pobedonostsev, Minister of Education Glazov, and Minister of Interior Bulygin had left their posts; and the others were soon to follow. But the retirement of the old order proved to be more easily accomplished than the introduction of the new. Not that Witte failed to make sufficient effort: he worked with unflagging energy to collect the new Council of Ministers. Thinking to begin with a well-known and respected liberal, he invited Dmitri Shipov to come from Moscow, intending to offer him the post of State Comptroller. Shipov responded immediately, arriving on the 19th via one of the first trains to leave Moscow since the beginning of the strike. And there followed extended discussions, not only with Shipov, but also with other prominent liberals—including Alexander Guchkov, Fedor Golovin, Fedor Kokoshkin, and Prince George Lvov—about the composition of the proposed council. At the end of a week, however, no hope remained that ministerial candidates were to be found among these men. Witte had agreed with Shipov's contention that the council would need men with a larger following among the liberals than he himself had—that is, men whose political positions were to the left of his. But he quickly found that the views of those to the left of Shipov—Kokoshkin, for instance—could not be adjusted to his own. Kokoshkin was representative of the membership of the Constitutional Democratic Party (members of which were known as Cadets), which he, along with Milyukov and other members of the Union of Liberation, had only recently formed.[7] The new party adhered to the old liberal demand for a constitutional assembly

[7] For the program of the Constitutional Democratic Party, *see* Appendix, p. 292.

and aspired to a constitutional state in which the Council of
Ministers would be responsible to the elected representatives
of the people assembled in the Duma. And the Cadets had
agreed to refuse all proffered posts in the Council of Ministers unless Witte would consent to the summoning of a constituent assembly. Since he had neither the authority nor the
desire to do this, Witte saw the door to agreement with the
Cadets closing. They were soon to become the strongest organization among the liberals, and their support would have
been of great advantage to him. But since neither he nor they
would compromise, he was forced back to his first tactic, to
seek an arrangement with the moderate liberals.

Even that move was forestalled when Witte recommended,
and the Tsar approved, the selection of Peter N. Durnovo
(not to be confused with Governor-General P. P. Durnovo, of
Moscow) as head of the Ministry of Interior.[8] Durnovo was a
bureaucrat, not a "public figure," a fact that lessened his popularity; and, though he was not a reactionary, he was regarded
so unfavorably by the liberals that his appointment precluded
further negotiations between Witte and the moderate liberals.
Witte's defense of the appointment was that it fulfilled the
need for a man with knowledge of police work (Durnovo had
served as head of the Department of Police from 1884 to
1893), who could assume the dual responsibility of preserving
public order and insuring the safety of the imperial family in
the current period of troubles; but rumor accused him of making the appointment to acquit himself of some kind of personal indebtedness to Durnovo.

Failing to attract the men he wanted for the remaining
posts, Witte had to be content with those he could get. The
resulting Council of Ministers was neither united nor impressive. As heads of the four ministries exempted from the au-

[8] From the Tsar's point of view, Trepov would have been an
excellent choice for this post, but he and Witte were so uncongenial
that they could not work together. After Witte's appointment,
Trepov resigned his post of Assistant Minister of Interior as well
as that of Governor-General of St. Petersburg, and the Tsar named
him as Commandant of the Imperial Court.

thority of the chairman, the Tsar retained the incumbent ministers: General Roediger for War, Admiral Birilev for Navy, Count Lamsdorf for Foreign Affairs, and Baron Fredericks for the Imperial Court. These men were nominally in the council and occasionally attended its meetings, but in their work they remained responsible only to the Tsar. The ministers in whose selection Witte figured were a mixed lot. Durnovo, as might be expected, was immediately identified in the public mind with the old police tradition. Some of the others, though not marked by the taint of association with reactionaries, were bureaucrats whose careers had been closely tied to that of the chairman. One such was Prince Alexis Obolensky, appointed as Over-Procurator of the Holy Synod, replacing Pobedonostsev (who crustily described him as a man in whose head "three cocks were crowing at the same time") ; another was Ivan Shipov, the new Minister of Finance, who had accompanied Witte to Portsmouth. Then there were those who, though including men competent in their fields, lacked both the popularity and the political dedication needed to change the traditional aspect of the council. By training and temperament, the chosen ministers were part of the bureaucratic world; politically they were somewhat to the right of the moderate liberals and to the left of their predecessors; they accepted the October Manifesto as an accomplished fact and were willing to lend their energies to the changed regime. Beyond that, they were of little political significance, for the most part failing to arouse enthusiasm for the new order either in the Tsar or in the public. Thus the first part of Witte's program, the building of a bridge between society and government, was an immediate failure. As a result, when the government tried in succeeding months to activate the specific promises of the October Manifesto, it was as ill-supported by the public as it had been in the days of Bulygin or Plehve. To be sure, those who had recently come into the Council of Ministers were less reactionary than their predecessors; but, since the public temper had undergone such a definite change toward the left in the preceding year, they proved to be just as unpopular.

INCREASE IN THE NUMBER OF QUASI-POLITICAL BODIES

And now Russia faced the paradox of the Revolution of 1905: that its most important product, the October Manifesto, preceded, rather than followed, the most serious revolutionary disturbances of the year. Instead of saving the government from revolution, it was serving the opposition as a means of stimulating further insurgence.

One of the indications of this situation was the ability of the St. Petersburg Soviet and other bodies born of the general strike to survive and grow after the strike was over. When ending the strike in the capital, the Soviet transformed itself into a continuing organ of labor, the main purpose of which was declared to be the continuation of the struggle for a constituent assembly. As far as was obvious, it was simply a body that had been improvised with little clear design in response to circumstances and, like many others, was now deciding to prolong its functioning. It appeared to be no more than it had been: a council of deputies elected by the trade unions and socialist groups, which in turn elected an executive committee of twenty-two that met frequently to make decisions on matters concerning the workers represented by the Soviet. On the day after the issuance of the October Manifesto, however, it began to demonstrate that it was a body with power. Without waiting for the government to work out the legislation necessary to provide for civil liberties, the Soviet decreed the end of censorship and, furthermore, made its decree effective by ordering printers to refuse to print newspapers that had been submitted to the censor. The decree was illegal, but it was effective. And it was the beginning of a practice that was to make yet another change in the development of the revolution.

The idea of soviets was not conceived in St. Petersburg, but the success of the one established in that city encouraged the growth of similar bodies already existing and inspired the establishment of others. In all, nearly fifty soviets of workers deputies, several peasant soviets, and a number of short-lived military soviets came into being in the fall of 1905. The Moscow Soviet, formed in November and representing eighty thousand workers, was next in importance to that in the capital. Almost all of these organizations maintained, or had the support of, workers' militias or fighting detachments, and that fact lent more than a little strength to their pretensions. In St. Petersburg at least six thousand workers possessed arms of some kind. Armed workers guarded the buildings of the Free Economic Society, in which the Soviet met; and in some districts, armed workers patrolled the streets for the declared purpose of dealing with Black Hundreds—and for the undeclared purpose of harassing the police.

The soviets were not the only form of self-appointed quasi-political authority. Socialist party committees, in a few cities, represented another. In Riga, the SD Federative Committee carried out police functions. In Vilna, the Bund, through its self-defense organization, assumed some of the duties of those responsible for public order. And in Kharkov, a joint committee of Bolsheviks and Mensheviks, having arrogated a measure of political power, successfully gave orders to the city's electrical stations and even invaded meetings of the municipal duma with demands for funds to aid strikers.

The soviets and kindred organizations soon began to establish ties among themselves, the St. Petersburg Soviet acting as the chief source of leadership and energy. Its representatives visited soviets of various cities; and representatives of other soviets, of socialist parties (including the PPS), and of local branches of the Peasants Union met from time to time with its leaders in St. Petersburg. Here was an embryonic form of a national organization of the labor, agrarian, and socialist movements, one that might become part-ally, part-rival to the Union of Unions. In fact, such an organization was envisioned by ambitious leaders, and an all-Russian congress of soviets was actually planned.

Though the soviets were not definite threats to the imperial government, for about two months after the October Manifesto was issued, those in St. Petersburg, Moscow, and several other cities were powerful enough to encroach boldly and with impunity upon established authority, and to operate openly in defiance of the law and the government. The chairman of the St. Petersburg Soviet, Khrustalev-Nosar, appropriated so much administrative control that observers saw more truth than humor in a local newspaper's statement that the odds were about even on the question of whether Witte would arrest him or vice versa.

POPULAR ARROGATION OF CIVIL FREEDOMS

These quasi-political bodies were, in fact, just one type of outlet for the spirit that was pervading Russia in the fall of 1905, a period often called "freedom days." At that time thousands of people were exercising the promised freedoms as if already permitted, and assuming certain rights, privileges, and exemptions not specifically mentioned in the October Manifesto. Everywhere the manifesto was being interpreted as if it were a charter of general political and social liberty. At the same time various groups and classes were audaciously pressing demands and wishes that they had been unable to realize —and, in some cases, had not even dared to voice—in the past. In short, a spirit of revolt was astir in the country, expressed in many ways.

Newspapers and magazines expressed it by ignoring the censors. In St. Petersburg the Soviet compelled them to do so, and elsewhere they did so of their own accord. When hapless censors began turning to the central government for instructions, they were told to ignore the acts of defiance; and, on November 24, temporary press rules were issued to end officially the practice of preliminary censorship. At once, Russian journalism took on a different look. What had once appeared only in the underground press was now printed without restraint. Socialist parties established and openly published newspapers; and as the novel idea of legal free expression spread, almost every shade of political opinion was put into print. Relief from preliminary censorship, however, did not mean complete freedom from regulation. Censors still read publications after their appearance, and the government legally could—and did— close down newspapers and imprison editors. But such measures could not stifle a vigorous and, on the whole, hostile press: the closing of a newspaper was usually soon followed by its reappearance under a different name.

Organizations that had been under legal restraint began to exercise the freedom of assembly and association immediately after the manifesto was made public—though the first official rules on that freedom did not appear until March, 1906. The labor movement pushed the establishment of trade unions to the extent that this period saw the real beginning of widespread unionization. Provincial cities hitherto unaffected by the movement were now being reached, and occupations hitherto untouched were being unionized. So encouragingly rapid was the trade-union growth that labor leaders began to plan a national congress for December.

Open political activity also mushroomed during the "freedom days." Liberal party organizations discarded the rather flimsy subterfuges they had used in earlier times. The socialists, however, were still being hunted by the police and therefore had to continue operating their party organizations clandestinely, even though openly participating in trade unions and engaging in such activities as the operation of newspapers. Many of their leaders returned from Switzerland and other countries, not only because the risk of arrest was reduced, but also because they felt that the decisive moment for the overthrow of the monarchy was close, and they wanted to take a more immediate part in the revolutionary work. In addition, some of those who had been imprisoned for political reasons were released by a government order of amnesty, issued on October 21. This order applied only to those whose guilt had been judged as agitation for a constitutional order— that is, mainly liberals—but many socialists believed that general amnesty could be wrested from the government, and they were ready to risk the effort.

National minorities also were soon caught up in the new spirit. And their belief that rights for nationalities were on the point of being officially recognized was encouraged by an imperial manifesto, issued on October 22, restoring to Finland the rights that had been submerged when Nicholas II started on his ill-advised campaign of Russification in 1898. In areas where nationalist sentiments were traditionally prominent, leaders had no trouble in rounding up support for organized action. Even in Lithuania, where the nationalist movement was in its infancy, a national congress calling for Lithuanian autonomy was held in November. And, in the same month, a Lettish national assembly met in Riga to prepare for a future Lettish parliament to govern Latvia (Courland and Livonia), the status of which had not been fully agreed upon: it might, or might not, remain in a federated Russian state—depending on future circumstances.

PEASANT UPRISINGS

At the beginning of "freedom days," the evidences of en-livened political consciousness were encountered principally among urban dwellers, but inevitably the mood communicated itself to the already-stimulated peasantry. As has been seen, agrarian disorders had become intensified during the summer of 1905, and the strength and influence of various groups and organizations among the peasants had increased. The result was that both officials and landlords were on the alert for any development reminiscent of the dread name "Pugachev," which, since the late eighteenth century, had signified "peas-ant uprising." At that time Emelyan Pugachev had led the peasants in an outbreak of such savagery that the very govern-ment was threatened and the country was left with a vivid fear of a repetition. Now, in late October and November, agrarian disorders appeared to be justifying that fear. Turbulence was growing in Congress Poland, while it continued to rage with-out letup in the Baltic provinces and in Georgia. But the most rebellious areas were in European Russia, specifically in nine-teen provinces located in the south-central part. In this area, more than 50 percent of the districts experienced waves of illegal agrarian acts ranging from the customary cutting of timber to the burning of manor houses and murder of land-lords. In seven of the provinces—Voronezh, Kursk, Poltava, Chernigov, Saratov, Tambov, and Penza—the unsettled state approached full-scale revolt. The names of many leading fami-lies were included in the list of those whose properties were burned or overrun and looted: Kasatkin-Rostovsky, Kochubei,

Orlov-Davydov, Apraxin, Vorontsov-Dashkov, Volkonsky, Katkov, Shcherbatov, Stolypin, Shuvalov, Leichtenberg, Shakhovskoi, Petrovo-Solovovo, Voeikov, Panin, Rodzyanko, and Musin-Pushkin. As the cry indicating the peasants' flaming retribution, "The red cock is crowing!" was relayed from estate to estate, the governors bombarded Witte with demands for additional troops to deal with the situation.

The armed force of the government was, of course, still superior to the physical fury of the peasants; but, since the troops available were limited in number and a detachment might have to serve in more than one area, the force was often too belated to prevent the dreadful consequences of the fury. Moreover, force was ineffectual in three important respects: it could not relieve the immediate feeling of desperation that usually accompanied the outbursts, it could not affect the deep-seated causes of the desperation, and it did not reach the outside sources that were encouraging the peasants' discontent. This, the first large agrarian revolt since the one led by Pugachev, was something new in the history of Russian peasant unrest. It had a degree of organization; it was influenced to some extent by political ideology; and it was related to the general disquiet and agitation among the country's urban population. Some of the peasants, by their own wits, drew political conclusions from the October Manifesto, but most of them followed the conclusions offered them by leaders in the Peasants Union, by SR and other socialist agitators, and by various zemstvo employees.

The manner in which peasants were generally introduced to things political may be illustrated by the course followed in Davydovskaya volost, in the province of Vladimir. A teacher in the local parochial school, twenty-two-year-old Vasily Sochikhin, aided by the volost clerk and the latter's assistant, took the lead, after October 17, in a successful program of political agitation throughout the volost. Their aim was to impress the peasants with arguments they could understand, based on the premise that the "enemies" were officialdom and the landlords. Rural Russians, they explained, needed no officials, needed to pay no taxes. They needed land, which must ultimately be taken by force. And as the first step toward strengthening themselves for the undertaking, they must form local branches of the Peasants Union. Here, as in other rural areas, a tendency toward anarchism was being fostered; the peasants were being encouraged to ask for independence from all superior organized authority. In some places, a definite program was laid out and accepted by them. In Olkhovskaya volost, in Saratov province, a group of peasants under the chairmanship of a local veterinarian, Abraham Yushko, had such a program. In it they disclaimed the need for churches, officialdom, and an army. They would convert the churches into schools and hospitals; they would retain the clergy, but on an elective basis; and they would replace the army by units of voluntary militia, organized for service only in the vicinity of their residence.

Between this political agitation and the disorders in the countryside there was an identifiable—though admittedly indirect—connection. Many, perhaps most, of the peasants still had little interest in political issues even when acquainted with them; but they wanted economic amelioration and, in the autumn of 1905, they were being led to believe that the possibility of achieving it was near. Mere suggestions of changes that might result from anticipated political measures could set off activity among them. Thus near the first of November, peasants in the Nizhne-Lomonovsky district, in the province of Penza, hearing rumors from neighboring Saratov province that partition of the nobles' land was at hand, reacted by turning their attention at once to the local Naryshkin estate, against which many of them had grievances. They began with demands on the estate administrators for grain and timber, threatening violence if they were refused. Unsatisfied, they increased both demands and threats, then began illegal cutting of timber. When local police interfered, the peasants beat them off with clubs and, in retaliation, looted and destroyed much of the landlord's property.

Such violence could hardly be called revolutionary in nature or purpose; but, without question, its increase followed closely the increase in the political sophistication of the peasantry. And that, in turn, followed the growth of the Peasants Union, which by November included over two hundred thousand members in twenty-six provinces. Another aspect of this interrelationship is noteworthy also: in the process of helping to spread political ideas among the peasants, the Union itself was affected. In many areas the local branch was marked by a growing radicalism that did not conform to the spirit of the central leadership. It was to be observed in the widespread talk about the immediate partition of the land. And in some provinces where the SR influence was strong—Saratov, for example—it was taking form in the organization of SR peasant fighting detachments, which set about their activities in a manner that was almost revolutionary, interfering in some instances with the operations of local officials.

Indications of this changing tone were to be seen in the Second Congress of the Peasants Union, which met in Moscow early in November. The *intelligents* (who were 42 to the 145 peasant delegates) continued to provide the guidance and to direct the central organization toward the principal goal of the Union of Unions, the convocation of a constituent assembly; and the sentiment of the majority of the delegates was still opposed to individual acts of violence, then becoming common, and to the use of force for political ends. Many of the peasant delegates, however, declared that if the hoped-for constituent assembly did not partition the land, they would counsel the use of force to that end. And, to satisfy the demand for some kind of immediate action, the congress voted to press at once for the free transfer of land to the peasants. If possible, this was to be accomplished by peaceful pressure, such as collective refusal by the peasantry to buy or rent land from the landlords. Should such pressure not produce satisfactory results, the union would call a general agrarian strike to coincide with a general urban strike, in the hope of forcing the desired response.

This Second Congress showed the Peasants Union to be now in the left wing of the Union of Unions and sympathetic to the spirit of the St. Petersburg Soviet—that is, resolved to continue the struggle with the government. Its position was implicit in its approval of a boycott of the coming Duma and its declaration that, if it were harassed by the government because of its activity, it would call on the peasantry to refuse to pay taxes or to serve in the armed forces. None of the measures adopted by the congress could be called revolutionary per se or favorable to the idea of armed uprising, but they strongly suggested that the Union was now among those organizations dedicated to keeping the oppositional movement alive and growing. Moreover the deliberations of this congress indicated that, for the first time in the country's history, there was a possibility that urban and rural discontent might be united in action against the government.

TURBULENCE IN THE ARMED FORCES

Practically all parts of the armed forces also, during the "freedom days," underwent an unmistakable change in attitude toward authority. The results were mutinous and disorderly conduct that ranged from minor infractions to quite ominous outbreaks. Generally they were without plan or preestablished aim, but they aided the opposition, particularly by the manner in which they weakened the government.

At the Kronstadt Naval Base and Fortress, both sailors and soldiers, having expressed themselves exuberantly in celebration of the October Manifesto, showed reluctance to resume their military decorum; instead they became more and more unresponsive and disrespectful to their officers. And, on October 26, when a group of sailors attempted to free some soldiers who had been imprisoned for refusal to obey orders, they led the way to open mutiny. Soon more than a fifth of the sailors and soldiers in the base and fortress were involved, and their insubordination grew into violence. They broke into the arsenals and, armed with rifles, rampaged through the streets of the base and ran riot in the town of Kronstadt, respecting neither life nor property. Disorganized though it was, the mutiny raged on for two days while officers tried vainly to check it, and, at Peterhof, just across the Gulf of Finland, the Tsar listened to the gunfire and realized that demoralization was reaching a most vital area. Finally sufficient outside forces were brought in to quell the mutiny and about three thousand of the mutineers were put under arrest. Trials by field courts-martial were scheduled, and military routine was resumed.

Had revolutionary plans for an armed uprising matched the calls for it, this Kronstadt mutiny might easily have been used to set it off. But as yet no definite means had been devised for getting such a movement under way. The St. Petersburg Soviet made public its approval of the mutinous acts and, as a broad gesture, called a citywide political strike to express sympathy for the imprisoned men and to denounce the proposed field courts-martial. The Union of Unions supported the strike. And, in all, about one hundred and twenty thousand workers responded. Although this demonstration was somewhat limited since the professionals and white-collar workers did not join, it was a manifestation of organized strength that the government was in no position to ignore. It ended on November 7, after the government had signified a degree of deference by announcing that the mutineers would be tried by regular military courts.

General insurgence among the naval forces seemed little affected by the outcome at Kronstadt. At the end of October, sailors joined soldiers in a mutiny at Vladivostok. And soon discipline in the Black Sea Fleet, based at Sevastopol, was facing another test. It started when the crew of the cruiser *Ochakov*, along with several units stationed in the naval garrison ashore, met and issued the customary call for a constituent assembly, accompanying it by a demand that enlisted men be granted the privilege of meeting freely. Then, on November 12, as a result of an attempt by a naval detachment to break up one of their meetings, they grew mutinous; and, having elected as their commander ex-Lieutenant Peter Schmidt, released from prison only the day before, they called on the rest of the fleet and the men ashore to join them in mutiny. A number of other crews (including that of the former *Potemkin*, now reclaimed and recommissioned as the *Panteleimon*) seized their ships, imprisoned their officers, and held elections to select delegates to the local soviet. Of the men attached to the garrison, a sizeable minority joined the mutiny, giving it the added advantage of shore support. Together the muti-

neers, though poorly organized, represented a serious problem
to the fleet commander, Admiral G. P. Chukhnin. Despite the
fact that most of the ships and most of the garrison remained
apart from the mutiny, he hesitated to test their loyalty by
using them against their fellow servicemen. He therefore appealed to St. Petersburg for help. The Tsar sent the sixty-one-
year-old General Baron Alexander Meller-Zakomelsky, whose
experience with tactics of constraint had begun with his participation as a young subaltern in the suppression of the Polish Revolt of 1863. But before the help arrived, Admiral
Chukhnin, either fearing the possible consequences of delay
or having regained his confidence, decided to handle the matter himself. He ordered his ship and shore artillery to fire on
the mutinous ships and the results, he felt, justified his taking
the step: all the crews surrendered, Schmidt and about two
thousand sailors were arrested,[9] and it was possible to begin
restoring order by the time Meller-Zakomelsky arrived. The
veteran was of assistance, however, in the task of clearing up
the mutinous situation, which he handled with a dispatch that
earned him the special respect of the Tsar.

These mutinies, added to numerous smaller instances of insubordination, made the navy practically worthless as a trustworthy fighting force and indicated that it might well be a
liability in the event of another war. Moreover, its personnel
was now recognized as a potential source of revolutionary danger. Complete reorganization seemed to be called for, and the
Tsar selected a commission to consider the general state of
the naval service and recommend measures for improvement.
That proved to be a longer assignment than anticipated; its
accomplishment took about six years.

Less demoralized than the navy, but not lacking in disaffection, the army had to deal with twenty-six mutinies or near-
mutinies during November alone. The units whose morale
continued to be of greatest concern to the authorities were
those that had been sent out to Manchuria. They included
almost a million men, the bulk of whom were still in Manchuria when the October strike began; and they were soon cut

⎯⎯⎯⎯
[9] Schmidt and three others were executed for their parts in the
mutiny.

off from Russia not only by the stopping of railroad service but also, for a time, by the lack of direct telegraphic communication (messages to the Far East having to be routed by way of Japan). The few units that were on the way home at the time were stranded at various points along the Trans-Siberian Railroad, where they were quickly affected by the radical sentiments among the railroadmen. For the government, the prospects were cheerless indeed. Much as the troops, particularly the reliable ones, were needed to handle the unrest on the home front, there was hesitation about pushing their return, for it was doubtful that the reservists among them would prove loyal under prevailing conditions. Yet, it was agreed, prolonging the period of inaction in Manchuria could only result in general lowering of morale. The situation was hazardous, but it had to be faced as soon as the railroaders went back to work after the strike. Large-scale movement of troops from the front began early in November. It was a tedious operation (not completed until the middle of 1906) to move so many men from such a distance on a single-track railroad—precarious also, of course, since radical union men were operating the trains. The results were such as the army had never before experienced: rebellious incidents increased in number as the trains moved westward, and unforeseen problems multiplied. The soldiers disobeyed officers and fraternized with civilian radicals in centers where authority was being broken down—particularly Harbin, Chita, Krasnoyarsk, and Irkutsk. Their contempt for discipline ranged from simple gestures of insubordination to quite serious excesses—such as their retaliation at Chita for a general's insult to some railworkers: they detached his coach and left him there.

Among troops in the interior, disaffection was not as marked, but it was on the increase. Even if they had been completely dependable, they were now insufficient in number to meet the governors' demands for troops to handle the agrarian troubles in the central and southern provinces. In short, there were good reasons for concern about the instrument upon which the regime would have to place its ultimate dependence, its armed forces.

PRESSURE FOR ACTION

The character of the irregularities faced by Russia in November of 1905 clearly indicated a revolutionary situation: mass movements enlarging as of their own accord, generating sufficient momentum to force opposition leaders into becoming bolder and more aggressive, regardless of their personal inclinations. In the weeks following the issuance of the October Manifesto, the various groups that had either been left dissatisfied by it or whose appetites had been whetted by it, had gradually gained more followers and expanded their aspirations. And planning had to be advanced accordingly.

Conditions in the labor movement were typical. Since the movement had not been able to register any substantial gains, its moral capital consisted of aspirations. Its leaders had no choice but to seek their realization. Almost everywhere the workers considered the achievement of the eight-hour day basic to the improvement of their condition; and the St. Petersburg Soviet, usually the leader in innovations, undertook to demonstrate a means by which to achieve the shorter day. It advised the workers of the city to leave their work each day at the end of the eighth hour; a *fait accompli*, it predicted, would be an effective weapon in this case. But it had failed to take into account a counterweapon that the employers now used against this highhanded action: the lockout. Thwarted, the Soviet was then forced to consider further aggressive measures in order to maintain the leadership of the St. Petersburg labor force and its status as a national model of effective labor administration. The growth of established unions and the rise of new ones provided another source of strength that caused labor leadership, sometimes unexpectedly, to keep moving ever farther toward the point of no return. The efforts at unionizing among the employees of the government telegraph and postal offices will illustrate. While a congress of their representatives, meeting in Moscow, was making preliminary plans for setting up an organization to promote not only better working conditions but also political reforms, the government interrupted. It condemned the effort, declaring that the October Manifesto did not signify the right of government employees to unionize, and then dismissed a number who were engaged in the undertaking. After this rebuff, the planners were faced with the now-common alternatives: retreat or go forward. They chose the latter: the First Congress of Postal and Telegraph Employees took the defiant step by calling a postal-telegraph strike to begin on November 15. In addition, it made a declaration of sympathy for the Russian labor movement, as led by the St. Petersburg Soviet.

The ensuing strike influenced rail workers and encouraged a new rash of railroad strikes which, in turn, reinforced other types of turbulence in various parts of the country. And again there were repeated instances of the masses pushing the leadership to new acts of defiance. In Vilna, the two thousand delegates to the Lithuanian nationalist congress declared that they did not recognize the legitimacy of the government under which they were living, asserted their willingness to unite with their Russian brothers against tsarism, and called for a general refusal to perform military service. In the Baltic provinces, rebellion and disorder gave rise to an exchange of drastic measures: on November 22, the Tsar declared martial law in Livonia; on the 24th, Riga retaliated with a general strike; on the 26th, the SD Federative Committee of Riga released an issue of what was intended to be the chief organ of the strike, "Bulletin of the Revolution, No. 1"; and on the 29th, the Tsar placed the three Baltic provinces under martial law and reinforced the government's control over them by the appointment of a governor-general pro tempore to administer them as a unit. In Chita, soldiers and Trans-Baikal Cossacks of the local garrison demanded for all men in uniform an eight-hour day and the right to organize, at the same time declaring their support of the Social Democrats and the call for a constituent assembly. In Kharkov, a citywide political strike set off by the Sevastopol mutiny openly upheld the action of the local military garrison. This whole spate of troubles, added to the disorders going on simultaneously in the agrarian region of the central and southern provinces, gave ample justification for alarm in the government.

Growing Readiness for
Armed Uprising

Certainly the situation in the latter part of November was far from what Witte had predicted as the outcome of the October Manifesto. Instead of being blessed by the anticipated pacification, the country was now confronted by near-revolution. Much of the warm feeling that had overspread the liberation movement before October 17 was gone and, with it, the informally united front that it had achieved.

The quasi-revolutionary movement that was replacing the liberation movement was something new. It had no over-all formal identity and no organization except what was implied in the general acknowledgement of the leadership of the St. Petersburg Soviet. It included socialists, radical nationalists, a large proportion of those connected with the burgeoning labor movement, and some liberals, peasants, and members of the armed forces. It was without a program and without common aims except to obtain, by whatever means were expedient, a constituent assembly. Moreover, in keeping with its tendencies as a kind of amorphous labor-socialist movement, it did not look to the liberals for cues, but was favorably inclined toward socialist leadership, not so much because of the socialists' ideology as because of their vigorous tactics—which now seemed to many the only means of influencing events and achieving new victories.

The existence of this new movement was attested by the high degree of interaction, particularly prominent in November, among such organizations as soviets and unions. Throughout the country, they were reacting in a similar and fairly predictable manner to the same stimuli: calling political strikes whenever they heard of strikes by other groups or in other localities, whenever they had reports of executions of mutineers, and whenever the government placed any area under martial law. Members of these bodies held certain beliefs in common: 1) the government was the "enemy," 2) the changes they sought could be realized only through a constituent assembly, and 3) political strikes and acts of civil disobedience, such as refusal to pay taxes or perform military

service, were legitimate responses to the conditions under
which they lived. Moreover, although they were not unani-
mously in favor of armed uprising, they were not appalled at
the possibility.

Time of Decision

This situation presented to both the radical opposition and
the government the need for action. Neither could expect any
advantage from waiting on events; yet neither was sufficiently
confident of its strength to dare an all-out offensive. Consequently each side feinted, struck occasional blows, watched
events, and acted from immediate necessity rather than in
accordance with broad plans.

Nicholas II interpreted the state of affairs as reflecting the
weaknesses of men in his government:

> He [Witte] did not expect on the whole to have so many
> difficulties.
> It is strange that such a clever man should be wrong in
> his forecast of an easy pacification.[10]

. . . .

> I hold a meeting of the Council of Ministers every week.
> . . . They talk a lot, but do little. Everybody is afraid of tak-
> ing courageous action. . . .
> In Petersburg, the authorities seem to have less courage
> than anywhere else; and this more than anything deepens
> the impression that the Government, out of fear and inde-
> cision, does not dare to state openly what is permitted and
> what is not.[11]

While the Tsar kept his head during this period, numerous
officials, high and low, were definitely disturbed by the fear
that open and armed rebellion was imminent. Many of the
nobility were disengaging themselves from the liberation
movement and demanding that the government take firm ac-

[10] Nicholas II to Maria Feodorovna, October 27, 1905, *The Secret
Letters*, pp. 191-92.
[11] Nicholas II to Maria Feodorovna, November 10, 1905, *ibid.*,
pp. 194-95.

tion against the peasant violence, which was now encroaching upon their own security. Of them, the Tsar later expressed his bitter judgment, seasoned by years of disheartening struggle to maintain the regime, when he declared that "in the terrible autumn of 1905," the nobility "thought that the end was coming and hardly a one came to the aid of the government."[12] Unwilling to endure the uncertainty, some of the grand dukes departed for the south of France; others began to set their affairs in order, against the chance of an uprising. At the Tsar's advice, the Dowager Empress continued her visit in Copenhagen instead of returning to Russia as she had planned. It was apparent that, all around, preparations were being made for a showdown. And, oddly enough, the monarchists were turning to the country's first constitutional "premier," depending upon his now assuming the role of slayer of revolutionary dragons: court circles were consoled to note that Witte was changing his opinion about the "political sense of Russian society," and they were willing at this time of extremity to accept him as champion of the regime. Actually Witte was being assigned greater importance, whether by credit among some or opprobrium among others, than he deserved. The Tsar himself was quietly, but resolutely, preparing the counterattack against the potential insurrection.

What had happened since October 17 had only confirmed Nicholas II in his personal views: that a strong monarchy was the right kind of government for Russia, that the country's troubles were the work of a minority, and that the only way to deal with sedition was by using a firm hand. He accepted the judgments of Meller-Zakomelsky and others that the *Potemkin* mutiny in June and the Sevastopol mutiny in November had been fomented by a handful of revolutionaries, predominantly Jews, and that strong-willed commanders could have checked them forthwith by meeting force with force. Other disorders, he believed, were likewise misguided efforts inspired by disloyal elements that could be handled best by traditional methods. And although he was faced by indecisiveness among

---

[12] Nicholas II to Maria Feodorovna, March 27, 1908, *Krasnyi Arkhiv*, L-LI (1932), 183-84.

responsible officials and unreliability among the armed forces, he was determined that the government should make an offensive move, if only tentatively. The fact is that he could hardly have planned otherwise, for the government's position was analogous to that of the opposition: it could not stand still, it had either to retreat or to attack. Out of this situation, with both sides maneuvering in an exploratory and haphazard manner, came the decisive struggles of the revolution.

ATTACK AND COUNTERATTACK

The Tsar drew first blood. Deciding to give priority to the central and southern provinces where peasant revolts were rampant, he assigned to certain of his adjutant generals[13] the task of pacifying the areas and determining the causes of unrest. All of the troubled provinces were to be included in the project, but the first efforts were to be limited to contiguous Saratov, Penza, Tambov, Kursk, Voronezh, and Chernigov. The "assignment to pacify" these six provinces was given to three men: F. V. Dubasov, who was sent with a punitive force to Kursk and Chernigov; A. P. Strukov, to Tambov and Voronezh; and former Minister of War V. V. Sakharov, to Saratov and Penza.

Empowered with almost dictatorial authority over the regions to which they were sent, but with forces wholly inadequate for the task of complete pacification, these men began their operations early in November. In St. Petersburg the daily reports of their progress were watched with anxiety. On the 22nd, General Sakharov was assassinated in the Saratov office of Governor Stolypin by a Socialist Revolutionary; he was replaced by another adjutant general, K. K. Maximovich, and the action continued without interruption.

"Pacification," as accomplished by campaigns of this kind, depended upon the administration of summary punishment to the peasants responsible for disorder. It was meted out pub-

---

[13] The title of adjutant general was given to a select few among the ranking generals and admirals. On becoming an adjutant general, a man retained his regular duties and, on special occasions, was honored as a member of the imperial suite.

licly, and usually brutally, in order to convince the guilty of
the folly of their misdeeds and to discourage others who might
be contemplating similar foolhardiness. Typically, if a village
were known to be the residence of troublemakers, troops
would arrive, order a village meeting, and demand that cul-
prits be given up. If the demand were not obeyed, Cossacks
would drag out the suspects and publicly beat them with
nagaikas. Then the suspects would be placed under arrest or,
at the villagers' general request (forced from them by threats),
the alleged evildoers would be driven into Siberian exile. The
peasants usually submitted to these indignities and were
thereby quieted, but occasionally they offered resistance. In
one instance, three thousand peasants (of Pógoritsky, Chernigov province), armed with axes and whatever weapons came
to hand, set upon a well-armed punitive unit in an effort to
release a number of their fellow villagers who had been arrested, and dealt some telling blows of their own before sufficient reinforcements arrived to subdue them. The retaliation
for such defiance could be expected to bring more arrests, the
burning of the peasants' homes, and the order that all the villagers humble themselves and, on their knees, beg for mercy.

These methods applied to village after village had given the
government the upper hand by the beginning of 1906 in the
six selected provinces, but the condition could not be called
complete pacification. Force had driven the peasant insurgents
into abeyance only, not into willing obedience or acceptance
of their lot. Even a degree of pacification, however, was welcomed by the government, for other troubles in other places
had been mounting, and agrarian unrest was now only one
aspect of a many-fronted struggle.

No one in the government seemed able—or willing—to decide just how to begin the larger offensive against the opposition, now clearly unavoidable in view of the growing
incidence of military disorder, the evidences of radical temper
among workers, the near-revolution in the Baltic provinces,
and the postal-telegraph strike. Nicholas II, nevertheless, was
set on his course: action was to be taken, and it was not to be
delayed. In dealing with urban problems he had to rely

largely on Minister of Interior Durnovo, who, although nominally subordinate to Witte, was in fact acting independently—
with the Tsar's approval.

Durnovo's decision on how to initiate the government's urban offensive was, in a sense, forced by the defiance of the
First Congress of Postal and Telegraph Employees in calling
a strike to begin on November 15. To recognize either the government employees' right to organize or their right to strike
would be a serious capitulation, not to be considered except
as an admission of defeat. Therefore, on November 18, he issued an order for the arrest of all who had agitated for the
strike, and followed it by another, dismissing all who had participated. To these orders, the congress responded by calling
for Durnovo's removal from office. And, on the 25th, he had
the members of the central bureau of the congress arrested.

This type of emphatic action made it necessary for the opposition also to make additional moves if it were not to lose
ground. There were no concerted plans for such moves, but
the very need seemed to call forth results. On the day that
Durnovo arrested the refractory bureau members, three further gestures of defiance were being planned by opposition
bodies. The Central Bureau of the Union of Railroad Workers voted to call strikes against the government for the court-
martial sentencing to death of engineer Sokolov and others for
their parts in a recent strike at Kushka Station on the Central
Asian Railroad. And two other schemes were being considered
at a meeting of the St. Petersburg Soviet. One concerned the
means by which peasants could best participate in the revolutionary movement—a subject brought up by peasant representatives from Chernigov and Tambov, where pacification was
then in progress. The second concerned a scheme, approved a
few days earlier, by which it was hoped to further weaken the
already unsteady fiscal position of the government.

The next day brought the first step in the counteroffensive
against the St. Petersburg Soviet—the arrest of Khrustalev-
Nosar. But for another week the opposition made no striking
response to that loss, though there were signs that the idea of
a general strike was gaining supporters, that the urge toward

armed uprising was growing stronger in some quarters, and
that the sentiment for action was becoming intensified in both
the St. Petersburg and the Moscow Soviet.

Finally, on December 2, the St. Petersburg Soviet took the
first and ultimately decisive step. With the support of the
Peasants Union, the Social Democrats, the SR's, and the PPS,
it issued the "Financial Manifesto," a declaration of the
planned financial war against the government. After lengthily
denouncing the government for the manner in which it was
obstructing the revolution, the manifesto stated that "the people" intended to "deprive it of its last strength" by 1) refusing
to pay any taxes or government debts, 2) demanding specie
payment in all dealings (gold for wages and for all except
minor transactions), and 3) withdrawing, in gold, all deposits
in government banks. Then it added a general warning that
since "autocracy has never had the confidence of the people,"
no loans "contracted by the Tsarist government" would be
paid while it was "openly at war with its own people."[14]

This manifesto produced some of the results intended by its
framers when, in the next weeks, extensive withdrawals from
banks brought some embarrassment to the government. But
the chief result was an unintended one: the provocation of an
open, direct, and large-scale conflict with the government.
Heretofore the authorities had been reluctant to arrest the
members of the Soviet for fear of a retaliatory mass rising. But
here was a challenge that could not be ignored. Durnovo immediately issued orders to close the eight newspapers that had
printed the manifesto in the city and to institute criminal proceedings against their editors. And on the following day, in
order to make further arrests, he had the Soviet's meeting
place, the building of the Free Economic Society, surrounded
by police, gendarmes, Cossacks, and guardsmen; some 250
were taken into custody, including all of the deputies of the
Soviet and almost all of the executive committee.

Now the radical opposition had no alternative but to meet
the government head-on under circumstances that neither side

[14] Akademiya Nauk, SSSR, *Vyshii Podem Revolyutsii 1905–1907
Gg.* (Moscow, 1955), I, 26. (For an English translation of part of
the manifesto, *see* Postgate, *Revolution from 1789–1906,* p. 385.)

had foreseen. The weapon chosen was the general strike. Those members of the St. Petersburg Soviet's executive committee who were still at large, supported by SD and SR representatives, issued a call to a nationwide political strike to start at noon on December 8. The Moscow Soviet, which had not always approved the methods of its older counterpart, now also recognized the need for a general strike. But it was at first undecided about whether or not to accept the Bolshevik proposal that the call to strike be accompanied by a call for a concurrent armed uprising. In the end, it adopted an alternative position, that of the Mensheviks, calling for a general strike to begin at noon on December 7 and ultimately to become an armed uprising. This call was approved by both the organization of the postal and telegraph workers and by the Union of Railroad Workers. In cooperation, the medical personnel of the city voted to organize medical aid for persons who might be injured while participating in the strike. And a large group of municipal employees, voting to join the strike, expressed their stand in true revolutionary style:

> We demand a constituent assembly!
> Long live the democratic republic!
> Long live the struggle of the proletariat under the banner of the RSDLP![15]

As the final test of the revolution approached, one aspect of the preparations was out of keeping with precedent: the St. Petersburg Soviet was not in the van of leaders. Enfeebled, deprived of its experienced leaders, and operating under cover, it could serve only in the auxiliary forces. Yet the strike proved to be a remarkable demonstration of revolutionary power. It began in Moscow on the 7th; in St. Petersburg, on the 8th; and, within a week, almost all cities in the empire were involved. Moreover, it served to fan the spirit of rebellion, already smoldering in some parts of the country.

The Moscow strike began with an impressive sweep. Within twenty-four hours, industry was at a halt, almost all trains were stopped, most municipal services suspended, and the

15 *Ibid.*, pp. 652-53.

schools closed. During that time, the reaction of F. V. Dubasov, who had just been appointed governor-general of the
Moscow province, was puzzling to observers. He arrested some
of the strike leaders but, keeping most of the police and the
troops off the streets, made no organized drive against the
strike. Ostensibly the Moscow Soviet was master of the city: it
had called for the idling of most of the local activities and
assumed direction over municipal services; and it quite evidently had the support of the people who thronged the
streets, awaiting developments. The strike leaders hoped—and
Dubasov feared—that the troops of the Moscow garrison would
join the strike. There had, in fact, been recent displays of mutinous sentiment among the soldiers, and the Second Grenadier Rostov Regiment had mutinied in the garrison only a
few days earlier.

As long as neither side would begin a physical offensive, it
appeared that the Moscow situation was to become just a repetition, in smaller compass, of what had been going on, here
and there throughout the country, for three months: the opposition, having reached threatening proportions, demonstrated,
asserted its position, but stopped short of seizing power; and
the government, unsure of itself, offered so little interference
that it seemed only a concerned observer. The stalemate, in
this case, was broken almost inadvertently, by developments
growing out of two relatively minor incidents. During the
night of December 8, Dubasov ordered police and reliable
troops to surround the Aquarium Theater, a huge structure
with many auditoriums, in which some twelve thousand persons were meeting in connection with the strike, and to arrest
as many leaders as possible. A number of armed persons and
some leaders were taken, while about fifty leaders managed to
slip out and hide in a nearby building. The next night, troops
invaded a meeting held at a private school and, after some
firing from both sides, arrested a few strikers, none of them
important leaders—as they were thought to be, at the time.

These incidents provoked the armed detachments of the
strikers, who so far had not taken part in any planned engage-
ments. Now they began to build barricades on the main boule-

vards—Tverskaya, Sadovaya, Bronnaya, and others—where they could be expected to impede the movements of troops and offer protection for fighters. As troops and police removed the barricades, strikers rushed to put up new ones, using barrels, iron telephone poles, and whatever else was available and movable. As this see-saw activity continued, feelings ran high, and finally shots were exchanged. Thus the local uprising, openly supported by the Moscow Soviet, got under way. It lasted for a week, most of it concentrated in the Zamoskvoreche, the Presnya, and the Rogozhsko-Simonovskoi districts —all industrial sections. The showing made by the few thousand workers, students, and municipal employees who took part, indicated that they had much determination but no offensive plan. When it became evident that they were not to get the hoped-for support from the local garrison (though they had witnessed many instances of soldiers' refusal to fire on them), their only recourse was to fight on, using hit-and-run tactics, hoping that other areas would take up the fight and thus give the armed uprising a chance to accomplish its purpose.

At first, neither side was in a definitely favorable position. The strikers, though they had the sympathy of a large part of the city's population, did not have their physical support. And the number of rebels would have been wholly inadequate to offer any serious resistance if Dubasov had dared use against them the fifteen thousand men available to him in the Moscow garrison. Two-thirds of the government troops, however, were judged unreliable; one whole regiment had actually undertaken to join the strikers before the fighting began, and had been prevented only by the interposing of loyal troops. And since only a third of the garrison troops, therefore, were drawn out, the strikers appeared to have at least a fair chance of holding their own for a while.

However, on the 12th, after two days of somewhat futile fighting, Dubasov telegraphed the Ministry of Interior:

> The situation continues to be very serious: a network of barricades is constricting the city ever more tightly; there are clearly not enough troops for counteraction. It is abso-

lutely essential to send a brigade of infantry from St. Petersburg, at least for the time being.[16]

Then, with the prospect of a reinforced opposition, the Moscow uprising was recognized by the rebels as a desperate struggle against high odds. They did not have the best of communications with other parts of the country, and the reports that did get through to them were not such as to give them much encouragement.

Few cities responded favorably when called to join the fight. In the St. Petersburg Soviet, where there was a definite sentiment for this part of the oppositional program, there was insufficient interested leadership at this time to turn sentiment into anything but scattered and ineffective local actions; and so the capital, admittedly one of the most militant cities of the empire, remained in its state of "quiet disturbance." In some centers, where revolutionary sentiment was already strong, the strike was accompanied by either an armed uprising or a relatively unopposed take-over of power. Notable among the places where authority gave way during this time were Novorossiisk, a busy industrial center and seaport on the eastern shore of the Black Sea; Krasnoyarsk, on the Trans-Siberian Railroad, where civilians and soldiers joined to take over power; Chita, also on the Trans-Siberian, where General I. V. Kholshchevnikov, military governor of the Trans-Baikal region, subordinated himself to the authority of the revolutionary strikers; and Kharkov, where unrest had been endemic for years.

By the middle of the month, this December strike had displayed more intensity, more bitterness, and more violence than had the October strike. Yet it failed to reach the dimensions of the earlier one. Its differences were, in part, a reflection of the manner in which it was instigated and the nature of its supporters. It came about in such a way that, once the issue was joined, it was often difficult for either side to retire without a definite test of strength; and a physical contest, violence, seemed the only resort in some places. As for its supporters, the December strike had a narrower representa-

16 *Ibid.*, pp. 676-77.

tion of society than did the earlier one. It was carried out largely by workers and students—though by no means all of the opposition in either category. Except in cities along the Trans-Siberian Railroad, the military forces rarely gave it open support. Some members of the professions and some government employees participated, but a larger number of them refrained from involvement. The liberals also, for the most part, withheld their support, though many of them remained sympathetic to the revolution. The agrarian element of the countryside, where the peasant revolt was in progress at the time, made practically no effort to identify itself with the strike. Here and there, some peasants took part in the urban uprisings or gave some other kind of direct support, but their number was small.[17] One consequence of these limitations in support was that the December strike, despite the fact that it was using many of the methods of the October strike, never managed to affect the life of the country as deeply. Communications between Russia and the outside were curtailed, but not cut off; and, within the country, the strike produced only partial paralysis. While many of the railroad lines were idled, many continued to function. Even the line between Moscow and St. Petersburg was kept open with the help of railroad battalions, though all others emanating from that center were immobilized. And, except in the cities where authority passed to the revolutionaries, municipal services and commerce continued.

Furthermore, this strike did not affect the Tsar's advisers as the October strike had, and they did not advise him to make new concessions because of it. Once it was clear that the various centers of strikes and uprisings could not be fused into one revolutionary whole, the government was able to turn from the mere containment of violence to planned measures of counteroffensive. Strategically, the suppression of the Moscow uprising was the most important part of this action; and it began in earnest on the 15th, with the arrival of the

[17] Even Soviet historians, who like to emphasize peasant support, particularly in the Moscow province, can present only slight and unconvincing evidence that it was of any consequence. *See* V. Yakovlev and Ya. Shorr, *1905 v Moskve* (Moscow, 1955), pp. 291-96.

Semenovsky Guards and other reliable units to reinforce the
Moscow garrison. Since the strongest of the rebel concentrations was in the Presnya district, the fresh forces moved at
once to clear that area. And there, for almost two days, the
rebels continued the resistance against artillery and rifle fire,
while noncombatants kept them supplied with medicine and
other needs. The troops, led by Colonel Mins, were under
instructions to be severe, and they were. Men surrendering or
captured with arms were shot after quick drum-head trials—
or, in many cases, without even that formality. The strikers
recognized the superior strength of their opponents, but they
fought on anyway; and when their will was finally broken, the
Presnya district had been reduced to a smoking waste. Elsewhere in the city, the defense was less enduring, and soon
none could doubt that the insurrection had failed. The Moscow Soviet acknowledged the defeat-at-arms and set December
19 as the day on which the strike would end officially. About
a thousand civilians were killed in the course of the fighting,
and many thousands were arrested, large numbers of them to
be later exiled to Siberia.

The termination of the Moscow uprising was the beginning
of the end, but the end was by no means spiritless. In many
places—notably Novorossiisk, Krasnoyarsk, Chita, and the
Baltic provinces—the fire of resistance continued to burn
brightly for days and, in some cases, did not actually die down
for weeks. But rebellion was now a struggle without hope. In
the latter part of December, the strikes ended one by one,
sometimes by formal action of local soviets or strike committees, sometimes by the unorganized resumption of work by
discouraged strikers. As the strike receded, local officials,
backed by police and troops, moved in to forestall the possibility of new outbreaks. They arrested members of the soviets
and other strike leaders, systematically searched and disarmed
workers, and closed radical newspapers. Often they received
the help of employers in intimidating workers; the management of the often-struck Putilov plant, for example, stopped
plant operations for three weeks beginning on December 21,
and then accepted the return of only those workers whose
records showed that they were not troublemakers.

There was no longer any question about the general strike's having failed to achieve its goal; the government had shown no sign of being even moderately impressed by the demand for a constituent assembly. And now the "freedom days" were about over. The Tsar had made his last major political concession and was ready to bring the country to heel, to reestablish the government's authority in the land by an all-out show of strength. Even Witte, who had staked so much on the possibility of conciliating society, was now far more concerned with pacification by force than with conciliation. The Tsar noted this change of attitude with a good deal of acerbity:

> As for Witte, since the happenings in Moscow he has radically changed his views; now he wants to hang and shoot everybody.
> I have never seen such a chameleon of a man. That, naturally, is why no one believes in him any more.[18]

For the first time since the furor had started over the Eleven Theses in November of the preceding year, the government was beginning to demonstrate a recovery of its command, to summon enough courage and strength for a counterattack against sedition and revolution. In fact, the tactics it used in the months following the collapse of the December strike were such as almost to justify an accusation made by the St. Petersburg Soviet in its "Financial Manifesto," that it acted toward the people like a conqueror in a foreign country. But in judging the government's harshness at this time, it must, in justice, be remembered that the "enemies" as seen by the Tsar and most of his officials were only a part of the Russian people. They included the intelligentsia, many of the urban workers, and substantial numbers of the national minorities. The Tsar still believed, however, in the innate loyalty of the Russian nobility and the peasantry. As he interpreted happenings, the former, though affected to some extent by liberalism, had recently begun to right its course; and the latter needed only time and proper assistance to do the same.

[18] Nicholas II to Maria Feodorovna, January 12, 1906, *The Secret Letters*, p. 212.

He believed that the Russian peasants, when they had attacked property and officialdom, were simply responding as
dupes of outside propagandists; and once these propagandists
—be they seditious zemstvo employees or leaders of the Peasants Union—were removed and the peasants were made to
understand that violence and theft would not be condoned, it
would be possible to turn to the peaceful reconstruction of
the countryside. As for the cities, it was expected that their
normalcy would be restored when the revolutionary organizations had been destroyed. And most high officials agreed with
the Tsar that this return to conditions of peace would be
forthcoming, not only because police and military measures
would be able to subdue sedition, but also because the people
would respond favorably, once the promised legislature began
to function.

The government's counterattack consisted of several operations. In the cities, in addition to the measures employed
against openly antigovernment organizations and newspapers,
steps were taken to expel from their positions all municipal
and zemstvo employees who had supported antigovernment
activities. At the same time, special rules regarding meetings
were rigidly enforced. Revolutionary meetings and outdoor
assemblies of all kinds were forbidden. Indoor meetings called
by moderates were permitted only under certain conditions;
they might not be held in buildings of higher schools, and
they might not be held anywhere unless a sufficient number
of police were present to close them in case of disorder or
in case members of the armed forces or secondary school
pupils were found to be in attendance. Such measures as these
were intended both to end the possibility of large-scale revolutionary activity and to demonstrate the government's firm
intention not to tolerate open attacks on its authority as it
had in the preceding year.

In the Russian countryside, in the borderlands, and along
the Trans-Siberian Railroad, the counterattack took the form
of punitive expeditions, in which the Cossacks and the Guards
were heavily represented. As the pacification already under
way in the south-central provinces continued, forces were

dispatched to the neighboring provinces where further agrarian disorder had to be handled. In addition, expeditions were sent to Transcaucasia and the Baltic provinces with orders to pacify, not just villages, but whole districts— occasionally entire provinces—in those areas.

The most savage of these punitive expeditions was the one sent to the Baltic provinces, where some three thousand attacks on German landlords and Russian officials and soldiers had been made during the worst of the recent outbursts there, about a thousand Germans and Russians had been killed, and whole districts had been taken over by Lettish and Estonian rebels. To lead the pacification the Tsar appointed his close friend Prince Alexander Orlov, the commander of the Life Uhlan Regiment. Orlov's instructions were to stop disorder, punish the troublemakers, start the trains moving, and get the workers back to their jobs. To accomplish these tasks he had the help of military units already in the area as well as the enthusiastic support of the German landlords. Even so, progress was very slow, pacification having to be carried out district by district. In the process, more than two thousand rebels were hanged or shot; hundreds of peasant homes were burned; and public floggings of rebels and mass arrests became commonplace. By early January, a semblance of order had been restored in several areas; and some of the Lettish leaders were sufficiently cowed to appear before Russian officials, sing the Tsarist national anthem, and announce their readiness to obey the government. A little later, the punitive expedition to Transcaucasia had also achieved a degree of success, and the condition of that area could be reported as "improving."

About the time that Orlov was leaving for the Baltic provinces, a very important operation involving two punitive expeditions was being set in motion to restore order along the Trans-Siberian Railroad. The Tsar ordered one expedition, under General Meller-Zakomelsky, to proceed eastward from Moscow and another, under General Rennenkampf, to proceed westward from Harbin; the place of their meeting would depend upon the obstacles they encountered and their success in overcoming them. Both progressed fairly rapidly, making liberal use of floggings and firing squads along the way. Often, news of the approach of the expeditions was sufficient to stop disorder and make it possible to restore authority. Two cities, however, were so deeply involved in revolutionary activity that they were considered special problems: Chita and Krasnoyarsk, where local railroad workers and soldiers of the Second Railroad Battalion had established soviets that now held almost complete power. Krasnoyarsk was first to yield—and that before the arrival of the Meller-Zakomelsky expedition, which would otherwise have had to deal with it. Credit for its pacification went to the Cossacks and units from the Omsk Regiment, which reached the city on December 24 and fought the armed rebels for over a week before subduing them. Chita, the remaining stronghold, where rebel civilians and soldiers were armed with an estimated twenty-five thousand rifles, was reputed to be ready to resist Rennenkampf when he reached the outskirts of the city, on January 21. But, for some reason, when the general let it be known that he planned to attack the city on the following day if arms were not surrendered, bravado was replaced by panic; and Chita became the last link in the restored Trans-Siberian line. Now the government was in a position to resume the evacuation of troops from Manchuria and to provide itself with adequate reinforcements for dealing with remaining areas of trouble in European Russia. And during the remainder of the year, it used the regained advantage to the full, holding to its gains and handling renewed disorders with dispatch and severity.

END OF THE REVOLUTION

No day can be specified as the end of the Revolution of 1905. Rebellion was not abruptly ended: it flickered out or was kept alive underground when further open protest became impossible or was deemed self-defeating. And many of the ambitions aroused but unrealized during this upheaval continued through the years, to find open expression again in 1917. However, the point of turning, the point at which this revolution ceased to be an actual threat to the government, can be dated: December 19, when the Moscow strike officially came to an end. Thereafter the government was concerned, not with the danger of being set aside, but with the problem of restoring equilibrium in the country and making the necessary adjustments to the changes that had been wrought by the revolution.

8

The Settlement

The manifesto of October 17th meant the capitulation of Tsarist autocracy, victory over servitude, victory of law over arbitrary rule—that is, all that five generations of sensitive Russians both dreamt of and sacrificed for, by going to prison or into exile, by dying in penal servitude or on the gallows; and by their sacrifices they are transmitting as their legacy to future generations the obligation to transform Russia into a country of liberty, law, and European culture.
> —Ivan Petrunkevich (liberal leader), *Iz Zapisok Obshchestvennago Deyatelya*, 1934.

So a constitution is granted [by the October Manifesto]. Freedom of assembly is granted, but the assemblies are surrounded by the military. Freedom of speech is granted, but censorship exists as before. Freedom of knowledge is granted, but the universities are occupied by troops. Inviolability of the person is granted, but the prisons are overflowing with the incarcerated. . . . A constitution is given, but the autocracy remains. Everything is given—and nothing is given.
> —Leon Trotsky (Social Democrat, inclined toward the Mensheviks at the time), *Izvestiya Soveta Rabochikh Deputatov*, 1905.

THE REVOLUTION OF 1905 did not expunge the issues that had brought the "two Russias" into conflict; nor, at the end of it, could either claim unqualified victory or defeat on any one of them. "Government" had made some concessions, and "society" had achieved some of its aims. Their relative positions had been changed—but only to a limited degree. Whether or not, from the new positions, the two could work together to produce successful reform in Russia was the big problem that faced the country as the violence of revolution receded.

CHANGES IN POLITICAL STRUCTURE

The Tsar had accepted constricting limitations on his authority and had been forced to part with some of his reactionary ministers. But he was still in power; and the character of the officials to whom he would now turn for assistance in framing and administering the promised reforms would be very important to the final outcome of the revolution. Had Witte's efforts at conciliating "society" succeeded, new blood would have been introduced into officialdom and cooperation might have followed; but because of his failure, the government was still administered by a bureaucracy that had changed only slightly in recent years. Some of the bureaucrats, it is true, welcomed the October Manifesto as the beginning of much-needed change; but their influence was overridden by that of their conservative colleagues, whose position was continually strengthened by the need to keep in check the anti-government agitation that persisted for many years after the revolution. On the whole, these bureaucrats were ill-equipped, both in training and conviction, to guide the creation of a new political order in which public opinion was to be recognized, and persons lacking any clear place in the bureaucratic order were to have a part in the scheme of government. Believers in "autocracy, orthodoxy, and nationalism," they were unlikely to make any great efforts to conciliate the public. The outlook for reform agreeable to those who made the revolution was obviously unfavorable. Changes were made, nevertheless; and they were significant ones.

The October Manifesto declared that Russia's autocratic government was to be transformed, and it was transformed in some respects. But the resulting political structure is difficult to classify. Using a Western European label, one might say, with reservations, that it was a constitutional parliamentary monarchy. Western labels, however, are not entirely adequate for a comprehensible definition of the form of government finally set up after the Revolution of 1905. That fact is illustrated by the change of the Russian entry in the *Almanach de Gotha*, the yearbook of European royalty: before 1906, Russia was classified simply as an absolute monarchy; thereafter, as a constitutional monarchy ruled by an autocrat—an ambiguous classification, to say the least.

The new political structure was, in fact, a hybrid, resulting from the efforts of the Tsar and the bureaucracy to carry out the letter of the manifesto while preserving the spirit of the autocracy. It was brought into existence by the work of three special conferences[1] held between December, 1905 and April, 1906. The personnel of each included a number of grand dukes, certain specially designated high officials, and the incumbent ministers. Their specific task was to work out the legal basis of the new order: 1) the fundamental laws defining the structure of the state and 2) the laws specifying the methods of election, the organization, and the powers of the new legislature. The only "outsiders" admitted to any of the sessions were Alexander Guchkov and Dmitri Shipov, who were invited to present their proposals for an electoral law but not permitted to participate in, nor to hear, the discussions that followed.

Even if the special conferences had been held in a period of calm, it is doubtful that the participants would have attempted to interpret the October Manifesto in a liberal sense. But deliberating as they did, when mutinies, political strikes, and agrarian disorders were daily reminders of what many of them considered the public disregard for law and order, they were even less inclined to such interpretations. Their principal aim, as it soon became evident, was to make the throne secure against encroachment by the legislature that they were committed to establish, not to provide the country with a constitution and a parliament.

This aim would be realized satisfactorily, they felt, through the type of legislature that they planned. As promised in the October Manifesto, the right to vote for deputies to the Duma

[1] A special conference (*osoboe soveshchanie*) was a meeting of persons selected by the tsar to consider problems that he deemed outside the competence or authority of established committees, ministries, or other government bodies. Usually the tsar presided over these conferences himself and took part in the discussions. Proceedings were secret, and any final decisions arising from them were the tsar's own.

was broadened to include persons from all classes, and that body's consent would be requisite to the conversion of any bill into law. But the Duma was to be adjusted to the existing regime by two definite limitations. One was the result of retaining the system of indirect election and unequal suffrage devised for the Bulygin Duma.² Another was the setting of a curb on the Duma's legislative power: the State Council was to be vested with legislative power equal to that of the Duma, and no bill was to become law without the approval of both bodies. Nothing in the October Manifesto had suggested that the Duma would be so limited but, in the period of disturbances following October 17, the notion had been advanced and officially approved. To that end, not only was the State Council to be transformed into a legislative body, but its members were to be so chosen as to insure its being even more conservative than the Duma. Half of them were to be appointed by the Tsar; and half were to be elected by votes of the Orthodox churchmen, the nobility, the zemstvos, the university faculties, and the associations of commercial and industrial leaders. Thus were set up the first lines of defense.

But precautions did not end there. The conferences devised four additional defenses for the autocrat. One accorded him the right of absolute veto over bills passed by both legislative bodies. Another provided that he have discretionary power in matters of finance, thus seriously circumscribing the power of the legislature: if the Duma and the State Council disagreed over budgetary matters, the Tsar was free to accept the views of either body or to employ the figures of earlier budgets. A third gave him the authority to issue emergency laws between legislative sessions, and to enforce them until such time as the legislature could meet and approve or disapprove them.

The fourth additional defense was a particularly vital one

² Before this complex system was put into operation, the people had ample time to analyze its limitations. Though the Tsar had stated in the October Manifesto that the Duma elections would not be postponed, the fact that the special conferences took months to complete their work necessitated delaying the beginning of the elections to March, 1906.

from the standpoint of an autocrat. It was that which limited
the power of the legislature over the executive branch of the
government. Provision was made that ministers could be inter-
pellated by the legislature; but, aside from the use of its
limited budgetary power as a means of influence, it had no
further power over the executive. The Tsar remained firmly
in control of the executive branch. He appointed and removed ministers. He exercised supreme command over the
armed forces. He appointed administrative officials and judges.
He retained the right to issue ukases. He could place areas
under reinforced protection, extraordinary protection, or martial law, thus depriving persons in these areas of some or all of
their civil liberties. He was still the defender of the Orthodox
Church—in actuality, its ruler. He maintained exclusive control over foreign affairs, including the right to make treaties
and to declare war. And he still had exclusive control over all
administrative machinery.

The basic nature of the new political structure was made
manifest in the revised Fundamental Laws, as they were
worked out by the special conference of April, 1906 and approved by the Tsar. And the legislature was accorded no
power to change that structure except by the Tsar's consent.
In fact, it was debarred not only from changing the Fundamental Laws but also from discussing them. They were to
serve, in a sense, as the "constitution" of the new Russia, defining both the nature of the legislature and certain essential
features of the state.

Article I of the revised Fundamental Laws indicated how
little real change was being allowed: "The Russian Empire is
One and Indivisible." In other words, the country remained a
unitary state with a single source of sovereignty, the Tsar. It
was further provided that, as in the past, the Russian character of that unity would be strengthened by the enforced use
of Russian as the language of the armed forces and administration. The inclusion of this provision in the revised laws
effectually precluded the possibility of any legislative consideration of a proposal widely endorsed by the opposition, that
members of national minorities be permitted to use their

mother tongue in national units of the armed forces and in administrative procedures.

Article IV of the revised laws, central to the new political structure, was finally approved, after very involved and extended deliberations, in this form:

> To the Emperor of All the Russias belongs the supreme autocratic power. Not only fear, but also conscience commanded by God Himself is the basis of obedience to this power.

This wording differed from that of Article I of the old Fundamental Laws, which it replaced, in that it omitted the words "and unlimited" from the older phrase "autocratic and unlimited power." The Tsar reluctantly agreed to the elimination of "unlimited" because he recognized that already, in the October Manifesto, he had accepted limitations by which he would be bound. But—and he made this explicit at the conference—he was still an autocrat, still the sovereign. As he indicated it, his intention was to observe the October Manifesto because he had promised to do so, not because he was so compelled. And he implied that, if he found it necessary, he would rescind or ignore it.[3]

After all the work of the three special conferences, one vexatious question remained to be answered: whether or not a ruler could be an autocratic monarch and, at the same time, a constitutional monarch. Nicholas II believed that he had not granted a constitution and that he remained an autocrat. Some of his ministers and most of his subjects believed that he had granted a constitution and that the term "autocrat" was simply a historical vestige of the kind that the British monarchy cherished. Arguments could be marshaled on each side; but the decision was to be derived from actuality, not from law or logic. Russia had a constitution of sorts in the revised Fundamental Laws; she had a legislature of sorts in the Duma and the State Council; and she had civil liberties fairly broad

[3] He actually ignored the October Manifesto when, on June 3, 1907, after dissolving an unruly Duma, he issued an emergency electoral law intended to insure a more cooperative Duma.

in principle but somewhat circumscribed by law and practice. In short, she had the beginnings of a constitutional, parliamentary system. Whether or not this system could fulfill its limited promise was to depend on the Tsar, the bureaucracy, the people, and the accidents of history.

CHANGES IN AGRARIAN POLICIES

Next in importance to the changes in the political structure of the country were the changes in its agrarian policies. In many respects the Tsar's shift in position on the latter resembled his shift on the former: each was, in fact, a retreat from one position to another in the face of a superior force until, having given up considerable ground, he found a firm position beyond which he could not be compelled to retreat. He faced the agrarian question later than the political one, and his stand on it was taken without the drama that attended the issuance of the October Manifesto; but it was a serious question, and the answer was of far-reaching consequences. The agrarian revolt, which forced the Tsar into reluctant retreat from one position to another between November, 1905 and November, 1906, was ultimately responsible for a radical departure in agrarian policy.

Outbursts in the rural areas, though lacking exact articulation, were seen to have certain common and fairly clear goals: 1) release from the control that land captains and other bureaucrats held over peasant life, 2) the termination of redemption dues, 3) the mitigation of taxation, and 4) the achievement of "black partition."

In the fall of 1905, a few frightened officials favored an effort to allay the peasant unrest by the distribution of noble lands; but, in the Tsar's reasoning, that would be a rash act, weakening the nobility, one of the main supports of the monarchy. Yet the peasantry, another essential support, could not be allowed to continue drawing away. It was therefore necessary to stop revolt and, at the same time, manage to retain the peasants' devotion to the throne, which the Tsar still believed to be deep and genuine. Punitive expeditions could not serve the purpose adequately; they could stop revolt, but they could not remove the causes of peasant distress, nor could they guarantee rural peace. One different approach was suggested by the reports of governors and adjutants-general that the peasant risings were prompted by outside agitators. To rid the countryside of these disturbers, the government began, in the last months of 1905, to dismiss zemstvo employees suspected of revolutionary connections, to break up the Peasants Union, and to arrest revolutionary agitators. At the same time it continued attempts to find a lasting solution to the problem of peasant distress without cost to the nobility.

The Tsar issued a manifesto on November 3, 1905, promising that the conditions of peasant life should be improved; but the promise did not specify even the general nature of the improvement—for the good, but unstated, reason that it had not yet been determined. On the same day, he announced that redemption dues for 1906 would be cut in half and that, after 1906, no further payments would be required. This was an act of good will and, to all appearance, one that would prove costly to the government. In fact, it was little more than a gesture; although, on the books, the cancelled redemption dues amounted to a billion rubles, peasant payments were so far in arrears as to make it unlikely that the government would ever have collected more than a small part of the sum. The debt cancellation, nevertheless, relieved the peasants of financial obligation and suggested to them that further relief would follow.

Another measure, more material in nature but still inadequate, resulted from the Tsar's efforts to answer the peasants' cry for more land. He proposed that four million acres of appanage land be sold to the government-operated Peasants Bank, which would in turn sell it on easy terms to the peasants who had been renting it. But this action could be taken only with the consent of the imperial family, some of whom, the Dowager Empress and the Grand Duke Vladimir in particular, opposed it at first—in contrast to the Grand Duke Nicholas Michaelovich, who blithely suggested giving the land away. The family finally acquiesced, and the Tsar ordered that the land be sold as planned and made available to the peasants. It was thought that other lands might be likewise released by some of the landed nobility, but none saw fit to follow the royal example. And even if they had done so, the peasant distress would not have been markedly eased thereby; the land of all the noble estates could not have solved the basic rural problem, overpopulation. The indisputable fact was that there was not enough land under cultivation to support the people of the countryside.

Some of the officials concerned with the agrarian dilemma began in the winter of 1905/06 to lean toward a solution based on the idea of weakening a rural institution that had traditionally been held sacrosanct—the village commune. In the past, a few officials had timidly suggested that the village commune, by giving its members an inalienable right to allotment land, rewarded the inefficient as well as the efficient farmer and was, therefore, a bar to agrarian progress. But they had been silenced by the reiteration of official policy: the aim of the government was to maintain the peasantry as a land-owning, and therefore conservative, class; and that aim was realized through the village commune. Now, in the midst of the agrarian revolt, the assumption behind the traditional policy seemed to be belied, and it became easier and politically safer for the government and the nobility to consider a new policy, permitting and encouraging the peasants to leave the commune and allowing them the privilege of receiving title to their allotment lands. Under such a policy, they would be enabled to operate as individual proprietors; and it was to be expected that the more diligent among them would prosper and, like the conservative French peasant proprietors, identify their interests with the *status quo*. While this rearrangement would probably bring bankruptcy and impoverishment to some peasants who, without the artificial prop of the village commune, would lose their land and have to become agricultural or industrial laborers, it seemed more desirable than the alternatives—continued agrarian revolt or confiscation of noble lands. Moreover, this new policy could be offered to the peasantry, not as one proposed by the opposition and reluctantly accepted by the government, but as one initiated by the government.

The change to the new policy was facilitated by the attitude of the man appointed, in July, 1906, to the chairmanship of the Council of Ministers, Peter Stolypin.[4] He had, for some time, been a firm but quiet opponent of the village commune; and his conviction that it was a pernicious institution had been strengthened by his experience as governor of Saratov, where he had seen the worst of the agrarian uprisings. He took office with the determination to bring about reform, and he was particularly favored by the assurance that his efforts would have the support of the Tsar.

Under his leadership, the new agrarian policy was put into effect and proved to be, along with the October Manifesto, one of the most significant achievements of the Revolution of 1905. It was embodied in two ukases issued by the Tsar—one in October, 1906, the other in November, 1906—and subsequently approved by the Duma and the State Council. The first lifted most of the legal restrictions that had subordinated the peasants to the village commune, and limited the authority of the land captains. The second, the more important one, permitted peasants to acquire title to the strips of allotment land they had held as members of the commune, to sell that land or buy allotment land, and to consolidate their several strips into unified farmsteads.

The Stolypin Laws, as these ukases came to be called, made a promising beginning of radical change in Russian agrarian life, a definite departure from the past; and that would assuredly bring improvement. But the laws, regardless of their promise, could not produce an immediate change in the rural way of life, nor could they bring immediate relief from agrarian pressures. Stolypin himself estimated that perhaps twenty years would pass before the full effect of the new policy would be realized.

[4] Witte, who must be credited, along with Stolypin, for handling much of the outstanding work of the government following the Revolution of 1905, resigned his chairmanship in April, 1906. He was followed by the ineffectual Ivan Goremykin, whom Stolypin replaced.

OTHER CHANGES

The other changes that the government granted as a result of the revolution were less sweeping. It made some concessions to the national and religious minorities: permitting subjects to choose any variety of Christian belief that they desired, lifting some of the restrictions on the use of the Polish and Ukrainian languages, restoring Finland's autonomous rights, and permitting Jews to vote in Duma elections. And it made two concessions of special satisfaction to thousands who had figured prominently in the revolution: granting labor the right to organize and to strike (providing that strikes were conducted in a peaceful manner), and restoring autonomous rights to the universities.

Though much of old Russia remained intact, the changes made and the concessions granted were, all told, considerable. The regime looked to them for the salvation of the monarchy, while the liberal opposition looked to them for the peaceful regeneration of the country. The two aspirations, the former focused on stabilization and the latter on change, were not necessarily mutually exclusive, though they appeared basically to be so: both accepted, as a prerequisite for the ideal status, domestic tranquillity.

GENERAL POSTREVOLUTIONARY ATTITUDES

Historians, the "prophets who look backward," would agree that the settlement following the Revolution of 1905 proved unsuccessful, but they would not agree that it was predestined to fail. The achievement of the condition of domestic tranquillity requisite to its success was dependent on the degree to which the hitherto disaffected were satisfied; on the capacity of the new political institutions to produce "government by consent," a sufficient consensus among the peoples of Russia to insure that the machinery of representative government be used for achieving the needed changes; and on the effective application of such policies as those embodied in the Stolypin Laws.

There is no way of measuring accurately the degree of satisfaction or dissatisfaction that remained in the postrevolutionary period, but some defensible estimates can be made. When the deputies to the first Duma were elected, in March and April of 1906, the temper of the voters could be judged by the political affiliations or leanings of those they chose to represent them. Of the 497 deputies elected, 340 were patently of the opposition (180 of them were Cadets), and less than 10 percent of them were of the right; the rest, mainly peasants, adhered to no party, but often voted with the opposition. Those results indicated to contemporaries that the opposition was still very strong and that there was considerable dissatisfaction in the country. But administrative officials took exception to that interpretation, arguing that the regime had been at a disadvantage in mobilizing electoral support since the parties of the right lacked both adequate organization and an active press, and that the Duma therefore did not reflect the real temper of the majority. Later developments, however, did not sustain their argument.

It is safe to say that in the postrevolutionary period a large part—perhaps a major part—of the population was dissatisfied with what had been achieved. Many were dissatisfied even though they had attained some of their pre- or early-revolutionary goals. Their ambitions had changed, having advanced with the revolution and expanded with each additional concession from the government, so that now they were likely to be aspiring to goals far ahead of those that had been reached. Moreover, the revolution had produced new attitudes in many and taught new methods of action. It had, for instance, given rise to the first soviets, called forth the first expressions of nationalism among some minorities, and planted the seed of political sense among the peasants. In fact, there was no class and no group that had not been somehow changed by it. And such changes had much to do with the manner in which individuals and groups responded to the postrevolutionary settlement. Assessment must be based, therefore, on changing factors, not constant ones.

ATTITUDES AMONG THE EDUCATED

The educated class, on the whole, continued to be disaffected. A fair representation of their general feelings could be seen in the political expressions of the Cadet Party: the new governmental arrangements left much to be desired, and neither the Tsar nor his officials were yet to be trusted wholeheartedly. The Cadets were willing to concede, nevertheless, that the settlement, imperfect as it was, marked a turn toward a better life for the country. Many felt as Petrunkevich did (p. 244 above), that the October Manifesto had provided a release from the suppressive features of the old regime and that, with the new freedom, Russians could now transform their country into one of "liberty, law, and European culture." This was an attitude quite different from the prerevolutionary attitude of the liberals: hope had replaced desperation. And, since they were no longer impelled by what they had considered the urgent need to force change, they were not inclined, as before, to ally themselves with the revolutionaries. Their disaffection had not been eradicated, and their loyalty had not been restored intact; but their opposition was to be of a different kind—more assured, more orderly, and perhaps more provoking.

Among the nobility, by the time the settlement was well under way, a marked change in attitude toward the throne seemed to be taking place. The appearance was somewhat misleading: there was a shift of many nobles from liberal to rightist positions, but their shift was not wholly responsible for the evidence that their class was now becoming more prominent on the political right. The fact was that the nobility as a whole was becoming better organized and more alert to national issues. During the revolutionary period, the liberal nobles had been the most energetic and outspoken of their class; those of decidedly rightist views had been poorly organized or erratic in response; and the remainder, apparently unperturbed, had refrained from involvement in public controversy. Some of the nobility continued to hold to liberal positions; but, with the organization of the Council of Unified

Nobility (in May, 1906), the class began to take on political prominence, and the tone of its sentiments became that of the right. The Council stood squarely for "autocracy, orthodoxy, and nationalism," condemning Jews and other minorities, and calling for the dissolution of the Duma. It urged the abolition of the village communes and denounced agrarian reform at noble expense. The emphatic expression of these views, certainly not new ones among the nobility, had been prompted by the attacks upon the nobility during the course of the agrarian revolt; and now it had the support, not only of the hitherto politically apathetic nobles, but of the government as well.

University students, by and large, changed little after the receding of the flood that had carried them to such revolutionary heights. They retained their interest in political affairs and expressed it with as much determination, though not as much dramatic action, as they had during the year of their direct implication in the revolution. The majority of them still eschewed the moderate views that their elders might have approved in them, and they gave little evidence of faith in the peaceful perfectability of the country's institutions. The general political disposition among students in the institutions of higher learning was now, as before, about the same throughout the country. It was indicated in the November, 1906 election (conducted on party lines) of delegates to the student-operated Central University Organization of the University of Moscow: 40 percent of the elected delegates were SD's, 23 percent were SR's, and 28 percent were Cadets.

Attitudes Among National and Religious Minorities

Among the minorities, many of whose problems had been brought into prominence by the revolution, few were satisfied with the settlement. The groups most nearly satisfied were those whose manner of worship had been freed from legal disabilities by the ukase of April, 1905: the Old Believers, the sectists, and the Uniats. Others had received some concessions, usually of such a nature as to provide little change in status; but their desires had not been thereby gratified—only stimulated.

The minorities still suffered under legal disabilities. The Jews, for instance, long held in a debased legal position, had received nothing from the settlement except the right to vote in Duma elections. And the yearning for personal and political rights, as long as unrequited, was going to keep some areas in a state of unease. Even more powerful than the demand for removal of disabilities was the demand for national rights. The only important response the Tsar had made to any demand for such rights was his concession to the Finns. And even that concession proved to be more effective in stimulating agitation among other minorities than in reviving the erstwhile Finnish loyalty to the throne. So far, the government had made no change to indicate any real deviation from its stubborn adherence to traditional policies and beliefs that recognized only a unitary state in which the Russians of the Russian Orthodox faith were the "state nationality." That meant to the minorities a continuation in their old status: they were expected to remain officially relegated to a position of comparative inferiority and untrustworthiness. Their aspirations, enlivened and encouraged by the revolution, were not to be easily submerged again; yet prospects would have to improve if they were to lead to anything beyond frustration. The most hopeful outlook was that the nationality problem might win some support and favorable attention through the moderation of some of the minority leaders. Neither wanting nor expecting another revolution, these potentially effective leaders sought to realize their aims by peaceful means, by cooperation with the Russian liberals in the Duma.

POSITION OF LABOR

Labor remained in a restive state after the revolution. A large proportion of the country's workers were not political dissidents, and they were inclined to be satisfied with the considerable gains that had come their way. But the conditions prevailing during the settlement and in the years that followed, combined to make even these workers discontented.

Because organized labor had taken a prominent part in the strikes and uprisings of late 1905, the government, understandably but unwisely, treated the unions thereafter with calculated severity, circumscribing the right to strike and to engage in other organized activities with debilitating, and sometimes crippling, restrictions. At the same time, management was conducting a campaign to end disorder and irregularities in industrial life, using such weapons as the lockout. And, in a further encroachment on labor's freedom, the Black Hundreds identified unions with sedition and included union members in their list of "enemies."

Such circumstances served to keep alive the memories of the experiences of 1905. The workers, therefore, instead of becoming supporters of the established order, were the more easily convinced of the need to hold onto their ties with the socialists.

POSITION OF THE PEASANTS

It was to be expected that the durability of the settlement would be determined largely by the extent to which it sufficed as a means of solving the agrarian problem. The government gambled on the chance of achieving that end through the Stolypin Laws. These laws, though they did not provide what the peasants wanted, embodied what the regime expected to be effective in the long run. "Long run" was the operative term: the government needed time—time during which there was no recurrence of violent disorder in the countryside. The hope for this extended period of calm was favored by the dying down of revolutionary ardor among the peasantry as a result of the failure of the peasant revolt and the harshness of the attendant pacification. And it was supplemented by the termination of redemption payments and the arrangements by which imperial lands were to be made available to the peasants.

On the other hand, there were considerations that made the

government's gamble somewhat precarious. The peasantry had acquired some political understanding during the revolution; and, though the authorities had managed to stop radical political activity wherever it was recognized in rural areas, they could not eradicate what had been learned. Then there were the fearful memories of the punitive expeditions; while they helped to produce a state of quiescence, they also left a permanent blemish on the peasants' picture of the Little Father. And finally, there was the continuing pressure of rural overpopulation—an almost overwhelming challenge to all concerned with the agrarian problem.

The "Two Russias"

The Revolution of 1905 opened up the prospect of evolution toward a state of equilibrium between the "two Russias." Before that prospect could be realized, however, old animosities would have to fade away, and "government" and "society" would have to become adjusted to the art of government by consent. Like the reforms among the peasants, these changes could be brought about only during a prolonged period free from major crises. But the outlook for such a period was not promising: reactions on both sides indicated that the settlement would provide, at best, a breathing space. And that, only because, on the one hand, the disunity and inexperience among the elements of the revolutionary movement would impede it for the time being; and, on the other, the strength and resilience of the government would help it retain its position of superiority for the time being.

The opponents, during this period of truce, would be unlikely to move any appreciable distance from their embattled positions. The government, inexperienced in the conduct of representative processes and with little propensity for acquiring the necessary experience, would not feel the need for further change as long as it retained the strong support of the extreme right, made up of men who favored the throne but not the ideas embodied in the October Manifesto. Nor would the opposition, lacking experience in cooperation with the

government and including in its ranks many who h;
sire to learn, be likely to alter its position greatly.

There were many who had no intention of allowing
spirit of the revolution to die. The socialists, for instance,
steeped in hatred for the old regime and accustomed to underground operations, had no thought of trying to make the
settlement succeed. For them, the uprising had been an in-
complete initial operation, to be followed by a future and con-
cluding act of the "bourgeois-democratic" revolution. They
treated the victories that had been won simply as new opportunities to advance their preparations for the next revolution,
and studied the history of 1905 for lessons to guide them
in the future. Lenin drew such a lesson from the Moscow
uprising:

> December confirmed another of Marx's profound proposi-
> tions, which the opportunists have forgotten, namely, that
> insurrection is an art, and that the principal rule of this art
> is that an audacious and determined *offensive* must be
> waged. We have not sufficiently assimilated this truth. We
> have not sufficiently mastered this art, nor taught it to the
> masses, this rule of attacking, come what may. We must
> make up for this with all our energy. It is not enough to
> take sides on the question of political slogans; we must take
> sides also on the question of armed insurrection. Those who
> are opposed to it, those who do not prepare for it, must be
> ruthlessly dismissed from the ranks of the supporters of the
> revolution, sent packing to its enemies, to the traitors or
> cowards; for the day is approaching when the force of events
> and the conditions of the struggle will compel us to separate
> enemies from friends according to this principle. We must
> not preach passivity, nor advocate "waiting" until the troops
> "come over." No! We must proclaim from the housetops the
> need for a bold offensive and armed attack, the necessity
> at such times of exterminating the persons in command of
> the enemy, and of a most energetic fight for the wavering
> troops.[5]

The Cadets, the chief liberal party, no longer flirted with
revolution, but their program and their methods made coop-

[5] V. I. Lenin, *Selected Works* (Moscow, 1947), I, 447-48.

eration with the government difficult, if not impossible. They insisted on the need for ministerial responsibility, the four-tail suffrage, national rights for minorities, decentralization of government, and a fairly radical agrarian reform. Since the government rejected these conditions out of hand and the Cadets refused to recognize any need for compromise, there was no position for the party to assume in the legislature but that of a bitter oppositional element.

As for the moderate liberals, who recognized the October Manifesto as an acceptable basis for future cooperation between people and government, they had only a secondary part in postrevolutionary political life. Though they unified and organized their efforts in the Union of October 17 (or Octobrist Party), their influence was quite limited. They won only 38 of the 497 seats in the first Duma; and even when their representation was increased, after June, 1907, their gain was the result of change in the electoral system, not of any marked increase in their popular support. The negligible showing made by these proponents of moderate political views indicated the extent to which Russia was still divided between political extremes.

The Revolution of 1905 had provided the *means* for finding a middle ground between the two extremes, but it had not created an atmosphere favorable to those who sought to find it.

Appendix

Documents Related to the
Russian Revolution of 1905

PROGRAM OF THE RUSSIAN SOCIAL DEMOCRATIC LABOR PARTY[1]

[Russian Social Democracy is an integral part of international Social Democracy, the historical mission of which is to lead the movement for the overthrow of capitalism by social revolution. Contemporary capitalist society is characterized by a growing proletarianization of the masses and a concentration of wealth in the hands of the few; it is further characterized by overproduction of goods and consequent periods of industrial crisis and stagnation, as well as by increasing rivalry among bourgeois countries in the world market.

The contradictions of bourgeois society lead to an increasingly bitter class struggle between the proletariat and the exploiters. At the same time, technological progress results in the concentration of increasingly large numbers of workers in industrial enterprises, thus creating the base for proletarian revolution. The first stage of this social revolution will be the establishment of the dictatorship of the proletariat—that is, the seizure of power by the proletariat to the degree necessary

[1] Source: *Polnyi Sbornik Platform Vsekh Russkikh Politicheskikh Partii* (St. Petersburg, 1906), 7-14. This program was adopted in 1903. The first three paragraphs, bracketed, are the translator's digest of the introduction; the remainder is a direct translation.

for insuring the ability to crush any resistance by the exploiters.

The task of international Social Democracy is to organize itself into an independent party to lead the proletariat. It invites into its ranks all elements of the toiling and exploited masses, providing that they accept the point of view of the proletariat. International Social Democracy has a common goal—the overthrow of capitalism; but the short-range goals of Social Democratic parties in various countries differ because not all countries are at the same stage of socio-political development. Russia, for example, has survivals of the precapitalistic order—based on enserfment of the toiling masses by the landlords, the state, and the tsar—which permit the state and the propertied classes to exploit the peasantry in a barbaric fashion and to keep the people in ignorance of their rights.]

Therefore, the immediate political task of the Russian Social Democratic Labor Party is to overthrow tsarist autocracy and to replace it with a democratic republic, the constitution of which should guarantee:

1. popular sovereignty—that is, the concentration of supreme political power in a unicameral assembly consisting of representatives of the people;

2. universal, equal, and direct suffrage at all elections as well as in the legislative assembly and all local organs of self-government, for all citizens who have reached the age of twenty; the secret ballot at elections; the right of each voter to be elected to all representative institutions; biennial parliaments; payment of the people's representatives;

3. extensive local self-government, also regional self-government for all those localities characterized by a specific way of life or ethnic composition;

4. inviolability of person and home;

5. unlimited freedom of conscience, speech, press, strikes, assembly, and association;

6. freedom of movement and trade;

7. abolition of classes, with complete equality of all citizens irrespective of sex, religion, race, or nationality;

8. the right of the people to be educated in their mother

tongue, this to be made possible by the establishment of the necessary schools at the expense of the state and the organs of self-government; the right of each citizen to express himself at assemblies in his mother tongue; the establishment of equality of the mother tongue with that of the state in all local, social [e.g., zemstvo], and state institutions;

9. the right of self-determination for all nations within the state;

10. the right of each person to prosecute any official, under common law, before a jury;

11. popular election of judges;

12. replacement of the standing army by the arming of the entire people;

13. separation of church and state, and of school and church;

14. general education, free and compulsory, for all children of both sexes up to the age of sixteen; the provision of food, clothing, and school materials for poor children—at the state's expense.

As a basic condition for the democratization of our national economy, the Russian Social Democratic Labor Party demands: *the abolition of all* [existing] *governmental taxes and the establishment of a progressive tax on income and inheritance.*

In order to save the working class from physical and moral degeneration and to develop its capacity for the struggle for liberation, the party demands:

1. limitation of the working day to eight hours for all wage earners;

2. legal establishment of a weekly period of rest, continuing without interruption for no less than forty-two hours for wage earners of both sexes in all branches of the national economy;

3. complete abolition of overtime work;

4. prohibition of night work (from nine p.m. to six a.m.) in all branches of the economy except where it is absolutely necessary for technical reasons that are approved by labor organizations;

5. prohibition of the use of labor of school-age children (up

to sixteen years of age) by employers, and the limitation of the working day for youths (sixteen to eighteen years of age) to six hours;

6. prohibition of work by women in those trades that are harmful to the female organism, also provision of leave with full pay for women four weeks before and six weeks after they give birth;

7. establishment of nurseries for infants and young children in all factories, mills, and other enterprises where women work; release of nursing mothers at least once every three hours for a period of no less than half an hour;

8. governmental insurance of workers for old age and for full or partial loss of the ability to work, payable from a special fund created by a general tax on the capitalists;

9. prohibition of payment of wages in kind; [provision of] weekly payment of wages for all workers, regardless of existing wage agreements, and payment of wages during work time;

10. prohibition of deductions from wages, by employers, for whatever reason they may offer or by whatever name (fines, breakage, etc.) ;

11. appointment of a sufficient number of factory inspectors in all branches of the national economy, and extension of the jurisdiction of factory inspectors to all enterprises—including governmental—that use hired labor (the work of domestic servants also to come under this jurisdiction) ; appointment of women inspectors in those branches where the labor of women is used; participation of workers' elected representatives, paid by the government, in supervision of enforcement of factory laws, also in determination of rates for breakage and for completed work;

12. supervision by organs of local self-government, with the participation of representatives elected by the workers, of inspection of sanitary conditions in, and internal regulations of, living quarters provided by employers—for the purpose of protecting hired workers from interference of employers in their lives and activity as private persons and citizens;

13. establishment of properly organized sanitary inspection in all establishments using hired labor, with complete independence of all medical-sanitary organizations from the em-

ployers; free medical aid, at the expense of the employers, for workers, with maintenance during time of sickness;

14. establishment of criminal responsibility for employers who violate laws protecting workers;

15. establishment in all branches of the national economy of industrial courts, consisting of an equal number of representatives of workers and employers;

16. establishment, by all local organs of self-government, of labor exchanges for local and out-of-town workers in all branches of the economy, with participation in their administration of representatives elected by labor organizations.

In order to eliminate the remnants of the serf order, which places a heavy yoke directly on the peasantry, and in the interest of the free development of the class struggle in the village, the party demands above all:

1. abolition of redemption dues and quit-rents, also of all obligations still imposed on the peasantry as on a poll-tax-paying class;

2. return to the peasants of all sums taken from them in the form of redemption dues and quit-rents; for this purpose, the confiscation of all monastery and church property, the appanage and cabinet estates, and those belonging to members of the tsarist family; also a special tax on the land of noble landlords who had the benefit of redemption advances [paid them by the government]; the placing of the sums realized in this way in a special people's fund for the cultural and welfare needs of agricultural societies [village communes];

3. establishment of peasant committees: a) for the return to agricultural societies (by means of expropriation or, in those cases where land has passed from hand to hand, through recovery by the government at the expense of large landlords) of those lands cut off from peasant holdings at the time of the abolition of serfdom and which serve the landlords as means of enslaving the peasantry; b) for giving the peasants in the Caucasus, property rights over those lands they now use and which are temporarily encumbered etc.; c) for the elimination of the remnants of serf relationships that still exist in the Urals, the Altai, the Western region, and other parts of the state;

4. the right of courts to invalidate land rentals set at an excessive rate, and to declare invalid one-sided agreements.

Seeking to attain its immediate aims, the Russian Social Democratic Labor Party supports all oppositional and revolutionary movements directed against the social and political order that now exists in Russia, at the same time categorically opposing all those reformist projects that in any way call for the extension or strengthening of police-bureaucratic control over the toiling masses.

As far as it is concerned, the Russian Social Democratic Labor Party is firmly convinced that full, consistent, and enduring realization of the aforementioned political and social changes can be attained only through the overthrow of autocracy and the calling of a Constituent Assembly, freely elected by all the people.

DRAFT PROGRAM OF THE RUSSIAN SOCIALIST REVOLUTIONARY PARTY[1]

[Contemporary civilization, characterized by the increasing power of man over nature, provides the possibilities for social progress and the complete development of human individuality. This power is conditioned, however, by both the creative and the destructive aspects of contemporary capitalism. As a creative force, capitalism unites wage earners into compact social groups, thus paving the way for the socialist organization of society. As a destructive force, it promotes class division, exploitation, economic irrationality, and the degeneration of moral values while the chief goal of life becomes the acquisition of money and men are encouraged in selfish competition for privilege and for the means of existence.

The contradictions within capitalism result in a sharpening class struggle; the toilers grow more restive and seek to change

[1] Source: *Revolyutsionnaya Rossiya*, May 5, 1904. Because the Socialist Revolutionary Party did not adopt its formal program until after the Revolution of 1905, this draft program (the wording of which was followed closely in the formal one) is the more appropriate for study of SR views at the time of the revolution. The introductory paragraphs, bracketed, are given here in digest. The remainder is a direct translation.

society while the exploiting classes, seeking to perpetuate their rule, grow more reactionary and more destructive.

The liberation movement of the toilers is an international one: its conscious expression is international revolutionary socialism—the fighting vanguard of the toiling masses—which seeks to end the power of the exploiting classes, to eliminate private ownership of natural resources and the means of production, and to end the division of society into classes. Only after these achievements, will mankind be able to develop its spiritual and material powers freely and to realize its goal of liberty, equality, and fraternity for all.

The Russian Socialist Revolutionary Party is part of the international socialist movement and shares its common goal. At the same time, it takes into account the peculiar feature of Russian life—the survival of the old patriarchal-landlord-bureaucratic autocracy within the new capitalistic society. This feature serves to aggravate the condition of the lower classes. The bureaucracy, the circumstances under which the serfs were liberated, and the development of a kulak class lead to the weakening of rural productive forces: the landlords and the kulaks ally themselves with autocracy in order to maintain power over the toiling masses. The labor movement also is hampered by the autocratic regime: the wealthy classes, more reactionary in Russia than elsewhere, ally themselves with autocracy to keep the proletariat down. Furthermore, autocracy seeks to maintain its position by subjugating national minorities and fomenting national and religious hatred. Autocracy is the major obstacle to progress in Russia and the world; its overthrow is necessary for the welfare of Russia and the world.

Despite the existence of a liberal-democratic opposition, the chief responsibility for the struggle against autocracy rests on the proletariat, the toiling peasantry, and the revolutionary-socialist intelligentsia.

The ultimate aim of the Socialist Revolutionary Party is the establishment of socialism: this assumes complete victory on the part of the working class, organized in a socialist revolutionary party, and, in case of necessity, the establishment of a temporary, revolutionary dictatorship. Since the organized revolutionary party is still a minority and cannot immediately realize its ultimate goal, it will strive for immediate, limited changes, making sure that these changes do not divert the working class from its ultimate goal; in fact, the party will support only those changes that increase the solidarity of the working class and strengthen its capacity in the struggle for liberation.]

As long as the reorganization of Russia is directed by non-socialist forces, the Socialist Revolutionary Party, basing itself on the aforementioned considerations, will, through revolutionary struggle, defend, support, or compel the following reforms:

A. In the political and legal sphere:

Establishment of a democratic republic, with broad autonomy for urban and rural areas, as well as for village communes; the organization of relationships among the nationalities on a federative basis insofar as it is possible; recognition of their unconditional right to self-determination; direct, secret, equal, and universal suffrage for all citizens aged twenty or over, irrespective of sex, religion, or nationality; proportional representation; direct, popular legislation (referendum and initiative); the election of all officials, who shall be subject to recall at any time and shall be legally responsible to the courts; complete freedom of conscience, speech, press, assembly, labor strikes, and unions; full and universal civil equality; inviolability of person and home; complete separation of church and state, and the recognition of religion as the private concern of individuals; establishment of compulsory, equal, and secular education at governmental expense; equal rights for all languages; legal proceedings at no cost [to the individual]; abolition of the standing army and its replacement by a people's militia.

B. In the economic sphere:

1. The Socialist Revolutionary Party favors labor legislation to protect the spiritual and physical powers of the working class and to improve its ability to continue the struggle for liberation; all narrowly utilitarian, immediate, local, and craft interests of the various labor elements should be subordinated to these aims. With these in mind, the party will support: decrease of the working day as far as the limits of surplus labor

permit; establishment of a legal maximum working day in conformity with norms set by medical science (most immediately, an eight-hour day in nearly all branches of production, and a correspondingly shorter one in those branches that are particularly dangerous and harmful to health) ; establishment of minimum wages by agreement between the organs of self-government and the trade unions; government insurance of all kinds (accident, unemployment, sickness, old age, etc.) at the expense of the government and the employers and on the basis of self-administration by the insured; legal protection of labor (insuring normal conditions of work, sanitary conditions on the premises, prohibition of work by those under sixteen, limitation of work by minors, prohibition of work by women and children in certain branches of production and for certain periods, adequate uninterrupted weekly rest, etc.) in all branches of production and commerce, in accordance with the demands of medical science, to be supervised by factory inspectors elected by the workers; organization of trade unions among workers and progressively increasing participation of unions in the determination of internal regulations for industrial establishments.

2. With respect to agrarian policy and land relationships, the Socialist Revolutionary Party recognizes the communal and general working traditions and habits of the Russian peasantry, in particular the view that land is the common property of all toilers—a view that agrees with the interests of socialism and of the struggle against bourgeois property concepts. Accordingly, the party supports the socialization of all privately held land—that is, the transfer of these lands from private and individual ownership to common ownership on the basis of equal use under the control of democratically organized village communes and territorial associations of village communes. In the event that this major, basic aim of the minimum agrarian program cannot be achieved at once by revolutionary means, the S.R.P. will be guided in its future agrarian policy by the possibility of attaining its final goal through intermediate steps: e.g., the extension of the right of village communes and their territorial associations to expropriate privately owned lands; confiscation of monastic, appanage, cabi-

net lands, *et sim.*; the use of these lands, together with state lands, to provide village communes with adequate land as well as to provide land for settlement and resettlement; limitation of rents for the use of land to the net profit of the household (gross receipts less the cost of production and normal payment for labor) ; compensation for improvements when land is being transferred from the use of one person to that of another; a special tax to convert rents into a source of income for village communes and organs of self-government.

3. With respect to fiscal policy, the party will support the enactment of a progressive tax on income above a certain level and on inheritance; the elimination of indirect taxes (except those on luxury goods), protective duties, and all general taxes imposed on labor.

4. With respect to municipal and zemstvo economy, the party will support the development of all kinds of social services (free medical aid; zemstvo agronomic organizations; communalization of water supply, lighting, transport, *et sim.*) ; extension to cities and villages of the broadest right to tax and confiscate real estate, particularly for the purpose of meeting the housing needs of the working population; communal, zemstvo, and governmental policy directed toward the development of cooperatives organized on strictly democratic bases.

5. The Socialist Revolutionary Party may support proposals for the nationalization of certain branches of the national economy within the confines of bourgeois society if the political structure and social relationships are sufficiently democratized and if the provisions [for nationalization] adequately guarantee the working class against becoming more dependent on the ruling bureaucracy. In general, the Socialist Revolutionary Party cautions the working class against this "state socialism," which is, in part, a system of half-measures for lulling the working class and, in part, a special form of state capitalism that concentrates the various branches of production and commerce in the hands of the ruling bureaucracy for its own fiscal and political purposes.

The Socialist Revolutionary Party, beginning a direct revolutionary struggle against the autocracy, agitates for the convening of a Zemsky Sobor (Constituent Assembly) freely elected by all peoples, irrespective of sex, class, nationality, or religion; for the liquidation of the autocratic regime; and for the reconstruction of the entire existing order. It will fight for its reconstruction program in the Constituent Assembly and will strive to carry it out directly during the revolutionary period.

PROGRAM OF THE UNION OF LIBERATION[1]

The Union of Liberation believes that the current foreign and domestic crisis which Russia is experiencing has become so severe that the people, in cooperation with the several social groups opposed to the regime, should take into their own hands the matter of resolving this crisis. Therefore, the Union of Liberation demands that a constituent assembly, elected on the principle of universal, direct, equal, and secret suffrage, be convened to prepare a constitution for Russia. Moreover, the Union of Liberation considers the general and direct aim of its activity to be the basic reformation of the Russian political structure according to the principles of liberty and democracy.

To establish the principles of liberty and democracy proclaimed by the Union, we demand the incorporation of human and civil rights in the fundamental laws of the state. The basis of these laws should be the equality of all before the law, irrespective of sex, religion, or nationality. All class distinctions and all limitations on the personal and property rights of Poles, Jews, and other groups of the population should be abolished. In addition, the inviolability of person and home should be insured. No one should be searched, arrested, or punished except in accordance with the general judicial process, providing suspects and accused with all means of defense at every stage of judicial inquiry. All citizens should have complete freedom of movement: the passport system should be abolished. Furthermore, it is mandatory that freedom of con-

[1] Source: *Osvobozhdenie*, May 7/20, 1905. The program was adopted in March, 1905

science be guaranteed. All religious persecution must be ended; no one should be required to accept a given faith or be compelled to belong to a given religious denomination; on the contrary, each person has the right to choose any religious faith and to join any religious association as well as the right to renounce any religion and to leave the church of which he has been a member. It follows from this enunciation of the principle of the freedom of conscience that, on the one hand, religious organizations should be freed from governmental control and that, on the other, the state should be freed from subordination to the interests of the church. The registration of acts of civil condition [e.g., birth, death, marriage] of all persons should be the business of the civil authorities. Likewise, freedom of the printed word is indispensable. Freedom of the press means complete abolition of censorship; it means the right to publish and distribute all kinds of printed material, periodical and nonperiodical, in all languages, without authorization, guarantees, or other restrictive conditions. For crimes or offenses committed in print, the guilty are answerable only to the courts, which should have no jurisdiction over any opinion expressed in print unless a violation of the criminal law is thereby involved. Finally, we demand freedom of the spoken word, public assembly, and association. All should have the right to make speeches, give lectures, and organize indoor or outdoor meetings. They should have the right to form permanent and temporary associations for any purpose that is not in violation of the criminal law and, moreover, the right to do so without preliminary authorization by the police. Associations and public meetings should have the right to address themselves, in conformity with established procedure, to the legislature with declarations and recommendations.

However, no people's legislature can express the thoughts and will of the land unless the law of the land irrevocably establishes equality of all citizens before the law, inviolability of person and home, freedom of conscience, freedom of press, and freedom of assembly and association; moreover, human and civil rights will not be guaranteed unless the executive branch is subject to the supervision of the people's legislature.

To achieve this, it is necessary that legislative authority be vested in a popular representative body, organized on the basis of universal, direct, equal, and secret suffrage, without regard to sex. (Regarding suffrage for women, the minority, for practical reasons, held to a different position, in view of which the congress recognized that this point of the program was not binding on the minority.) The people's representatives should have the right of legislative initiative. Approval of the state budget should be the inalienable right of the people's legislature. No one should be required to pay taxes or duties when they are not included in the budget or when the budget has lost its legal force. The ministers, the highest authorities of the executive branch, should be responsible to the legislature, which should have not only the right to review the actions of ministers and their subordinates and demand explanations from them, but also the right, if it is aware of notorious conditions, to bring the ministers to trial.

We not only demand that the legislature be organized on the basis of political equality, but we also seek to have the reorganized political structure of Russia based on broad local and regional self-government. . . .[2] Liberated Russia should consciously and decisively end the subjugation of the borderlands as well as bureaucratic centralization. It follows therefore that, first of all, the Finnish constitution, guaranteed by special state statute, should be completely reinstituted and solemnly inscribed in the fundamental laws of the Russian Empire. Henceforth, all measures affecting both the Empire and the Grand Duchy of Finland should be decided by agreement between the legislative agents of the Empire and those of the Grand Duchy. In any case, the broadest regional self-government should be granted to those parts of the Empire that are specially characterized by their own way of life and historical conditions—e.g., Poland, Lithuania, Little Russia,

[2] This ellipsis mark occurs in the text printed in *Osvobozhdenie*. In later versions of the text, there is no such mark, and the succeeding sentence begins with the words "The aforementioned organization of the legislature implies our demand that Liberated Russia," then follows the wording of this earlier text.

and Transcaucasia. Without condition, we recognize the right of all nationalities within Russia to cultural self-determination. The right of all nationalities within the Russian State to the use of their native tongues in primary schools and in all local institutions should be unconditionally recognized in principle. At the same time effective, independent self-government, on the basis of universal suffrage, should be established throughout the country—in villages, townships, districts, provinces, and cities—having authority over all matters of local concern, including the police.

But the political reconstruction of Russia should not be limited to fundamental political reorganization. Political reform also is necessary in order to permit basic cultural, legal, and economic reorganization. The first place belongs to school reform: we must proceed immediately to the organization of universal, purely secular, primary education throughout the country, and then make it obligatory. Secondary and higher schools should be organically reformed. We demand autonomy for universities and other higher schools and the complete transfer of primary and secondary education to the jurisdiction of local self-government. The programs of the lower, secondary, and higher schools should be so coordinated as to guarantee students the opportunity of moving consecutively up through the levels of the schools. Instruction in all local and state schools should be tuition-free. With respect to the courts, we consider it necessary to reestablish the judicial code of 1864 in its entirety and to have this code completely implemented. The courts should be equal for all; the creation of exceptional courts, by whatever means, should not be permitted. Therefore, officials should be brought to trial and tried according to common rules. The institutions of land captain and of volost peasant court should be abolished. The public character of courts should be completely reestablished, and the closing of doors for political reasons should not be permitted. Judges should be independent and, therefore, irremovable and unpaid. Judgment by juries should be established as widely as possible, with exclusive jurisdiction in criminal cases. The press law should be reviewed, and those articles in it that are in contradiction to the principles of political liberty should be repealed. The death penalty, which is used almost exclusively for the purpose of supporting the existing regime, should be unconditionally abolished.

The entire economic life of Russia is basically distorted as a result of the political slavery in which she lives. Liberated Russia must break with the system of foreign aggrandizement and with the financial and economic policies that are ruining the country. Supervision by the representatives of the people over the expenditure of the national wealth should end the customary practice of squandering that wealth. With respect to taxation, we demand: 1) the abolition of redemption dues collected from peasant lands; 2) the development of direct taxation and the gradual diminution, and then abolition, of indirect taxes; 3) the reform of direct taxation on the basis of progressive income tax. In line with the change in fiscal policy, it is mandatory that special favors for certain enterprises and entrepreneurs be ended and that support of the development of the people's productive force be increased. Gradual diminution of tariffs should not only aid the rural population but also contribute to the healthy growth of industry itself.

Agrarian reform should go hand in hand with the termination of unreasonable protectionism. The political liberation of Russia should bring the simultaneous completion of the emancipation of the peasantry. (We use this term to denote economic status, not class, including under "peasantry" small landholders who work their own land.) To accomplish this, it is necessary to have: 1) a new allotment of state, appanage, and cabinet lands to peasants who have very little or no land and, where such lands are not available, to allot lands of private landlords, who shall be compensated for them; 2) the establishment of a state land fund for the widespread organization of peasant resettlement, with state aid, on these lands; 3) the enactment of land rental laws which will guarantee to the land users the fruits of their improvements, and the establishment of arbitration boards for the regulation of land rentals in the interests of the toilers and for the settlement of disputes and differences between renters and landlords; 4) the

extension of labor legislation to agricultural workers, with
modifications suitable to agricultural conditions.

With respect to the labor question, it is necessary first of all
to create conditions favorable to the development of independent collective action by the workers: the right to strike
and openly to form labor societies and unions.

Furthermore, we consider as mandatory: 1) reform of labor
legislation and inspection in order to remove their present bureaucratic character, and the extension of legislation and inspection to all phases of hired labor; 2) legislative regulation
of the working day by the introduction of the eight-hour day
immediately where it is possible, and gradually elsewhere; 3)
abolition of overtime, except where it is technically necessary;
4) development of protection for working women and children; 5) legislative regulation of all wage relationships that
can be thus standardized; 6) establishment of arbitration
boards, consisting of an equal number of representatives of
labor and capital, to hear all questions concerning wage agreements that are not subject to government standardization; 7)
guaranteed continuous compensation to workers by employers
for loss of ability to work caused by accident or occupational
disease; 8) introduction of governmental insurance covering
death, old age, sickness, and inability to work; workers and
employers to participate in administration of the insurance
boards on the basis of equality.

This program represents the consensus of all groups in the
Union of Liberation; obviously it cannot include all individual views and opinions expressed in the course of preparing it. Furthermore, since the decisions of the Union were
dictated by political conditions current at the time of their
discussion, these decisions may be considered binding only as
long as political conditions remain unchanged. The Union of
Liberation considers admission of temporary and circumstantial elements into its program as an unavoidable and necessary
condition for any political program that is guided by practical
politics. Only the further course of political life can demonstrate what changes and additions to this program seem necessary; and the very necessity of leaving several matters for

decision temporarily open shows that, in those matters, the various members and groups of the Union have the freedom to choose those actions and decisions that their consciences and social convictions dictate.

The Eleven Theses of the First Zemstvo Congress, November, 1904[1]

The private Zemstvo [Congress] which met November 6-8 in St. Petersburg, having considered the general conditions necessary for the proper development of our public and government life, has reached the following conclusions:

1. The abnormal conditions of the present system of governmental administration, which began to manifest itself with marked vigor in the 1880's, has led to a complete separation of the government and the public and to the disappearance of that mutual confidence that is indispensable for political life.

2. The relationship of the government to the public has been governed by fear of the development of popular initiative and by the constant desire to prevent the public from participating in the operation of the state. Consequently, the government has sought to centralize power over all branches of local government and to place all phases of public life under its control. The government has interpreted its relationship to the public as meaning only that the activities of public institutions must be made to conform to its views.

3. By separating the central authority from the population, the bureaucratic system makes possible widespread administrative abuse and the exercise of personal interpretation. Such a system not only deprives the public of the constantly needed assurance of protection for its lawful rights but also undermines its faith in the government.

4. The proper development of governmental and public life is possible only through active and close contact and unity between the government and society.

[1] Source: D. Shipov, *Vospominaniya i Dumy o Perezhitom* (Moscow, 1918), pp. 261-65.

5. To avoid the possibility of administrative abuse, it is necessary to establish and maintain the principle of inviolability of person and home. No one should be subjected to search or restricted in his rights except by order of a court, independent in its authority. To achieve the above ends, it is necessary to provide also for the practical implementation of the principle of administrative legality by establishing procedures for civil and criminal prosecution of officials who violate the law.

6. In order to make possible the complete development of the spiritual resources of the people, the full exposition of public needs, and the free expression of public opinion, the following are indispensable: freedom of conscience and religion, freedom of speech and press, and freedom of assembly and association.

7. All citizens of the Russian Empire should have equal personal (civil and political) rights.

8. The independence of public activity is the chief requirement for the proper and successful development of the political and economic life of the country. Inasmuch as a significant majority of the Russian population belongs to the peasant class, it is necessary, first of all, for that class to develop initiative and energy, which can be obtained only by a radical change in the present inequitable and degraded position of the peasantry. To achieve these ends, it is necessary:

    a. to make the personal rights of the peasants equal to those of other classes,

    b. to free the rural population from administrative tutelage in all phases of its private and public life, and

    c. to provide it with the protection of properly constituted courts.

9. Zemstvo and municipal institutions, in which local life is chiefly concentrated, ought to be so constituted that they can successfully carry out the responsibilities that properly and broadly belong to established organs of self-government. For this the following are essential:

    a. that zemstvo representation not be based on class principles and that, insofar as it is possible, all elements of the local population be admitted to participation in zemstvo and municipal self-government;

b. that the population be brought into more intimate contact with zemstvo institutions through the establishment of small [i.e., having a small territorial base] zemstvo units, organized so as to guarantee their real independence;

c. that the whole sphere of local welfare and needs be brought under the jurisdiction of zemstvo and municipal institutions;

d. that these institutions be granted stability and independence, without which the proper realization of their potential is not possible; and that proper cooperation between governmental and public institutions be established and local self-government be extended to all parts of Russia.

10. *Majority opinion*

For the establishment of constant and close contact and unity between government and society on the basis of the abovementioned principles, however, and in order to guarantee the proper development of governmental and public life, it is absolutely necessary that representatives of the people, in an independent elective institution, take their proper part in the exercise of legislative power, the preparation of a budget of income and expenditures, and the checking of the legality of administrative actions.

Minority opinion

For the establishment of constant and close contact and unity between government and society on the basis of the abovementioned principles, however, and in order to guarantee the proper development of governmental and public life, it is absolutely necessary that representatives of the people, in an indepedent elective institution, take their proper part in the making of laws.

11. Keeping in mind the seriousness and difficulty in domestic affairs now being faced by Russia, the private conference expresses the hope that her sovereign authority will summon freely elected representatives of the people so that, with their help, it can lead our people along a new path of political growth marked by the establishment of the rule of law and by cooperation between the government and the people.

IMPERIAL UKASE TO THE GOVERNING SENATE, DECEMBER 12, 1904, CONCERNING PLANS FOR THE IMPROVEMENT OF THE SOCIAL ORDER[1]

In accordance with the hallowed precepts of Our Crowned Forefathers, and increasingly mindful of the sacredness of the Power entrusted to Us by God, We, in adherence to the principles of the Fundamental Laws of the Empire, regard the task of administration to be unremitting concern for the needs of the country, distinguishing between those matters that are truly germane to the interests of the Russian people and the frequently mistaken tendencies that arise from temporary circumstances. When, however, the need for a given change seems advisable, We consider it necessary to proceed with the execution of that change, even though it leads to substantive innovations in the law. We have no doubt that the results of this process will be received with sympathy by those of good will among Our subjects who honestly recognize that there is benefit for the Fatherland both in supporting the political order and in continuing to satisfy the needs of the people.

Our chief concern is the improvement of the way of life for Our numerous peasant class. We point out that the matter is already under consideration in accordance with Our directions: in addition to the exhaustive review conducted in the several localities concerning the proposals of the Ministry of Interior, a special conference of the most experienced persons of the central administration is now meeting to study the chief problems of peasant life on the basis of the evidence presented before the local investigating committees concerning the needs of the agricultural industry. We herewith order that these efforts produce, for inclusion in the general laws of the Empire, legislation concerning the peasantry that will make it easier for members of this class to enjoy the status of "agricultural inhabitants with full rights," as stipulated for them by the Tsar-Liberator.

In addition, after reviewing the general area of further pop-

[1] Source: *Pravitelstvennyi Vestnik,* December 14, 1904.

ular needs, We recognize the following as urgent for maintaining the proper course of Our Fatherland:

1. to take active steps for preserving the full power of the law—the most important support of the Throne in an autocratic State—in order that all authorities and all localities subject to Us regard the strict and uniform execution of the law as their paramount duty: failure to carry out such duty must entail direct legal responsibility for all arbitrary acts; and, in such cases, the attainment of justice for those persons who have suffered from such acts must be facilitated;

2. to permit zemstvo and municipal institutions the broadest possible participation in the administration of all phases of local welfare, granting them (within the limits of the law) the necessary independence and, on the basis of uniform regulations, admitting to participation in them, representatives of all groups of the population interested in local affairs; for the purpose of speedy satisfaction of the aforementioned needs, to organize, in addition to existing provincial and district zemstvos, and in close relationship with them, social institutions to administer matters relating to local welfare in smaller areas;

3. for the purpose of assuring equality before the law for persons of all conditions, to effect the necessary uniformity in the organization of the judicial branch of the Empire and to provide the independence necessary for judicial institutions at all levels;

4. for the further development of measures already taken by Us in order to guarantee the welfare of workers in factories, plants, and trades, to attend to the establishment of government insurance for them;

5. to review exceptional laws issued at a time of persistent criminal activity by the enemies of the established order, the application of which has been attended by a marked expansion of the discretionary power of administrative authorities; and, in this connection, to attend to the limitation, as much as possible, of the number of localities to which these laws are applied, as well as to provisions whereby limitations on the rights of private persons are restricted to cases in which state security is actually being threatened;

6. in order to strengthen the heartfelt wish We expressed in the manifesto of February 26, 1903, that religious toleration be preserved as ordained in the Fundamental Laws of the Empire, to review the legislation concerning the rights of schismatics [Old Believers] and of persons belonging to unorthodox and to heterodox faiths; and, independently of this, to take immediate administrative action for the issuance of measures necessary to free religious life from all limitations not prescribed by law;

7. to review the existing regulations that limit the rights of *inorodtsy*[2] (persons of foreign origin) and of *urozhentsy*[3] (natives) in various parts of the Empire, and to retain only those regulations that serve the vital interests of the State and definitely benefit the Russian People; and

8. to remove unnecessary limitations from the press regulations and define clearly the legal limits within which the press may operate, thus giving the responsible press, acting in accordance with advances in enlightenment, the opportunity of fulfilling its lofty purpose as the true spokesman for the wise and beneficial aspirations of Russia.

Anticipating, in view of the above, a number of important internal changes in the near future—some of them already receiving preliminary study on the basis of instructions previously given by Us—We recognize the necessity of establishing the order of consideration according to the variety and importance of these changes, in order to allow their most rapid and complete realization. Among Our State institutions, the Committee of Ministers has the task of handling the close coordination of the several branches of the administration; therefore, We order the Committee of Ministers to begin a review of the problem of how best to realize Our intentions in connection with all the abovementioned subjects and to present Us, as soon as possible, their conclusions concerning the future course, within the established order, of necessary measures.

The Committee shall report to Us concerning the progress

[2] A legal category that included Jews and certain nomadic and mountain peoples in Transcaucasia, Siberia, and Central Asia.

[3] A legal category that included various settled native peoples in such areas as Siberia and Central Asia.

of subsequent work on these matters. The Governing Senate
shall issue the instructions necessary for the execution of this
[ukase].

PETITION OF WORKERS AND RESIDENTS OF SAINT PETERSBURG FOR SUBMISSION TO NICHOLAS II ON JANUARY 9, 1905[1]

We, workers and residents of the city of St. Petersburg, of
various ranks and stations, our wives, children, and helpless
old parents, have come to Thee, Sire, to seek justice and protection. We have become beggars; we are oppressed and bur-
dened by labor beyond our strength; we are humiliated; we
are regarded, not as human beings, but as slaves who must
endure their bitter fate in silence. We have endured it, and
we are being pushed further and further into the depths of
poverty, injustice, and ignorance; we are being so stifled by
despotism and arbitrary rule that we cannot breathe. Sire, we
have no more strength! Our endurance is at an end. We have
reached that awful moment when death is preferable to the
continuation of intolerable suffering.

Therefore we stopped work and told our employers that we
would not resume work until they complied with our demands. We asked for little. We desire only that which is indispensable to life, without which there is nothing but slavish
labor and endless agony. Our first request was that our employers discuss our needs with us, but this they refused to do;
they denied that we have a right to speak about our needs, on
the grounds that the law does not recognize such a right. They
also treated as illegal our other requests: to reduce the working day to eight hours, to establish wage rates in consultation
with us and with our consent, to investigate our grievances
against lower administrative personnel of the factories, to increase the daily wages for unskilled working men and women
to one ruble, to abolish overtime, to administer medical aid

[1] Source: Akademiya Nauk, SSSR, Institut Istorii, *Nachalo Pervoi
Russkoi Revolyutsii* (Moscow, 1955), pp. 28-31.

carefully and politely, to construct workshops in which it would be possible to work without danger of death from miserable drafts, rain, and snow.

All this seemed illegal to our employers; each of our requests was treated as if it were a crime, and our desire to improve our situation was considered an act of insolence and insult.

Sire, there are many thousands of us here; we have the appearance of human beings but, in fact, neither we nor the rest of the Russian people enjoy a single human right—not even the right to speak, think, assemble, discuss our needs, or take steps to improve our situation.

We have been enslaved, with the help and cooperation of Thy officials. Any one of us who dares to speak up in defense of the interests of the working class and the people is jailed or exiled: it is as if it were a crime to have a good heart or a sympathetic soul. Even to feel for one who is beaten, deprived of his rights, or tortured is a grave crime. The entire people—workers and peasants—are at the mercy of the bureaucratic administration, which consists of men who rob the government and the people, men who not only ignore, but also scorn, the interests of the people. Government by bureaucracy has devastated the country, has involved it in a horrible war, and is leading it further and further into ruin. We, the workers and the people, have no voice at all in determining how the huge sums extracted from us are spent; we are denied the means of participating in the levying of taxes or deciding how they are to be spent. The people have no opportunity of expressing their desires and demands. The workers are denied the opportunity to form unions for the defense of their interests.

Sire! Is this in accordance with God's laws, by the grace of which Thou reignest? And is it not possible for us to live under such laws? Is it better to die—for all of us, the toiling people of all Russia, to die, allowing the capitalists (the exploiters of the working class) and the bureaucrats (who rob the government and plunder the Russian people) to live and enjoy themselves? This is the choice we face, Sire, and this is why we have come to the walls of Thy palace. Here we seek our last chance of salvation. Do not deny Thy people help;

lead them out of the depths of injustice, poverty, and ignorance; give them the chance to direct their own fate and rid
themselves of the unbearable bureaucratic yoke. Tear down
the wall between Thyself and Thy people and let them rule
together with Thee. Hast Thou not been placed on the throne
for the happiness of the people, and has not this happiness
been denied to us by the bureaucrats, leaving us only un-
happiness and humiliation? Examine our requests dispassion-
ately and carefully: they are not evil in design, but are meant
to help both us and Thee. We do not speak from insolence,
but from a realization of the need to find a way out of the
unbearable situation in which we find ourselves. Russia is too
great, its needs too varied and profuse, to be governed by bureaucrats alone. Popular representation is essential. The people must help themselves and govern themselves. It is only
they who know their true needs. Do not refuse their help;
accept it; and immediately order the summoning of representatives of the Russian land from all classes and all strata, including representatives of the workers. Capitalists, workers,
bureaucrats, priests, doctors, and teachers—let them all, who-
ever they may be, choose their own representatives. Let all
have a free and equal vote; and toward this end, order the
election of a constituent assembly on the basis of universal,
secret, and equal suffrage.

This is our chief request; in it and on it all else is based;
this is the chief and only means of healing our painful
wounds; without it, our wounds will fester and bring us to our
death.

But one measure alone cannot heal our wounds. Additional
ones are indispensable. Directly and frankly as to a father,
Sire, we tell Thee, in the name of all of the laboring class of
Russia, what they are.

Indispensable are:

I. measures to eliminate the ignorance and disabilities of the
Russian people

    1) the immediate release and return of all those who
       have suffered for their political and religious convic-
       tions, for strikes,˙ and for peasant disorders

    2) the immediate declaration of freedom and inviolabil-

ity of person, freedom of speech and the press, freedom of assembly, and freedom of conscience with
respect to religion

3) universal and compulsory popular [primary] education
at the expense of the state

4) responsibility of the ministers to the people and the
guarantee of legality in administration

5) equality of all, without exception, before the law

6) separation of church and state

II. measures to eliminate the poverty of the people

1) abolition of indirect taxes and their replacement by
direct, progressive income taxes

2) abolition of redemption dues, [establishment of] cheap
credit, and gradual transfer of land to the people

3) placement of orders for the Navy in Russia, not
abroad

4) termination of the war in accord with popular demand

III. measures to eliminate the tyranny of capital over labor

1) abolition of the system of factory inspectors

2) establishment in the factories and mills of permanent
committees elected by the workers, which, together
with the administration, will examine all claims of individual workers; no worker to be discharged except
by decision of this committee

3) freedom to establish consumers' and producers' [coop-
eratives] and trade unions—as of now

4) the eight-hour working day and regulation of overtime

5) freedom of labor to struggle against capital—as of now

6) wage regulation—as of now

7) participation of working class representatives in the
preparation of a bill for government insurance of
workers—as of now.

These, Sire, are our chief needs, concerning which we have
come to Thee. The liberation of our motherland from slavery
and poverty is possible only through the satisfaction of these
needs; only thus can she flourish; only thus will it be possible
for workers to organize in protection of their interests against

high-handed exploitation by the capitalists and the plundering
and oppressive governmental bureaucrats. Order these measures and take Thine oath to carry them out. Thou wilt thus
make Russia both happy and famous, and Thy name will be
engraved in our hearts and in those of our posterity forever.
And if Thou dost not so order and dost not respond to our
pleas, we will die here in this square before Thy palace. We
have nowhere else to go and no purpose in going. We have
only two roads: one leading to freedom and happiness, the
other to the grave. . . . Let our lives be a sacrifice for suffering
Russia. We offer this sacrifice, not grudgingly, but gladly.

> George Gapon, priest
> Ivan Vasimov, worker

Most Humble Report of State Secretary Count Witte, October, 1905[1]

Your Imperial Majesty has been kind enough to give me
Your Imperial Majesty's directives with respect to the policy
that the government should follow in studying the present
situation in Russia and, in this connection, to instruct me to
present a most humble report.[2]

Therefore, I have the honor of most humbly presenting the
following:

The unrest that has seized the various classes of the Russian
people cannot be regarded as the product of the partial imperfections of the political or social order or as the product of the
activities of organized extremist parties. The roots of unrest
are deeper: they are to be found in the disparity between the
high-minded aspirations of Russian intellectual society and
the framework within which it exists. Russia has outgrown her
political framework and is striving for a legal order based on
civil liberty.

Therefore, the framework of Russian political life must be

---

[1] Source: *Pravitelstvennyi Vestnik*, October 18, 1905.

[2] It was customary to characterize all reports to the Tsar as
vsepoddaneishii, "most humble."

changed to make it conform to the ideas that animate the moderate majority of society. The first task of the government is to fulfill the wish for the establishment of a legal order based on personal inviolability and the freedom of press, conscience, assembly, and association; and to do it immediately, without waiting for the legislative sanction of the State Duma. Normal legislative procedure should be employed in strengthening these foundations of the political life of society, as well as in the work of making all Your Imperial Majesty's subjects equal before the law, irrespective of religion or nationality. It goes without saying that the civil liberties granted to the people must be limited by law so as to safeguard the rights of all persons and the peace and security of the state.

Another task facing the government is that of establishing those institutions and legislative principles that are in accord with the political ideals of the majority of Russian society, at the same time providing a positive guarantee that the blessings of civil liberty so granted shall not be alienated: this means the establishment of a legal order. In keeping with the aims of reestablishing peace and security in the body politic, the economic policy of the government should be directed toward the good of the masses and, at the same time, safeguarding those property and civil rights that are recognized in all civilized countries.

The aforementioned bases of governmental policy will require much legislative work and consistent administrative reorganization. It is evident that some time must elapse between the statement of a principle—even though sincerely stated— and its transformation into law, and that even more time must elapse before the new legislative standards become part of the habits of society and of the practices of governmental officials. The principles of a legal order can be activated only to the extent that the population becomes accustomed to them and acquires civic responsibility. And no government can overnight prepare a country of 135 million people, of varying origins, living under a most complex administration, and educated in various ways, to recognize and adopt the principles of a legal order. The government must not only proclaim the idea of civil liberty; it must also work diligently and show

unremitting firmness and consistency if it is to establish order
in the land.

To accomplish its aims, the government must be uniform in
its composition and unified in the pursuit of its objectives; a
ministry consisting, insofar as possible, of persons having similar political convictions, should do its utmost to insure that
the ideas animating its work are the ideas of all other government officials also, from the lowest to the highest. The government should, by its practices, promote the realization of
civil liberty. The situation demands that the government use
methods that will demonstrate its candor and sincerity; it
should scrupulously refrain from interfering in the elections
to the State Duma; and it should, among other things, sincerely seek to implement the measures outlined in the ukase
of December 12.

With respect to the future State Duma, the government
must be careful to support that body's prestige, to show confidence in its work, and to give it proper status. The government should not oppose the Duma's decisions as long as they
are not basically alien to Russia's millenial grandeur—an incredible likelihood. The government should be guided by the
thoughts expressed by Your Imperial Majesty in the Manifesto
concerning the formation of the State Duma: that the regulations regarding that body can be altered in the future if
imperfections appear or if the times pose new demands. In
clarifying and settling these matters, the government should
definitely be guided by the ideas of the majority of society and
not by reverberations of demands, however sharply put, made
by isolated groups—demands that cannot be met because they
are constantly changing. But it is imperative to satisfy the
wishes of the broad groups of society by means of formal enactment of civil rights and the establishment of a legal order.

It is most important to reform the State Council so as to
make possible the prominent participation in it of an elected
element; only in this way will it be possible to establish normal relations between this institution and the State Duma.

Without listing specific measures, which should be left to
the future as circumstances change, I suggest that the state be
guided at all levels by the following principles:

1. frankness and sincerity in extending the benefits of civil liberty to all walks of life and in enacting guarantees of such liberty;

2. the aim of eliminating exceptional legislation;

3. coordination of the activities of all organs of government;

4. elimination of repressive measures against activities that clearly do not threaten society and the state; and

5. counter-measures, based on law and in harmony with the ideas of the moderate majority of society, against activities that do clearly threaten society and the state.

It is evident that the abovementioned tasks can be carried out only through extensive and active cooperation with society and under conditions of calm that will permit concentration on fruitful work. We must have faith in the political sense of Russian society and believe that it does not want anarchy, with its attendant threat of the horrors of strife and political disintegration.

PROGRAM OF THE CONSTITUTIONAL DEMOCRATIC PARTY[1]

I. Fundamental Civil Rights

1. All Russian citizens, irrespective of sex, religion, or nationality, are to be equal before the law. All class distinctions and all limitations on the personal and property rights of Poles, Jews, and all other groups of the population must be abolished, without exception.

2. Freedom of conscience and religion is to be guaranteed to every citizen. No persecution for professing any religious faith or conviction, change in religion, or withdrawal from a religion shall be permitted. The practice of religious beliefs and their dissemination shall be unrestricted as long as the activities connected with them are not offenses against existing

---

[1] Source: *Polnyi Sbornik Platform Vsekh Russkikh Politicheskikh Partii* (St. Petersburg, 1906), pp. 54-63. The program was adopted in October, 1905.

criminal law. The Orthodox and other faiths should be freed
from government control.

3. Every person is to be free to express his thoughts orally
and in writing, as well as to publish and disseminate them
through the press or by other means. Censorship in any guise,
general as well as special, shall be abolished and may not be
reestablished. For crimes and offenses committed in speech or
in print, the guilty shall answer only to a court.

4. All Russian citizens shall have the right to organize public meetings, indoors as well as outdoors, for the discussion of
any subject.

5. All Russian citizens shall have the right to organize associations and societies without the necessity of asking for permission.

6. Individual citizens, as well as any group, association, etc.,
shall have the right of petition.

7. The person and home of everyone must be inviolable.
Entry into a private dwelling, search, seizure within it, and
the opening of private correspondence are permissible only in
cases stipulated by law and only on court order. Any person
arrested in a city or other place where there is a judicial authority must be freed or turned over to judicial authority
within twenty-four hours; and in other parts of the empire, no
later than seventy-two hours from the time of arrest. Any arrest made without adequate reason or continuing beyond the
legal limit shall entitle the aggrieved party to compensation
by the government for losses sustained thereby.

8. No one may be prosecuted or punished except on the
basis of law—by judicial authority and before a legally constituted court. No extraordinary courts are to be permitted.

9. Every citizen shall have freedom of movement and of
travel abroad. The passport system shall be abolished.

10. All the abovementioned rights must be included in the
fundamental laws of the Russian Empire and guaranteed by
judicial protection.

———————

11. The fundamental laws of the Russian Empire should
guarantee to all members of national minorities in the empire
full equality with all other citizens in civil and political rights,

also the right of free cultural self-determination—i.e., complete freedom to use different languages and dialects in public life; and freedom to establish and maintain schools and all kinds of assemblies, associations, and institutions for the purpose of preserving and developing their language, literature, culture, et sim.

12. The Russian language should be the language of the central institutions and of the army and the navy. The use of local languages along with the general state language in governmental and social establishments, in state-supported schools, and in organs of self-government should be regulated by general and local laws and, within their limits, by the establishments themselves. The population of each locality should be guaranteed primary education, and other education insofar as possible, in its native tongue.

II. The Political Structure

13. The constitutional structure of the Russian state shall be defined by the fundamental laws.

14. The representatives of the people shall be elected by universal, equal, direct, and secret suffrage, without regard to religion, nationality, or sex. (Note: with respect to the immediate extension of suffrage to women, the minority held to a different position, as a consequence of which the congress recognized that the party decision on this question was not binding on the minority.)

The party permits within its ranks differences of opinion as to whether or not the legislature should be unicameral or bicameral, the second chamber consisting of representatives of the organs of local self-government (which shall be extended to all Russia and reorganized on the basis of universal suffrage).

15. The legislature shall participate in exercising legislative authority, in determining the state budget, and in checking the legality of all activities of higher and lower administration.

16. No regulation, decree, ukase, directive, or document of any kind not based on legislative decision shall have legal force, regardless of what it is called or by whom it is issued.

17. The state budget, which should include all receipts and expenditures of the state, shall be confirmed by the legislature for a period not exceeding a year. No taxes, tariffs, or duties for use by the government, nor any government loans, shall be instituted except by legislative process.

18. Members of the legislature shall have the right of legislative initiative.

19. Ministers are to be responsible to the legislature, the members of which shall have the right of inquiry and interpellation.

III. Local Self-government and Autonomy

20. Local self-government should be extended throughout the Russian state.

21. The population should have more direct representation in organs of local self-government, realized through the creation of smaller, self-administering units, which should be based on universal, equal, direct, and secret suffrage, irrespective of sex, religion, and nationality; the assemblies of the higher self-governing associations may be formed by election from the lower ones. Provincial zemstvos should have the right to form temporary or permanent associations among themselves.

22. The jurisdiction of local self-government should extend over the entire area of local administration (including the security and ordinary police), with the exception of those matters which, in the circumstances of contemporary political life, should be in the hands of the central authority; part of the revenues now in the state budget should be set aside for use by the organs of local self-government.

23. The legality of the actions of local representatives of the central authority should be subject to supervision by the organs of local self-government; the final decision with respect to disagreements and ambiguities arising in this connection shall be made by the courts.

24. After the right of civil liberty and a regular system of representation, with constitutional rights, have been established for the whole Russian state, legal means based on general legislation should then be provided for the establishment

of local autonomy and regional representative assemblies, having the right to participate in legislating on specific matters of concern to the local population.

25. Immediately after the establishment of democratic, representative government, with constitutional rights, for the whole empire, an autonomous regime shall be granted to the Kingdom of Poland, with a Sejm elected on the same basis as the central legislature—this not to affect the maintenance of state unity and participation in the central legislature on the same basis as other parts of the empire. The borders between the Kingdom of Poland and neighboring provinces may be rectified in conformity with ethnic composition and the wishes of the local population, the Kingdom of Poland being obliged to enforce the general guarantees of civil liberty and the right of nationalities to cultural self-determination and to guarantee the rights of minorities.

26. *Finland.* The Finnish constitution, guaranteed by special state statute, should be completely reinstituted. All further measures affecting both the empire and the Grand Duchy of Finland should be decided by agreement between the legislative agents of the empire and those of the Grand Duchy.

IV. The Courts

27. All deviations from the principles (irremovability, independence, and equality before the court) of the Judicial Code of November 20, 1864, which established separation of the judicial authority from the administrative, that have been introduced since that time—and even those permitted at the time of the framing of the Code—are to be rescinded. To this end, it is necessary that: a) there be no qualification of the rule that no one may be punished except by sentence of the proper court; b) all interference by the Ministry of Justice in the appointment of court officials, in the transfer of judges, and especially in court records, shall be ended; c) judges shall not be compensated; d) responsibility of officials shall be determined by general rules; e) the jurisdiction of juries shall be determined by the severity of the punishment, fixed by law without respect to the kind of case involved (excepting cases

of political crimes and crimes against the press laws, which shall always be under the jurisdiction of juries) . Courts based on class representation are to be abolished. The jurisdiction of elected justices of the peace shall include the volost. The institutions of land captain and volost court are to be abolished. Property qualifications for service as justices of the peace and as jurors are to be abolished; the principle of unification of the court of cassation is to be reestablished. The bar is to be organized according to the principle of genuine self-administration.

29. The most immediate tasks are: the complete review of the Criminal Code, the repeal of decrees that contradict the principle of political liberty, and the revision of the draft of the Civil Code.

V. Financial and Economic Policy

30. Review of governmental expenditures, with the aim of eliminating those that are unproductive because of their purpose or their size and of increasing expenditures necessary to meet the real needs of the people.

31. Abolition of redemption dues.

32. Development of direct taxation in place of indirect; general diminution of indirect taxation and the gradual abolition of indirect taxes on necessities.

33. Reform of direct taxes on the basis of progressive taxation on income and estates; establishment of a progressive tax on inheritance.

34. In consideration of the situation in various branches of production, the lowering of tariffs so as to reduce the cost of necessities and raise the technological level of industry and agriculture.

35. Employment of the resources of savings banks for the development of small-scale credit.

VI. Agrarian Legislation

36. Increase in the amount of land held by those who cultivate the land themselves; the distribution of state, appanage, cabinet, and monastic lands to peasants with little or no land,

as well as to various kinds of small landholders; and, insofar as is necessary for the purpose, the distribution of land alienated from private landlords and paid for by the government at equitable, not market, prices.

37. The placing of alienated land in a governmental reserve, the basis of the transfer of land from this reserve to those who need it to be determined by the practices of land ownership and land use in various parts of Russia.

38. Broad organization, with government help, for settlement, resettlement, and the organization of peasant economic life. Reorganization of land surveying, completion of demarcation of boundaries, and other measures for improving the welfare of the rural population and rural economy.

39. Legal regulation of land rental relationships by guaranteeing the right of renewal of rentals, by assuring the renter who transfers the land before completion of his lease that he will be compensated for expenditures on improvement, and by the establishment of arbitration boards for the regulation of land rentals and the settlement of disputes and differences between renters and landlords. Legislation to permit courts to lower abnormally high land rentals and to invalidate agricultural agreements of a one-sided character.

40. Repeal of existing rules governing payment of agricultural laborers, and extension to them of labor legislation conforming to the technological peculiarities of agriculture. Establishment of agricultural inspection to check the correct observance of laws protecting labor in this employment, and provision for the criminal liability of landlords who violate the rules for protection of labor.

VII. Labor Legislation

41. Freedom of trade unions and workers assemblies.

42. The right to strike. Accountability for infringements of law committed during strikes or in connection with them to be determined according to general principles—in no case to be increased.

43. Extension of labor legislation and independent labor in-

spection to all phases of wage labor; participation by elected representatives of labor in supervision of the execution of laws protecting the toilers' interests.

44. Introduction of the eight-hour day by legislation. Immediate establishment of this norm wherever possible, and gradual establishment elsewhere. Prohibition of night work and overtime except where necessary for technical or social reasons.

45. Development of protection for working women and children, and the enactment of special measures to protect men working in unhealthful trades.

46. Establishment of arbitration boards, consisting of an equal number of representatives of labor and capital, to standardize all wage relationships not regulated by labor legislation and to settle disputes and differences arising between workers and employers.

47. Compulsory governmental insurance covering sickness (for a specified period), accidents, and occupational diseases—with proportionate contributions by employers.

48. Government insurance covering old age and inability to work, for all who live by their own labor.

49. Establishment of criminal responsibility for violation of laws protecting labor.

VIII. Educational Questions

Popular education should be organized according to the principle of liberty, democratization, and decentralization, as incorporated in the following:

50. Admission to schools unrestricted by limitations connected with sex, origin, or religion.

51. Freedom of private and social initiative in the opening and organizing of all types of educational institutions, and in the realm of extra-mural education; freedom of instruction.

52. Establishment of direct relationship among schools of various levels and categories in order to facilitate movement from a lower to a higher level.

53. Complete autonomy and freedom of instruction in uni-

versities and other higher schools. Increase in their number. Decrease in tuition. Organization, by the higher schools, of educational work for the entire populace. Freedom of student organization.

54. Increase in the number of secondary schools in accordance with the needs of society; decrease of tuition in such schools. Broad participation in educational affairs by local social institutions.

55. Establishment of universal, free, and compulsory primary education. Transfer of primary education to the jurisdiction of the organs of local self-government. Provision by the organs of local self-government of material assistance for needy pupils.

56. Creation of adult educational institutions—elementary schools for adults, people's libraries, and people's universities —by the organs of local self-government.

57. Development of vocational training.

Bibliography

In English

I. Bibliography

Shapiro, D., *A Select Bibliography of Works in English on Russian History, 1801–1917*. Oxford, 1962.

II. Primary Sources

Baring, M., *A Year in Russia*. London, 1907.
Bing, E. J., ed., *The Secret Letters of the Last Tsar*. New York, 1938.
Feldman, K., *The Revolt of the "Potemkin."* London, 1908.
Gapon, G., *The Story of My Life*. London, 1905.
_____, "The Story of My Life," *The Strand Magazine*, XXX (1905), 3-33, 169-180, 304-317, 363-377, 483-496.
Kaplan, S., *Once a Rebel*. New York, 1941.
Kokovtsov, V., *Out of My Past*. Stanford University, 1935.
Kuropatkin, A., *The Russian Army and the Japanese War*. 2 vols. London, 1909.
Maklakov, V. A., *The First State Duma*. Bloomington, 1964.
"The Peterhof Conference of 1905," *Russian Review*, November, 1913, 87-120.
Urusov, S. D., *Memoirs of a Russian Governor*. London, 1908.
Witte, S., *The Memoirs of Count Witte*. New York, 1921.

III. Secondary Sources

Ames, E., ed., *The Revolution in the Baltic Provinces of Russia*. London, 1907.
Baron, S. H., "Plekhanov and the Revolution of 1905," in *Essays in Russian and Soviet History*, ed. by J. S. Curtiss. New York, 1963.
Fischer, G., *Russian Liberalism*. Cambridge, 1958.
Gurko, V., *Features and Figures of the Past*. Stanford University, 1939.
Hough, R., *The Potemkin Mutiny*. London, 1960.
Karpovich, M., "Two Types of Russian Liberalism: Maklakov and Miliukov," in *Continuity and Change in Russian and Soviet Thought*, ed. by E. J. Simmons. Cambridge, 1955.
Keep, J. L. H., *The Rise of Social Democracy in Russia*. London, 1963.

King, V., "The Liberal Movement in Russia, 1904–1905," *Slavonic and East European Review*, XIV (1935), 124-137.

Lane, D., "The Russian Social Democratic Labour Party in St. Petersburg, Tver and Ashkhabad, 1903–1905," *Soviet Studies*, XV (1964), 331-344.

Laue, T. H. von, "Count Witte and the Russian Revolution of 1905," *American Slavic and East European Review*, XVII (1958), 25-46.

Lenin, V. I., *Two Tactics of Social Democracy in the Democratic Revolution*. Various editions.

Levin, A., *The Second Duma*. New Haven, 1940.

Luxemburg, R., *The Mass Strike*. Detroit, 1906.

Milyukov, P., *Russia and Its Crisis*. Chicago, 1905.

Olgin, M., *The Soul of the Russian Revolution*. New York, 1917.

Pares, B., *Russia and Reform*. London, 1907.

Spector, I., *The First Russian Revolution: Its Impact on Asia*. Englewood Cliffs, N.J., 1962.

Treadgold, D., *Lenin and His Rivals*. New York, 1955.

Trotsky, L., *Our Revolution*. New York, 1918.

Wolfe, B. D., *Three Who Made a Revolution*. New York, 1948.

Zilliacus, K., *The Russian Revolutionary Movement*. New York, 1905.

In Languages other than English

I. Bibliographical Guides

Akademiya Nauk SSSR, *Istoriya SSSR, Ukazatel Sovetskoi Literatury za 1917–1952 Gg.: Istoriya SSSR v Period Kapitalizma (1861–1917)*. Moscow, 1958.

"Bibliografiya o Zubatovskikh Soyuzakh, 'Legalnom Rabochem Dvizhenii,' Gapone, i 9-om Yanvarya," *Krasnaya Letopis*, No. 1, 1922, 75-80.

Kommunisticheskaya Akademiya, *Pervaya Russkaya Revolyutsiya: Ukazatel Literatury*. Moscow, 1930.

Pankratova, A. M., ed., *Pervaya Burzhuazno-Demokraticheskaya Revolutsiya v Rossii 1905–1907 Gg., Kratkii Ukazatel Literatury*. Moscow, 1954.

Wolzenburg, O. E., *Bibliograficheskii Putevoditel po Revolyutsii 1905 Goda*. Leningrad, 1925.

Zlatoustovskii, V. V., *Pervaya Russkaya Revolyutsia 1905–1907. Kratkii Ukazatel Literatury*. Moscow, 1941.

II. Primary Sources

Akademiya Nauk SSSR, Institut Istorii, *Revolyutsiya 1905–1907 Gg. v Rossii; Dokumenty i Materialy*. 15 vols. Moscow, 1955–1963.

Chernov, V., *Pered Burei.* New York, 1953.

Drezen, A. K., ed., *Tsarizm v Borbe s Revolyutsiei 1905–1907 Gg.: Sbornik Dokumentov.* Moscow, 1936.

Gapon, G., *Istoriya Moei Zhizni.* Leningrad, 1925.

Garvi, P., *Vospominaniya Sotsial-Demokrata.* New York, 1946.

Gerasimov, A., *Der Kampf gegen die erste russische Revolution.* Frauenfeld, 1934.

Hessen, I. V., "V Dvukh Vekakh," *Arkhiv Russkoi Revolyutsii,* XXII (1937).

Khrustalev-Nosar, G. *et al., Istoriya Soveta Rabochikh Deputatov G. S.-Peterburga.* St. Petersburg, 1907.

"K Istorii Borby Samoderzhaviya s Agrarnym Dvizheniem v 1905–1907 Gg.," *Krasnyi Arkhiv,* LXXVIII (1936), 128-160.

"K Istorii 'Krovavogo Voskresenya' v Peterburge," *Krasnyi Arkhiv,* LXVIII (1935), 39-68.

Kondratev, V. A. and Pashchetnova, I. M., "Ochevidtsy o 9 Janvarya 1905 G. v Peterburge," *Istoricheskii Arkhiv,* No. 1, 1955, 73-90.

Kovalenskii, M. and Morokhovets, E., eds., *Russkaya Revolyutsiya v Sudebnikh Protsessakh i Memuarakh.* Vol. IV. Moscow, 1925.

Maklakov, V. A., *Vlast i Obshchestvennost na Zakate Staroi Rossii.* 3 vols. Paris, 1936.

Milyukov, P., *Vospominaniya.* 2 vols. New York, 1955.

Nicholas II, *Dnevnik Imperatora Nikolaya II.* Berlin, 1923.

"Perepiska Nikolaya II i Marii Fedorovny (1905–1906 Gg.)," *Krasnyi Arkhiv,* XXII (1927), 153-209. Translated into French as *Lettres de Nicolas II et de Sa Mère,* ed. by D. Léon. Paris, 1928.

Petrunkevich, I., "Iz Zapisok Obshchestvennago Deyatelya," *Arkhiv Russkoi Revolyutsii,* XXI (1934).

Pokrovsky, M. N., ed., *1905. Materialy i Dokumenty.* 8 vols. Moscow, 1925–1928.

Polnyi Sbornik Platform Vsekh Russkikh Politicheskikh Partii. St. Petersburg, 1906.

Semennikov, V. P., ed., *Revolyutsiya 1905 Goda i Samoderzhavie.* Moscow, 1928.

Shipov, D., *Vospominaniya i Dumy o Perezhitom.* Moscow, 1918.

Spiridovich, A., *Les Dernières Années de la Cour de Tzarskoie Selo.* Vol. I. Paris, 1928.

Sverchkov, D., *Na Zare Revolyutsii.* Moscow, 1921.

Tagantsev, N., *Perezhitoe: Uchrezhdenie Gosudarstvennoi Dumy v 1905–1906.* Petrograd, 1919.

"Tsarskoselskiya Soveschaniya," *Byloe,* Sept. 1917, 217-265; Oct. 1917, 183-245; Nov.-Dec. 1917, 289-318.

1905 God v Ocherkakh i Vospominaniyakh Uchastnikov. 2 vols. Moscow, 1927.

Varnashëv, N., "Ot Nachala do Kontsa s Gaponovskoi Or-
ganizatiei (Vospominiya)," *Istoriko-Revolyutsionnyi Sbor-
nik*, No. 1, 1924, 177-208.
Vuich, N. I. and Obolensky, N. D., "K Istorii Manifesta 17-go
Oktyabrya," *Arkhiv Russkoi Revolyutsii*, II (1922), 5-13.
Witte, S., *Vospominaniya*. 3 vols. Moscow, 1960.
Zakonodatelnye Akty Perekhodnogo Vremeni, 1904–1908. 3rd.
ed. St. Petersburg, 1908.
Zelikson-Bobrovskoi, Ts., ed., *Pervaya Russkaya Revolyutsiya
v Peterburge 1905 G.* 2 vols. Leningrad, 1925.

III. Secondary Sources

Akademiya Nauk SSSR, Institut Istorii, *Revolyutsiya 1905–
1907 Gg. v Natsionalnykh Raionakh Rossii*. Moscow, 1955.
Angrand, P., ed., *La Révolution russe de 1905*. Recherches
Soviétiques. Cahier 5. Paris, 1956.
Anweiler, O., *Die Rätebewegung in Russland, 1905–1921*.
Leiden, 1958.
_____, "Die russiche Revolution von 1905," *Jahrbücher
für Geschichte Osteuropas*, NF III (1955), 161-193.
Avenard, E., *Le 22 janvier nouveau style*. Cahiers de la Quin-
zaine. Cahier 5. Paris, 1905.
Borba Obshchestvennykh Sil v Russkoi Revolyutsii. 4 vols.
Moscow, 1907.
Doklady i Soobshcheniya Instituta Istorii AN SSSR, 1955–56.
Various articles.
Grinevich, V., *Professionalnoe Dvizhenie Rabochikh v Rossii*.
3rd. ed. Vol. I. Moscow, 1923. Translated into German as
Die Gewerkschaftsbewegung in Russland. Berlin, 1927.
Gurevich, L., "Narodnoe Dvizhenie v Peterburge 9-go Yan-
varya 1905 G.," *Byloe*, No. 1, 1906, 195-223.
Istoricheskie Zapiski, 1954–1956. Various articles.
Istoricheskii Arkhiv, 1955. Various articles.
Izgoev, A. S., *Russkoe Obshchestvo i Revolyutsiya*. Moscow,
1910.
Krasnaya Letopis., No. 1, 1922. (Entire issue deals with Janu-
ary 9, 1905.)
Leontovitsch, V., *Geschichte des Liberalismus in Russland*.
Frankfurt am Main, 1957.
Martov, J., Maslov, P., and Potresov, A., eds., *Obshchestven-
noe Dvizhenie v Rossii v Nachale XX Veka*. 4 vols. St.
Petersburg, 1909–1914.
Mitelman, M. *et al., Istoriya Putilovskogo Zavoda*. 2nd. ed.
Moscow, 1941.
Milyukov, P., *God Borby*. St. Petersburg, 1907.
Muratov, Kh., *Revolyutsionnoe Dvizhenie v Russkoi Armii v
1905–1907 Gg.* Moscow, 1955.

Naida, S. F., *Revolyutsionnoe Dvizhenie v Tsarskom Flote, 1825–1917*. Moscow, 1948.

Pankratova, A. N., *Pervaya Russkaya Revolyutsiya 1905–1907 Gg.* 2nd. ed. Moscow, 1951.

Pokrovsky, M. N., *La revolución rusa*. Madrid, 1931.

————, ed., *1905: Istoriya Revolyutsionnogo Dvizheniya v Otdelnikh Chertakh*. 3 vols. Moscow, 1925–1927.

Sverchkov, D., *Georgii Gapon*. Moscow, 1930.

Trotsky, L., *Die russische Revolution 1905*. Berlin, 1923.

Veselovsky, B. B. *et al.*, eds., *Agrarnoe Dvizhenie v Rossii v 1905–1906 Gg.* 2 vols. St. Petersburg, 1908.

Vestnik Akademii Nauk SSSR, 1955. Various articles.

Voprosy Istorii, 1955. Various articles.

Weber, M., "Russland's Übergang zum Scheinkonstitutionalismus," *Archiv für Sozialwissenschaft und Sozialpolitik*, XXII (1906), 165–401.

Yakovlev, V. and Shorr, Ya., *1905 God v Moskve*. Moscow, 1955.

INDEX

Index

the Probs inevitably led to Rev,